Library of
Davidson College

VOID

Sheldon H. Blank

PROPHETIC
Essays and Addresses
THOUGHT

Hebrew Union College Press
Cincinnati, 1977

Published with the assistance of the
Henry Englander — Eli Mayer Publication Fund,
established in their honor by
Esther Straus Englander and Jessie Straus Mayer

© Copyright 1977 Hebrew Union College Press
Jewish Perspectives, Volume Two

Library of Congress Cataloging in Publication Data

Blank, Sheldon H.
 Prophetic thought.

(Jewish perspectives ; no. 2)
"Bibliography of the writings of Sheldon H. Blank": p.
1. Bible. O. T.—Criticism, interpretation, etc.—
Addresses, essays, lectures. 2. Sermons, American—
Jewish authors. 3. Sermons, Jewish—United States.
I. Title. II. Series.
BS1171.2.B55   221.6   77-5898
ISBN 0-87820-501-2

Manufactured in the United States of America
Distributed by KTAV Publishing House, Inc.
New York, New York 10013

Contents

Foreword by Samuel Sandmel ix

Acknowledgments x

ESSAYS

The Relevance of Prophetic Thought for the American Rabbi 1

"Of A Truth the Lord Hath Sent Me" An Inquiry into the Source of
the Prophet's Authority, The Goldenson Lecture for 1955 11

The Prophet as Paradigm 23

The Dawn of Our Responsibility 35

The Theology of Jewish Survival According to Biblical Sources 45

Irony by Way of Attribution 55

"Perish the Day!" A Misdirected Curse (Job 3:3) 61

An Effective Literary Device in Job 31 65

The Nearness of God and Psalm Seventy-Three 69

Some Observations Concerning Biblical Prayer 77

Men Against God, the Promethean Element in Biblical Prayer 91

ADDRESSES

Starting from Where You Are
Sermon for Service of Ordination, 1959 105

A Foundation is to Build
Founders' Day Address, 1963 111

Coming of Age in America
Opening Day Address, 1966 117

Spoken in the Scheuer Chapel on June 7, 1967 — the Close of
the "Six Day War" 123

To Care Enough
"Vietnam Commencement," University of Cincinnati, May 23, 1968 125

Spoken in the Scheuer Chapel, October 1969: Vietnam Moratorium Day . . 129

"The Voice of Mirth and the Voice of Gladness, the Voice of the
Bridegroom and the Voice of the Bride"
Founders' Day Address, 1970 133

A Frontier is a Lonely Place
Ordination Address, 1971 141

"Know Before Whom Thou Standest" 147

Spoken at the Memorial Service for Merle Marcus, 1965 151

Spoken at the Special Convocation Honoring Robert Frost, 1960 153

The Sukkah — its History and Promise 155

Bibliography of the Writings of Sheldon H. Blank 159

To Samuel Wolk and
Martin E. Katzenstein
in grateful memory

and to those about me
whose friendship I cherish

Foreword

The spirit of one's teacher is as much cherished by his students as is his mind. The scholarly essays of Sheldon H. Blank have appeared where his academic peers have had opportunity to learn and deeply to respect his mind. The publication of this volume provides the opportunity for students and colleagues to grasp his spirit, and to do so in full measure.

For most of us the sporadic encounter with Sheldon Blank's spoken message promptly disclosed the unique combination of gentleness and gentility. One noticed that he treated his chosen theme with respect, indeed as though he might through some inadvertence damage it. He chose his words carefully, and was sparing of adjectives, especially extravagant ones, as if an excess might weaken the telling force of those he chose to use. Warm as is his manner, and strong as his voice can be, he has always been enough soft-spoken that it has been the content of what he has said, devoid of all histrionics, that has conveyed his convictions. His chosen themes have always reflected his concern that he speak on matters of some consequence. His literary style is completely unsuited for the pedestrian, or the obvious, and he has never succumbed to confusing mere human foibles with the basic intrinsic issues confronting society. He has been able to dissent without scorn for those he has dissented from, and what he has advocated has stemmed from a basic regard for the sensibilities of those to whom he has spoken. His manner has been unfailingly courteous, yet he has always been a man of sturdy conviction.

If one might speak of him as possessing a shy wit, it is to stress the wit and the agreeable humor characteristic of him, and the commendable restraint he has always displayed against overstatement. Jocosity has never been his way, nor has he felt it his obligation to tell pointless and irrelevant jokes. His wit is in a good sense sly, as well as shy, and as one has listened, one has become progressively aware that there lurked in his words a humor that gave striking emphasis to the substance of his message. One is quickly persuaded that ideas, which spoken otherwise might seem frighteningly radical or outlandish, in his way of presenting them appear both prudent and right.

In reading the papers here collected, it has been gratifying to me, Sheldon Blank's student as well as his colleague, to see that the written, and now the printed words, capture his person as effectively as had his spoken words.

His spirit has been a rare one. Our school has greately been enhanced by his presence among us, and by his unique part in what is our totality. How good it is for wider audiences to benefit from the printed word as we have been enriched by the spoken. How moving it is to have become acutely conscious of the presence in our midst of a truly spiritual giant.

—Samuel Sandmel

Acknowledgments

Over the years a good number of the essays and addresses reproduced in this volume have appeared in print in a variety of publications — some more, some less accessible:

"Some Observations Concerning Biblical Prayer" in the *Hebrew Union College Annual*, volume 32 (1961); "Men Against God, The Promethean Element in Biblical Prayer" in the *Journal of Biblical Literature*, Volume 72 (1953); "The Relevance of Prophetic Thought for the American Rabbi" in the *Yearbook* of the Central Conference of American Rabbis, volume 65 (1955); "The Theology of Jewish Survival According to Biblical Sources" and "A Foundation is to Build" in the *Central Conference of American Rabbis Journal*, volume 15 (1968) and volume 11 (1963); "The Prophet as Paradigm" in *Essays in Old Testament Ethics (J. Philip Hyatt, in Memoriam)*, KTAV Publishing House (1974); "The Dawn of Our Responsibility" in the *Report of the Twelfth International Conference* (of the World Union for Progressive Judaism) *Held in London, July 6th to July 13th, 1961*; "Irony by way of Attribution" in *Semitics*, volume I (University of South Africa, 1970); "An Effective Literary Device in Job 31" in *The Journal of Jewish Studies*, volume 2, (London 1951); "The Nearness of God and Psalm Seventy-Three" in *To Do and To Teach* (Lexington, Ky., The College of the Bible, 1953); "The Sukkah—its History and Promise" in *Pointer* (London 1966). "'Of a Truth the Lord Hath Sent Me'", the Goldenson Lecture for 1955, was originally published in booklet form, and later (1969) as a part of the collection *Interpreting Prophetic Tradition*, both by the Hebrew Union College Press.

The respective editors or publishers have graciously permitted republication of these pieces in this present volume, which permission I gratefully acknowledge.

—Sheldon H. Blank

Essays

The Relevance of Prophetic Thought for the American Rabbi

It is not because Moses prohibited them that you and I refrain from murder and theft and adultery. The expression, "the relevance of prophetic thought," or for that matter, "the relevance of the Bible," does not mean "the authority of prophetic thought" or "the authority of the Bible." The Bible and, within its covers, the prophets may have relevance for the American rabbi without having authority. It is relevance that we are seeking. We want to know what meanings prophetic thought may hold for us.

A listing and refining and grouping of these meanings suggest their treatment as four pairs of themes or ideas. Three of the four can be presented with exemplary brevity; only one (the third pair), because, in part, it is new, will require more extended treatment.

I

The first two themes to be paired are *religious ceremonies* and *ethical living*. In a prophetic context it is proper to pair religious ceremonies with ethical living because, again and again, the prophets so paired them. Amos (5:21—25) and Hosea (6:6) and Isaiah (1:10—17) and Jeremiah (7:1—11) and others (1 Sam. 15:22 f. and Ps. 40:7, 9), among them the author of Micah 6:6—8, all spoke of the two together, designating the one what God requires of men as against the other which he rejects.

About the worth and propriety of religious ceremonies there is controversy now as then. And as we consider this theme, we need to observe our initial distinction between relevance and authority. In the matter of ritual, I may discover that I do not agree with Amos. Well and good! He is not my authority. When I am sick, I do not consult the book of Leviticus; I see a physician. I want to enrich my religious life with more ceremonies; so—I do not consult Amos.

How nearly absolute the prophetic repudiation of ceremonialism really was has long been a matter of dispute. I am among those who believe that it was absolute and unconditional. As I read the pertinent utterances, they comprise an unambiguous rejection of ceremonialism as something irrelevant, too easy, and perhaps even an insult to God. But, granting the possibility of a more moderate view, one would nevertheless admit that, in the prophetic literature, a modern anti-ritualist can find texts in abundance to illustrate, if not to support, his position. Therein Reform found a veritable arsenal of barbed words for its polemic with Orthodoxy—and yet does; for, though the current trend is in the direction of ceremony, no code or guide of Reform Jewish practice is ever likely to rival the *Shulḥan Arukh*. Let us not lose perspective; the distance between Reform and a new, ceremonially oriented Reform is only a fraction of the way from Reform to Orthodoxy. And so, to add biblical warrant for the free, selective, and individual nature of our own

Paper read at the Convention of the Central Conference of American Rabbis, June 1955, Asbury Park, New Jersey.

approach to the תרי"ג מצות, we shall probably continue to invoke the prophets' reservations towards the cult of their day.

One who doubts that the prophetic rejection of ritual was absolute will say, for one thing, that although some prophets may have taken that position, others actually favored ritual so long as it was of a proper sort. And, certainly, he is right, and somewhere this needs to be said: that in so brief a paper, again and again one offends against truth by generalizing. Such respectable prophets as Haggai, Zechariah, and Malachi, and even Ezekiel, if he wrote the final chapters of his book, are surely to be counted among the advocates of a legitimate temple ritual. It is as wrong to say: "The prophets stood for this or that" as it is to say: "The American rabbis stand for this or that." Unanimity characterizes neither group, and the ritualist as well as the anti-ritualist can find פסוקים among the prophets. All such generalizations are faulty.

The extreme position, again, is the view that the prophets (generally speaking) rejected ritual in favor of morality, saying: God does not want the one, he wants the other instead. The moderate position here understands the prophets rather to mean: God does not want the one as much as he wants the other; he prefers the one above the other. Whether or not this latter view was the prophets' view, it is more or less our view today. In this religious area we think in terms of relative values. Though we may sometimes get very much worked up about the *kiddush* or the *tallith* or temple attendance, nevertheless we retain a sense of proportion and, in calmer moments, readily admit that in our scale of religious values morality outranks ceremony. In our sober scale of values it is worse to take advantage of a servant than it is to miss a Friday evening service. What American rabbi thinks otherwise? But, thinking so, he walks with Amos—a part of the way.

We also walk with Amos and his kind—for, if Amos was not "the son of a prophet," he was, at any rate, the father of an illustrious succession—we walk with them when we pursue the business of our Commission on Justice and Peace and the business of the Commission on Social Action, in which we join hands for social endeavor with the Union of American Hebrew Congregations.

In fact, in a sense, we go beyond the prophets when, to the ministry of preaching, we add the dimension of social action. It is good that we do so, but speech in itself is good. And we should not be contemptuous of resolutions and pronouncements, statements and platforms. They are distant relatives of prophetic utterances. The prophet's role was to make God articulate; it was his function to speak for God—with words and symbols to condemn and warn, to approve and encourage. Be it admitted that words then had more substance than now, the fact still remains that articulation was the prophet's function. Similarly, resolutions and pronouncements and platforms create the climate for action. When the American rabbi undertakes, as he does, to create such a climate, he adopts a role which partly parallels the prophet's role.

Yes, it is good not only to keep on phrasing and articulating and repeating the basic truths and fundamental ethical principles and to keep noting their relevance in the shifting social scene, but also to preserve and intensify, even at times to create concern among men when these same truths and principles are flouted and ignored. Complacency is a subtle foe, and to create concern among men is our business.

So much for the first pair of ideas, the place of ceremonies and the importance of ethical living.

II

Intolerance and *the critical spirit* make up the second pair.

We are prone in our day to be tolerant. Having tasted the bitter waters of intolerance, as Jews we cherish and safeguard the virtue of tolerance. A liberal man, we insist, must be tolerant; and Reform Judaism, as a liberal religion, takes pride in its tolerant spirit. As a consequence, we say: "Different religions, Judaism, Christianity, are different roads to the same destination." We say: "Hats or no hats, confirmation or *bar mitzvah, bath mitzvah*, the Union Prayerbook or the Adler Prayerbook, what do these signify?" And speaking thus, we talk ourselves into a problem. For eventually we have to ask: Must we not somewhere draw a line? Do our principles never limit our tolerance? How far can a religion go, how far can Judaism go, how far can Reform Judaism go in the toleration of differences and still retain its character? A conflict eventually arises between what we call principles and the virtue of tolerance.

The purpose of these remarks is to introduce the observation that the prophets were characteristically intolerant men. A strange kind of relevance, one might say; the relevance of the prophets for us in this particular is the fact that they and we are different; they were intolerant, and we are tolerant. But, given a fitting situation, the observation could have added significance. It could say to us that if, contemplating the chaos, we should ever feel the need to stand firm, intransigent, unyielding, we could then remember Amos' uncompromising answer to Amaziah (Amos 7:14–17), Isaiah's apparently irrational insistence that Assyria's withdrawal was no cause for rejoicing (Isa. 22:1–14), Jeremiah's simple affirmations in the face of his accusers ("It was the Lord who sent me": Jer. 26:12–15), and know, at least, that we are in good company—and, incidentally, hope that we may fare better than they did.

Call it fanaticism, a martyr complex; call it inspiration, a spirit of dedication, idealism, sober conviction—whatever its name, it made them recklessly uncompromising. And they were no more prudent than they were tolerant.

It is enough to take note of this thought, and store it up for future reference should we ever need to stand firm, and want company. Tolerance is a virtue, and prudence is our way of life, and we do not pretend to be prophets.

Prophetic intolerance was no orthodoxy. And so it is not strange to see it combined with a critical spirit, the second factor in this second pair of prophetic concepts. Prophets queried, questioned, challenged, re-examined what passed for dogma. They irritated, annoyed, disturbed, frightened their contemporaries by making them think. According to the then authorities, they uttered blasphemy and heresies. They asked whether on the "day of God" Israel would really be victorious, whether Jerusalem was in fact impregnable, whether the pact between Israel and God was truly eternal; they questioned the Sinaitic origin of sacrifices, God's interest in the cult, the sanctity of sacred places; they challenged all comforting, inherited notions, and they quite upset a lot of people. They, too, prized peace of mind, but they did not equate it with apathy.

And so it has been with us. It is of the very essence of Reform that it cannot rest content; that, unceasingly, it must rethink its fundamentals. By definition, Reform may never enjoy the luxury of belief stabilized into a finished system. A characteristic of early Reform was the spirit of inquiry, inherited from the prophetic movement. Older grown, are we becoming set in our ways? Is our Reform in danger of becoming another orthodoxy? If so, we might do well to drink again at the fountain of prophetic religion, thus to renew our youth and the zest for spiritual adventure.

III

The next thoughts to be paired concern *the dimensions of God* and *the responsibility of man*. Leaving the second aside for a while, what the first amounts to is a recognition that God is greater by far than the human imagination has ever conceived. His thoughts are not our thoughts (we know it now); high as the heavens are above the earth, so are his thoughts higher than our thoughts.

No doubt, it was in dim antiquity that men started thinking of the greatness of God. But to the contemporaries of Amos, God somehow seemed manageable. There were formulas; his people could "get around" him. Then God's question resounded like a thunderclap: "Are you not to me as the Ethiopians, O children of Israel?" (Amos 9:7). It came as a declaration of divine independence—the first of a series of hammer blows by which, through the prophets, God drove home the thought of his true greatness. Although this thought is not particularly new to us, it has a special relevance, if not indeed a grim significance today, and to meditate on it is profitable.

Amos was not the whole of the prophetic movement, but he gave it the impetus which carried it on to large achievement. He began the reinterpretation of the doctrine of Israel's choice. Through him, God said of his people: I know you well, yes; therefore I will punish you (3:2). This was another shock, but Amos was charged with yet more: What do you want with the day of God? It is darkness and not light (5:18). What he said added up to the incredible: far from being possessed by them, their "Portion," God was his own master and, exercising his uncommitted will, God had cast his people off.

What is incredible is not believed; so prophets have to say it again. Hosea, Micah, Isaiah, Jeremiah, Ezekiel—they kept saying it again and again until it needed no more saying, because it had happened. With sublime detachment, God had looked the other way, and his temple lay in ruins. The generation that heard it was shocked by the prediction; the generation that survived it was stunned by the event.

Have you tried to imagine what this meant? Have you seen in the eyes of the chained priests of Jerusalem their "wild surmise" as they viewed the demolition of the Sanctuary? There have been comparable moments in history. Consider the panic that swept over Europe only a little more than three hundred years ago (How strangely recent!) when the certainty dawned that the earth is planet to the sun and that, as a consequence, man on earth is not at all the center of a starry universe created for his sake—the panic that threatened Galileo with torture. Or consider today's near panic, the fall-out of the mushroom cloud—our new awareness that man, the subduer and lord of creation, but little lower than the angels, is capable of self-destruction, can and may in fact write "finis" to his destiny. In the unwritten annals of prehistory, it has occurred that men have ceased to be. If *pithecanthropus* and *australopithecus* had not had collaterals, what now is a future possibility would be a prehistoric reality, with none to reflect upon it. But now we are one world, and *homo sapiens*, without collaterals, has it in his power to extinguish *homo sapiens* for good.

What then of God (to say nothing now of the "brotherhood of man" or the "mission of Israel")? What of God on an emptied planet?

But why should we think about it? The whole notion is utterly ridiculous; it is quite incredible that God could ever let mankind become extinct—incredible as was that earlier crazy notion that he would ever look the other way, unconcerned, while the uncircumcised trampled his holy courts and carried off the golden cherubim.

This ironical remark is intended to suggest that some good men should do some good thinking in our times about the theological aspects of man's new-found means of self-destruction.

Now, in any such thinking, we, here assembled, have the advantage that, historically speaking, we have been over this ground before. We have survived an analogous experience; we have already had to adjust our theology to a fact quite as dismaying as is our prospect today. Prepared by the eighth and seventh century prophets, we were cushioned against the shock that came in the sixth, and could gain from it new insights into the dimensions of God.

If those prophets had given us nothing but perspective, it would have been enough. And what has greater relevance today than the perspective they gave? The terms have changed—of course; but only recently, and our thinking still retains some measure of parochialism.

Nevertheless, though only recently, the terms have changed. It is not Jerusalem or Canaan but this planet Earth, not the family and court of Zedekiah or any royal sanctuary but the species known as man, not "Yahveh" but God, that have now to be brought in relation. And the change in terms reflects our growing perception of the dimensions of God. From an Amos we learned that God was not limited by his traditional commitment to his people Israel. From an Einstein we may perhaps be learning that God is not limited by any presumed commitment to his creature, man. If we are to withstand this latest shock, we will need to draw upon our deepest spiritual resources.

And this leads to the second of the thoughts here paired: the matter of man's responsibility. For Amos and his line, man's acceptance of responsibility was a corollary of the independence of God. Though he might do so, God was not constrained to look the other way—there was an alternative, and men might choose.

This idea has been around for twenty-five centuries or more, and so, of course, its repetition engenders no excitement. It does, however, have a certain topical interest. And its significance becomes more evident when we recognize the possibility of a different corollary to the greatness of God. We could, of course, say: So great is God that only resignation befits our desperate case. This is, in fact, a statement (an extreme and inadequate statement) of a theological position which one hears now and then, and which has frequently been examined at this Conference. It is particularly as against this attitude of absolute dependency that the other position has meaning.

If we adopt this other position that men may choose, then courageously and resolutely we set out to seek a formula for survival. And Israel, abandoned, comes into the picture again. For, God needs Israel if his creation is not to collapse. The classic prophetic expression of the thought is Deutero-Isaiah's, and it goes by the name of "the mission of Israel." Far form being outmoded, today the mission concept has only just become fully meaningful in terms of resources which may be available to preserve our species. If ever we had a mission, we have it now—and not in the sense of grief to endure but in the sense of a task to perform.

The unnamed prophet who set the task also provided the encouragement for desperate times like these. It is just as if he had our decade in mind when he named God

> "The creator of the heavens, the Lord,
> The artisan of the earth, its maker,"

and said of him

> "He himself founded it.
> Not to be an empty waste did he create it;
> To be inhabited he formed it..."
> לא תהו בראה לשבת יצרה

(Isa. 45:18).

This claim is the reverse of the anticipated apocalyptic cataclysm of Isa. 24, and it is the opposite of our current fears. No burnt out planet, but, if we let God have his way, a place of habitation. These are words to inscribe on a banner: לא תהו בראה. Before creation the world was a *tohu*; it is not now God's intent to undo his work and bring back primeval chaos. Prophetic thought is reassuring on this score and still lends us strength to support God's purpose: לשבת יצרה, "for habitation he formed it."

For Deutero-Isaiah, "the mission of Israel" and "the servant of the Lord" were facets of the same idea. There is a point, indeed, where they seem to part company, though probably because of faulty exegesis. They cease to be the same idea when the servant of the Lord becomes "the suffering servant" in the sense in which we use the latter term—which is the wrong sense.

What we mean, when we speak of the suffering servant, is not what he meant who wrote the justly famous "fifty-third chapter." Nor is what we mean, when we use the term, applicable either to the American Jew or to the American rabbi. The term and the present reality are incongruous. Israel here and now is hardly suffering. And, devoted though he is and definitely overworked, the American rabbi would hardly call himself a suffering servant. The term is out of place in the current scene.

And as for the fifty-third chapter, its meaning in this respect is, to say the least, ambiguous. First and last, Deutero-Isaiah was a prophet of consolation. With his opening words, he established the mood: "Comfort, yea comfort my people" (40:1). He had come to say that Israel suffered more than enough. By no means destined to suffer for mankind's redemption, Israel might now look forward to an amazing rebirth, a glorious restoration. That is the theme, the theme of the song of the so-called suffering servant

(52:13—53:12) no less than the theme of the remaining chapters which go by the name of Deutero-Isaiah.

When Deutero-Isaiah spoke, the memory of suffering was fresh, and, too, there was present misery (40:2; 41:14; 42:22; 49:7; 50:6; 52:14; 53:9). But he announced an end to gloom—to do so was the reason for his coming; he was the bearer of good tidings. He says it on every page, and even in the fifty-third chapter (a composition which properly begins with 52:13, a few verses earlier). There, at the very outset, he states the theme: "Lo, my servant shall prosper" (52:13), and near its end God still is speaking of restoration and future glory: "He shall see his offspring; he shall live long. And what God desires shall succeed at his hand" (53:10).

The confusion concerns the "when" of the suffering, whether past or future. In the thought of the prophet, the suffering was past or present; unfortunately, his language is not wholly clear and he has been understood to refer to the future, to destined suffering, a part of God's design for his people's future.

Perhaps only the temperament of the exegete finally determines which of the two admittedly possible meanings he finds in the controversial chapter. Its prophetic author unambiguously says that the servant of the Lord has suffered beyond all measure. He also says, though somewhat less clearly, that the suffering of the servant has benefited other nations. He may be understood to say, though here legitimate doubt is in order, that Israel by past suffering has atoned vicariously for the sins of others. Finally—and this is where the temperament of the exegete becomes decisive, the prophet can be made to say that what happened once may happen again, that suffering is the servant's lot, that, indeed, Israel is a perpetual atonement. Just overlook a textual obscurity (What is the meaning of the second colon in 53:10a?), insist on the future tense of a couple of verbs (in 53:11b and 12b), disregard all resulting inconsistencies (with the current interpretation of the "suffering servant" contrast what is said in 52:13; 53:10b, the beginning of v. 11, 12a; and also 49:7 and 42:4, to say nothing of the exuberant tone of the whole Deutero-Isaianic context of the chapter) and you have one biblical passage (but only one) that seems to envisage for Israel a destiny of vicarious suffering. But the peg is too weak to support the whole philosophy.

To be sure, we can still have the philosophy yet forego the biblical peg. Yes, let us keep the philosophy—and pray we may never need it again—the philosophy that martyrdom is the recurrent lot of Israel and that behind our suffering a higher meaning lurks, one linked with man's redemption. Time after tragic time, events in Jewish history have prompted its philosophers to have recourse to these thoughts. Only too recently, the horrified victims of Nazi madness, we sought to understand God's ways in such terms as these. We were in sore need of light. Let us keep the philosophy, but look for no biblical peg to support it. Though phrases in our chapter may have suggested it, it lies beyond the area of prophetic thought and the limits of this study.

Partly by our history, partly a misinterpretation of a historically significant chapter of the Bible, we have been diverted from our true objective. It may be we have too readily accepted a role to which others assigned us, making Isaiah 53 our excuse. It may be we have preferred passivity and so resigned ourselves to sorrow with a pious word: גם זו לטובה, "this too is for the best."

It is not, in fact, in the fifty-third chapter, misunderstood, that the American rabbi finds a meaningful thought for our day, but in what the Second Isaiah did say about Israel's role in history. According to this prophet's vision, Israel, the servant of the Lord, was a people of prophets, possessed of a redeeming truth, God's witnesses, commissioned by God and sent forth to perform a task—active, not passive; not martyrs, but missionaries. We do the prophet an injustice if we understand him otherwise. He came with an affirmation to arouse the spirit and not a negation to hide under. He assigned to Israel a mission and the task is with us still.

Who, as a matter of fact, are more surely charged with the responsibility to support God's purpose than men such as we? Who, as we, can step outside the smaller circles that dissect and divide, the economic, the political, the sectarian (if we will), and look with a broad perspective at the human problem? Who also, as we, have no axes to grind, nothing to sell, no borders to defend, no social lines to hold, but can approach the problem with an interest merely in man's salvation? As men of religion, we have the opportunity; as Jews, we have the vision; as Americans, we have the freedom; and as American rabbis, we have the responsibility. This is the form the mission of Israel takes today.

> "You are my witnesses, saith the Lord
> And my servant whom I have chosen."

> "And I will make you a light to the nations
> That my salvation may reach
> To the ends of the earth."

> "Near is my triumph, salvation has gone forth;
> My arms shall arbitrate among nations.
> Isles put their hope in me. . . "
>
> (Isa. 43:10; 49:6; 51:5).

Stated in the simplest language, what, as a missionary people, we have to say is merely this: that there is no divided counsel on high and there need be no divisiveness on earth; or, positively stated: God, unrivalled, wills a world at peace. This is our evangel and our goal.

IV

Finally, a few words only about *reactions to frustration* and *the quest for certainty*. These last two thoughts are personal. They have less to do with systematic theology or "what Jews believe" and more to do with a man's own religion.

One after another, the prophets reveal their sense of complete frustration; their inability to communicate; their losing battle with human nature wilfully obtuse, in the guise of a stiff-necked people. And how at least one of them dealt with his problem is on record. The "confessions" of Jeremiah reflect that prophet's agony and his triumph.

To the extent to which one is able to identify with the prophets, one can share in or appropriate for oneself today their answers. The answer which Jeremiah found appears in his confessions as a divine word addressed to him (12;5; 15:19 f.). "Who told you," God seems to be saying, "that the task would be simple or easy? And, considering its magnitude and urgency, should you be taking time off to indulge in self-pity?" Add to Jeremiah's confessions the little chapter forty-five, "the confession of Baruch," and God appears to ask a further question, the perspective-building question: "What, O man, is your little grief compared to mine?" Jeremiah's first reaction was to run away, to escape: Why did not my mother's womb become my grave! (20:14−18). Oh, that I had a desert lodge and could get away from it all! (9:1). That was his impulse, but in the end, after how great a struggle! he achieved renewed dedication and an access of courage.

In the similar matter of certainty, it is again Jeremiah who, among the prophets, is the most articulate. Doubtless all of them had need of credentials and tried in some way to give evidence of their authority; probably they all tried likewise to sound the depths within themselves, to learn for themselves with what certainty they spoke for God, but none permits us to follow his quest as does this Jeremiah.

As all who speak of God must do, he struggles for adequate expression. That he experiences God as person to person (1:9), that he is admitted to intimacy with God (23:22), that his indignation is divine indignation (6:11; 15:17; 23:9) and his compassion divine compassion (12:7 with 8:18−23)—these things he knows and by virtue of them he can speak: "Thus saith the Lord," but, though he tells us much more than the others, we can understand even him only to the extent that our own experience of God agrees with his.

Whatever his experience, it lends him certainty and it enables him to write to his people exiled in distant Babylonia: God is approachable. This is God's word to you: Seek me and you will find me. If you but seek me with your whole heart, be assured I prove responsive (29:12−14). It enables him to outface a king (37:17) and to stand before a mob and quietly say: I am in your hands; do as you will. Only know, if you kill me, it is innocent blood you spill . . . for of a truth God sent me (26:14 f.).

Perhaps, when all is said and done, what has for us the greatest relevance is merely this: the prophet's certainty, born of his experience of God.

Of a Truth
the Lord Hath Sent Me

*An Inquiry into the Source of the Prophet's Authority
The Goldenson Lecture for 1955*

I am truly most grateful—grateful to Temple Emanu-El for establishing the Dr. Samuel H. Goldenson Lectureship; grateful to you, Mr. President, for inviting me to offer under its auspices this year the first of the projected annual lectures on the thought of the prophets; grateful to Dr. Goldenson for being what he is, a man whose religion is the religion of those prophets. I would wish that from year to year the value and the significance and the relevance of these lectures might grow, that they might thus become a worthy tribute to a worthy son of this Hebrew Union College.

There is a kind of link between us. Both of us—at different times, to be sure—were students of Moses Buttenwieser, and we share a reverance for his memory. Of him, Dr. Goldenson has written:

> "No man on the Faculty meant more to me...I became close to him from the very first year at College...For two years I lived at his home at Mt. Auburn and during many summers we had adjacent cottages in Southampton, Ontario...I think I saw everyone of his books in manuscript and he and I had many, many discussions on current problems from the standpoint of prophetic insight and teaching" (quoted from a personal letter).

These feelings were, of course, mutual. There was no student in whom Moses Buttenwieser took greater pride, none for whom he had more affection. And, indeed, Samuel Goldenson is a disciple to swell the heart of any teacher. His life is dedicated to prophetic ideals; and it is with an eminent sense of fitness that Temple Emanu-El, establishing a lectureship in his honor, designated prophetic thought the subject.

It is also fitting that the first of the lectures honoring Dr. Goldenson should center upon that one among the prohets for whom his revered teacher's enthusiasm was boundless, the prophet Jeremiah. Furthermore, in view of our search in a liberal seminary for the sources of religious authority, one in particular of the many facets of Jeremiah's varied life and thought, namely: his own attempt to discover and proclaim the source of his authority, holds for us both lasting and topical interest. Studying his problem over again, and following his quest, we would be inquiring into his religious experience and his personal religion—a task indeed worth undertaking.

But, first, before embarking on the study, a word to students past and present. I wonder whether students know (I think they do) the role they play in the life of a teacher. I want to express my own indebtedness. What I have to say here this evening was written in the classroom—it took form amidst the open give and take of the classroom. The student's comments spoken and unspoken, his questions, arguments, objections and suggestions, the stare, the puzzled frown, the perceptive, or even the confused answer in an examination, the nod, the compliment, even the too ready adoption of a new idea—all these are stimuli to a teacher's growth. They are the warnings and the guideposts on the way to deeper insights, clearer definitions. Dead classes are stupefying; they are fortunately rare on our campus, where almost any student, if coaxed (and some without coaxing), would be ready to change places with the teacher. Yes, I think my friends on the Faculty will agree with me that in the classroom, in the very process of communication, as a part of the serious, difficult business of communication, we achieve our own greatest growth. We owe thanks to all students, past and present, who make us go on thinking.

And now, the problem: How convince the unwilling? Even to the sympathetic, it is hard enough to demonstrate the truth of any proposition; how much more difficult to convince the unwilling! And the prophets' contemporaries were unwilling, and the prophets had their problems. The bitter fact that nobody listened to them—that nobody that was anybody listened—was the common denominator in their experience (Jer. 6.10, 17). Whether spoken to arouse the complacent or to comfort the despairing, their words appeared equally futile. Not only the first Isaiah whose metallic tones struck fear (6.9f.) but even the gentle, rhapsodic Isaiah of the Exile had to complain of a people of unseeing eyes and ears that did not hear (43.8; 42.19). Ezekiel's sarcastic comment betrays that prophet's bitterness; God told him, he says: "To them you are only as one who sings ditties with a pleasant voice skillfully; they hear your words, yes, but do nothing whatever" (33.32). The first Isaiah sensed the cause of their deafness: the deaf, he had said, were not able to hear simply because they preferred not to hear (28.12; 30.9, 15). Man's ability to shut out the unpleasant—not to see, not to hear—may be a biological necessity, but it is the prophet's Sambatyon. He stands thwarted on the hither shore. And none had a greater sense of frustration than Jeremiah.

Despite the tradition that he was a priest, we will neither call Jeremiah a "cult prophet" nor suggest that what he said carried weight simply by virtue of any office or any title of his. On the contrary, he enjoyed no respect which he had not earned, no authority beyond what he could win for himself. His was a kind of nightmarish nakedness: he had no framed diplomas, no transcripts of academic records, no recourse to colleagues in a conference. By nothing extrinsic could he command belief.

But he must be heard! Since the fate of his people depended upon his success with them and, specifically, his ability to make them see that he brought them an urgent message from their God, and since there was so little time, his mission had a grim earnestness and his argument was no collegiate debate, no matching of wits for empty honors.

To be sure, an argument is a deceptive course, in which it is often hard to determine whom one is trying to convince, one's opponent or oneself. No doubt, at times, Jeremiah, like all who argue, was battling his own uncertainties, and what he achieved in the process was not so much the favorable verdict of the market place (which was never his in his lifetime) as it was fortitude and a moral courage which enabled him to proclaim the word, regardless of the adverse opinion of others. He came out of the controversy stronger than when he went in, for it was in fact "a controversy for the sake of Heaven."

Jeremiah's supreme attempt to assure his people that God had sent him, and his own quest for certainty, they are not really two things but one. The others ask him how he knows and, agonized, he seems to ask himself in turn, How, indeed, do I know?

Jeremiah wrestled persistently with the twofold problem. His book is not alone the record of his concern to convince the eyebrow lifters that, though the form was the form of Jeremiah, the voice was the voice of God, but, especially in the confessions and elegies, the record also of his own seeking.

He did not prepare a legal brief, did not muster his arguments: "one, two, three, four a, four b." And yet, on page after page, his book reflects the ongoing controversy, and his reasoning emerges. The questions his opponents raised (which were at the same time his own questions); the doubts the unworried merchant expressed, and the tolerant minister, the prosperous farmer, and the well-paid prophet (which were at the same time his own doubts) led him through mental anguish and the stress of conflicting emotions, not to a reasoned answer, but to the stuff from which at this great distance we can, with some assurance, distill his answer—the answer which he, the prophet Jeremiah, managed to live with, however well or ill it satisfied his scoffing generation. His book contains matter for the whole variety of his arguments. Isolate and sift the material, translate it into such terms as we use, and then arrange it—it makes a strong case.

That is to say: It makes a strong case in the framework of religious experience. Reasoning is possible only among persons who start with the same assumptions. Suppose we would discuss the question: What does God want of man? Obviously we can discuss it only with persons who speak the language of the question. (Can two talk together, except they be agreed?) And so it is if we ask: Did Jeremiah truly speak the word of God? Only we can discuss it who speak the language of our question. It is fortunate that this is our language here; otherwise what follows would be meaningless. As it is, in the framework of religious experience, Jeremiah's case, as we can reconstruct it, carries conviction.

And this is his case, restated, rephrased, and set forth in the form of six propositions:

I

The argument which was, and is still, no doubt, the most convincing to the greatest number is the argument based upon fulfilled predictions, the proposition that a prophet can be accepted as authentic when what he prophesies comes to pass. But to Jeremiah the pragmatic test was probably the least satisfying of his several criteria.

We know that in those days prophets gave "signs" to prove their authenticity. These were their credentials. In a stratum of the Exodus narrative, which is probably later than the Second Isaiah and shows his influence, the true and highly reputed prophet Moses performs successful signs before Pharaoh to validate his message (see my "Studies in Deutero-Isaiah," *HUCA*, XV, p. 46, n. 88). In a law in Deuteronomy the possibility is envisaged that, as a test of Israel's devotion, even an heretical prophet may propose a sign and the sign come true (Deut. 13.2f.). To convince a king, the legendary Isaiah said that the shadow on a sundial would move backwards—and it did move ten steps backwards (Isa. 38.7f.).

And it would be false to say that even Jeremiah was contemptuous of facts and laid no store by successful predictions. Once, in prison, he had a premonition that a cousin would come to him and offer him the chance to purchase a certain field. When, the next day, his cousin comes to the prison on that same errand, Jeremiah himself sees in the act the will of God—because it happened as, in advance, he knew it would happen (Jer. 32.6–8).

On another occasion, when he has an opening, he says: I told you so. Zedekiah the king has sent for him, fetched him from prison to learn God's word. And why? Because, of all the prophets, Jeremiah was the one who said the Babylonians would come, and they had come. Jeremiah is human; he does not resist the temptation or fail to point the moral: "Where now are your prophets who said: The king of Babylon will not attack you or this land?" (37.19). He gloats here, even as on yet another occasion he challenges: "As for the prophet that predicts peace, when that prophet's expectation is realized, it will be known that God truly sent him" (28.9, cf. 17.15; 44.28; Ezek. 13.6b). By the light that is in him, Jeremiah foresees the disappointment which all such prophets must experience, whereas he, predicting war, will triumph. There is little to distinguish his challenge here in anticipation from his I-told-you-so in retrospect. He is not averse to the proof of fulfillment—only that this proof comes for him too tragically late. It is grim satisfaction to be proved right by an occurrence which frantically you strove to prevent. Thus Jeremiah had little enthusiasm for the argument based on fulfilled predictions—though he made use of it, too, needing all the support he could muster. Nevertheless, what men might call "success" seemed to him a prop too frail to buttress his conviction.

II

Apparently for Jeremiah his strongest argument is no argument at all but a simple affirmation. His only plea before the court when, charged with the capital offense of heresy, he fights for his life is a simple affirmation. This argument amounts to an affidavit—just this and nothing more, a bare statement in court:

> "It is the Lord who sent me to prophesy to this house and to this city all the words which you have heard...I am in your hands; do to me as seems good and proper to you. Only, know that if you kill me you incur the guilt of spilling innocent blood...for, of a truth, the Lord hath sent me to you to speak in your hearing all these words" (26.12–15).

No careless statement this; considering the circumstances, we suspect that the prophet had no stronger argument in his arsenal than this certain knowledge that he spoke for God. I am impressed anew whenever I read this simple statement: "It is the Lord who sent me...Of a truth the Lord hath sent me." What more can a man say?

If chapter twenty-six is an "affidavit," chapter one is the nearest thing to a "diploma." "God told me, Say not: I am a lad; for wherever I send you you shall go, and whatever I command you you shall speak...Then God put forth his hand and touched my mouth. And God said to me, Behold! I have put my words in your mouth" (1.7, 9). It is like a diploma, yet not a diploma; it bears no one's seal or signature but his own: "God said to me," "God told me" (cf., also 15.16, 19).

This passage is one of several descriptions of his experience with God. According to these, Jeremiah's conviction was not the conclusion of a syllogism but the result of a religious experience—his Sinai. He has "stood in God's private council" (23.22), been admitted to intimacy with God, shared and mirrored his moods, divine indignation, divine disappointment:

"My heart breaks, I shudder all over;
I am as one drunk, overcome with wine,
Because of the Lord, yea, the words of his holiness."

"I am filled with divine indignation,
Exhausted with holding it in"(23.9; 6.11).

Not in public utterances alone, but in prayer as well, he speaks in this manner:

"Because of your overpowering hand I sat alone,
Because you had filled me with gloom" (15.17).

Withal, Jeremiah very much remains Jeremiah. What he describes is not a mystical union but a sharing: Jeremiah sharing with God.

This is his second and strongest argument: his reference to the immediacy of his experience, his solemn assurance, his deposition that, sharing God's mood, he truly and faithfully speaks God's word.

III

His quest for the source of his message next involves the elimination of possible sources other than God. His voice, he says—and this is his third proposition—is not the *vox populi*, Jeremiah speaks indeed the unpopular word. He leaves all cliches to the plagiarizers, to the dealers in used oracles of whom God says: "They contrive to make my people forget my name with their dreams which they repeat one to another" (23.27) and "Therefore, lo! I am against the prophets...who pilfer my words a man from his fellow. Lo! I am against the prophets who appropriate phrases and oracularly boast 'Behold, an oracle!'" (23.30f.)

Jeremiah pointedly dissociates himself from the popular prophets. He has not borrowed his words as they have done, nor does he echo the rumblings of the crowd. Indeed, so much at odds with common belief is his own word that he passes for a madman (*meshugga'*, 29.26). He stands "the test of ridicule"—yet is discredited.

Of this he complains to God, the very cause of his grief:

"Thou, O God, hast enthralled me
    and I am enthralled..."
(this is Buttenwieser's perceptive translation)...
    "I have become a constant target for laughter:
        every one mocketh me...
    The word of God but serveth to bring upon me insult
        and derision without end" (20.7f.).

On another occasion, in a similar context, gently he reproaches his God:

"Know that for your sake I have borne disgrace" (15.15).

He mentions the taunt which he hears on all sides:
"Lo! they say to me:
'Where is this word of God? Let it come to pass!'" (17.15).

The implications of the record must be clear: the source of Jeremiah's word is obviously not the crowd. His voice is not the *vox populi*. What is it then but the *vox dei*?

IV

Or does another presumptive source suggest itself? Could he be deceived; could it be his own voice that he mistakes for the voice of God? His repudiation of this alternative is his fourth argument. For two reasons he must rule out the possibility that the words he speaks are his, not God's:

a) They are not his words because no one would be such a fool as to invite the disasters which his speech entails. What has it got him, this speaking for God? Curses (15.10) and a flogging (37.15), another flogging and exposure in stocks (20.2), taunts (15.15; 17.15; 20.7f.) and accusations (26.11; 37.13; 38.4), arrest and imprisonment (37.15; 38.6), the plight of a fugitive (36.5), of a pariah (16.5, 8; 15.17), a life of loneliness (16.2).

To speak of "disinterest" would be to understate the case. To the question: *cui bono?* he could reply: Certainly I have no profit from my labors. Quite the contrary; the message I bring is my ruin.

This is an argument which, if Plato may be trusted, Socrates also used a couple of centuries later in his futile attempt to prove that God had sent him:

"That I am given to you by God is proved by this:—that if I had been like other men, I should not have neglected all my own concerns . . . and have been doing yours . . . And had I gained anything, or if my exhortations had been paid, there would have been some sense in that; but now . . . not even the impudence of my accusers dares to say that I have ever exacted or sought pay of anyone; they have no witness of that. And I have a witness of the truth of what I say; my poverty is sufficient witness" (from Jowett's translation of Plato's *Apology*).

Like Jeremiah, Socrates asked in whose interest, then, he spoke; certainly not in his own. From his condition, each concluded that it was not he but God who set his dolorous way.

b) Jeremiah for another reason must repudiate the implication that his words are his own invention. He would say quite different things were he to obey his own impulse. His speech is not, indeed, automatic; nevertheless it is beyond his power to refrain from speech. He is possessed with a sense of inevitability:

"If I say, I will not remember him
Or speak any more in his name,
Then there is in me, as it were, a raging fire

Pent in my bones;
I weary myself to contain it—
But in vain" (20.9; cf. v. 7 and 11; also 6.11).

Similar again is Socrates' claim and similar his desperate inability to evoke belief. This is how he puts it:

"Some one will say: Yes, Socrates, but can you not hold your tongue . . . Now I have great difficulty in making you understand my answer to this. For if I tell you that this would be a disobedience to a divine command . . . you will not believe that I am serious; and if I say again that the greatest good of man is to converse about virtue . . . and that the life which is unexamined is not worth living—that you are still less likely to believe. And yet what I say is true, although a thing of which it is hard for me to persuade you" (from the *Apology*).

Two men claimed they had to speak: the one lost his case and drank the hemlock; by some magic, the other escaped.

Yet, sad is Jeremiah's plight: he has to speak; and when he does, he only says the wrong things, for in very fact he loves this people.

"Would my head were water," he laments,
"And my eyes a spring of tears,
  That I might weep by day and night,
  For the slain of the daughter of my people!" (8.23).

And again:

"If you will not hearken
  My soul must cry in secret
  For the arrogance, and weep,
  And my eye shed tears
  When God's flock is taken captive"
(13.17; cf. 10.19).

Is it conceivable that he could wish down judgment on the people whom he loves with such tender affection? Quite the contrary! When he is Jeremiah and not God's agent, he intercedes for them with God. When he is speaking not for God but to God in prayer, he prays for them. Though forbidden:

"Pray not for good for this people!" (14.11),

and

"Pray you not for this people,
  Nor take up any cry or entreaty,
  Nor intercede with me,
  For I will not hear you" (7.16)—

though twice forbidden, he yet dares to pray and in one of his "confessions" he admits his insubordination:

> "Is good to be rewarded with evil?" he asks.
> "Remember how I have waited on you,
> To speak good on their behalf,
> To avert your anger from them" (18.20).

He speaks of it twice:

> "Indeed I interceded with you in a time of calamity,
> And in a time of disaster on behalf of the enemy"
> (15.11b; cf. Isa. 1.21, 24).

And it is on record that once the king and once the people sought him out to pray for them (21.2; 42.2), which they would hardly have done had their errand seemed implausible.

There is one passage in which the prophet appears to recognize the ambiguity of his position. Here, again in the context of a "confession," he says:

> "I have neither sought to escape serving you
> Nor desired the grievous day" (17.16).

Serving God he has announced, but being Jeremiah he has not desired, "the grievous day."

And this is the fourth of his proofs. Even as his voice was not the voice of the crowd, so it was not the wish child of his own heart, being the contrary of his wish for his people.

He admits no further alternatives; it must then be the voice of God.

V

The fifth and the sixth of his propositions may be paired. Together they differ somewhat from the others, being based on the content of the message. He seems to be shifting ground now and putting it this way: If you do not choose to believe me, and refuse to accept my life as a proof; if you will not let me say: "It is true because it is God's word," then let me say: "It is God's word because it is true."

As concerns the content of his message, he denies, first of all, that it is heresy, and aligns himself with predecessors tried and true. He commends the ancient, tested ways:

> "Stand by the ways and observe,
> And inquire of the ancient paths
> Which way is the good way, and follow it,
> And find your security" (6.16).

(He may have repeated this thought in 18.15, but the text is in disorder and the meaning uncertain.) Jeremiah agrees: God spoke to the fathers when he brought them from Egypt—it is only that a false, a formalistic tradition has arisen concerning what he then said (7.22f.).

Rejecting the current slogans, Jeremiah yet espouses no new heresy; he represents a tradition. It is the others who are out of step. In the present situation, it is the prophets of peace who have left the road—those prophets who "too lightly heal the hurt of the daughter of my people, crying 'Peace!' though peace is lacking" (8.11; cf. 4.10; 14.13; 23.17). Jeremiah regards himself as one of a succession of prophets "from of old" who "prophesied to many lands and great kingdoms of war and disaster and disease" (28.8). No newfangled notion, no heresy his; he stands with those prophets squarely facing reality, grim though it be.

From what he says, from its normative character, one may know that of a truth God sent him.

VI

And his final argument is similar. What Jeremiah says for God is ethical and rational and thus comports with the nature of God; it is what such a God as he knows must naturally say. The words are the words of a just and constant God, whose purpose expressed by his prophet is to turn his people, through knowledge of him, into ways of righteousness. "Of this one may boast," says God through Jeremiah, "that he understands and knows me, as one who acts on earth with constancy, justice, and righteousness and that these are what I desire" (9.23; cf. 5.28f.; 7.5f.; 22.3). "Knowing" God he elsewhere equates with doing justice and righteousness, judging the case of the poor and needy (22.15f.).

In *The Prophets of Israel*, Moses Buttenwieser, speaking of Amos and Micah, Isaiah, Jeremiah, referred to "the great basic truths or principles of which they were cognizant through their moral consciousness, and which, constituting their revelation from God, formed the centre and essence of their prophecy" (p. 152). Pointing to such "basic truths," the substance of his knowledge of God, Jeremiah can say: By these I know, by this you may know: "of a truth the Lord hath sent me."

In Jerusalem Jeremiah has seen adulterous, lying prophets strengthening the hands of malefactors (23.14). But God has not sent them, he says. Had they "stood in God's council," they would be exhorting the people in words designed not to confirm them in wickedness but to divert them from their evil way (23.21f.).

Unlike them, Jeremiah is a prophet who has enjoyed the intimacy of God, and as proof now speaks a fitting word—"a faithful messenger" to him who sent him. His words bear the imprint of their author.

Once the prophet even seems to say: He is no parochial, regional God whom I represent; universalize my words and they will stand the test. They are the words of a God transcending people and land, who says:

"Am I a God nearby and not a God far off?
... Do I not fill the heaven and the earth?" (23.23f.).

So Jeremiah rests his case with the prima-facie evidence of the message itself as the final test of its authenticity and his own veracity.

He has made a good case. He has probably reached a satisfying conclusion, laid a foundation on which to build a life. The knowledge of God is inscribed on Jeremiah's heart.

Related perhaps to this answer which he found is the vision of the end of days that goes by the name of the "new covenant." There is, to be sure, some legitimate doubt, though this vision appears in his book, that the prophet Jeremiah is its author. But whether it is his own or not, it seems to be an implication of Jeremiah's quest for certainty. He (or another), reflecting upon his experience, the source of his authority, the source of his certainty, reached out beyond the personal to the universal, made general the particular experience, and so attained to that imposing vision. It is such certainty as his that, in the end of days, each will have, when *torah* is written on every man's heart, when a man must teach his neighbor no longer saying "Know the Lord," for each will know him, small and great (31.31–34). Jeremiah's quest quite naturally led to this ultimate in messianic expectation.

The analysis which, properly speaking, was the goal of our study is complete. We have read the record of a man's quest for certainty; we have explored the grounds for his "Thus saith the Lord." On this score there is no more to say. But it would be well before leaving the matter to briefly note two thoughts for our times.

The first is this: that the case which Jeremiah makes for the authority of his words is very much the same as the case for the authority of Scripture as a whole. For us, at least, who regard the Bible as a record of the religious experiences of great men, and of Jeremiah as not the least among them, that prophet's defense of his "inspiration" serves at the same time as a defense of the inspiration of Scripture. Jeremiah was not the only one to defend his calling. Amos, when challenged, asked simply: "When a lion has roared who can but fear? If the Lord God has spoken who can but prophesy?" (3.8); and he claimed: "God took me from behind the flock and said to me: Go, prophesy to my people Israel" (7.15). And there were others like Amos but none with such clarity as Jeremiah. And the most leave us quite in the dark. We wonder what proofs better than Jeremiah adduced, those nameless ones called "J" or "D" or "P", could have offered to support their claim that of a truth the Lord sent them, or what any writer—the author of Job, of Proverbs, of Psalm 73, or the nineteenth chapter of Leviticus (they were people, whether or not we know their names)—what else any of them experienced that lent their words authority and themselves conviction. Jeremiah, the articulate prophet, must speak to us for them all.

And lastly now: as rabbis or as candidates for the Reform rabbinate, we ourselves pose a comparable problem. Though we are neither prophets nor prophets' disciples, like Jeremiah we too seek conviction, if not indeed authority. Where are we to find certainty, and what virtue do our words possess that men should lend them credence?

Or, not as rabbis, but simply as Reform Jews, we sometimes wonder: with no dogmatic tests, no catechism, not being told what we must believe, what *do* we believe? What are our own convictions, and what their source, and what their authority, not now for others, but for ourselves? "How am I to know?" we ask, and lo! we are involved in the prophet's quest.

I suppose this final thought is not so much a thought as a question. Can we fight through our doubts, each for himself as our liberal religious orientation demands—a way more difficult than orthodoxy—and by what experience can we find our sure knowledge of God? And by what means can those of us, who may be called to leadership, find the heart to say: Of a truth the Lord hath sent me?

The Prophet as Paradigm

A "paradigm" is a bore we tolerate when we approach a new language by way of deductive grammar; it is a declension of a representative noun or a conjugation of a typical verb, designed to serve as a sample of what normally happens to such vocables in the language under review. A "paradigm" is also, in a broader and less tiresome sense, an example or a standard, as when, for example, one speaks of a Job as a paradigm of virtue wronged: "Have you considered my servant Job? You will find no one like him on earth, a man of blameless and upright life, who fears God and sets his face against wrongdoing" (NEB).

A puzzle which confronts a student of the biblical Book of Jeremiah is the presence in that context of the compositions known to the trade as "confessions." On inspection these "confessions" turn out to be Jeremiah's private prayers and it seems strange to find such personal musings included in a collection of his prophecies. If they appeared in the Book of Psalms, we would undoubtedly wonder about this or that detail, but we would not question their appropriateness in that devotional context.

The obvious difference between the prophecies and the prayers in Jeremiah is the addressee. Predominantly in prophetic literature the speaker is the prophet and he addresses his people—or certain persons among them, a king, a merchant prince, a priest or liar-prophet. To be sure, prophet and God here speak as one; but the addressee is normally people or the people. This is not the case in the prayers. There Jeremiah the prophet speaks for himself only and the addressee is God, his refuge or his adversary. It is a private matter between them—Jeremiah and God—and we hardly expect to find it reported along with the prophecies. Moreover, what the prophet says to his God is not in the public domain. No one else was there, and if Jeremiah had not himself put his words on record we would have no access to them.[1]

Why did Jeremiah tell his prayers? I suggest that in doing so he made of himself a paradigm.

In essence the confessions are prayers, and the one praying is Jeremiah. Until recent times these two statements were unchallenged assumptions; today they are questioned.

The confessions under consideration are those usually so called: parts of Jeremiah 11; 12; 15; 17; 18 and 20.[2] We must say: they are prayers "in essence," because in two of the confessions a prefatory verse[3] introduces the prayer itself, and because a response[4] follows close on three of the prayers—and implicitly a fourth (20:11)—but the confessions are essentially prayers. These prefatory verses and discovered responses are intimately linked to the respective prayers in thought or phrase. A "therefore so God says" (לכן כה אמר יהוה) joins 11:21–23 to the foregoing prayer and promises the precise vindication which the prayer demands. The symmetry in 11:20 and 22 corresponds to the symmetry in 20:10 and 11. In the former, the promise: "I will punish them" (הנני פוקד עליהם, v. 22) is an orderly response to the plea: "Let me see your vengeance on them" (אראה נקמתך מהם, v. 20), and in the latter, the assurance "But God is with me... therefore my persecutors will stumble and fail" (על כן רודפי יכשלו ולא יוכלו . . . ויהוה אותי, v. 11) properly balances—even with a form of the same verb—the complaint: "(They say) 'Perhaps we can beguile and overpower him'" (אולי יפתה ונוכלה לו, v. 10). Incidentally this comparison is particularly instructive, suggesting the route by which the answer comes to one who prays. The response in 20:11 is only implicit; it is not introduced as in 11:21 by a "Therefore so God says." It is a "this-I-know" conclusion. The speaker simply concludes his prayer with the serene assurance that he has been heard, God is with him. He does not need to be told; he knows.

In the confessions in chs. 15 and 12 we note again the symmetry between plea and response. In the one, the response (15:19–20) is linked to the prayer with a "Therefore so God says," while no such phrase joins 12:5 to the prayer in vv. 1–4. The prayer is over. "You" is no longer God in v. 5: "Running with men you get all worn out; how, then, will you race with horses? If only in a land at peace you could feel safe, how will you do in Jordan's dense thicket?" This is as surely a response to the preceding prayer as is the one explicitly so labeled in 15:19–20.

The symmetry here in chs. 15 and 12 is also obvious, but it is on a level different from that of the preceding pair. The response now is not supportive and reassuring. God does not here promise ruin for the adversaries, vindication for the petitioner; he makes new demands, tightens the reins. But rebuke is an appropriate response to both prayers. The speaker has said to God: "Know that for your sake I have borne disgrace" (15:15), "I sat alone because of your irresistable power" (15:17), "You indeed behave towards me as a deceptive stream, as undependable waters" (15:18)—to which evasive tactics ("copping out") the response attributed to God seems a proper reaction: "Therefore so God said: 'If you come back I will receive you; you may minister to me.'" In ch. 12 the rebuke already quoted (v. 5) follows the expression of similarly evasive sentiments. The speaker points the finger at God, an arbitrary power: "You have to be in the right, O Lord, if I argue with you," he says; "nevertheless I must bring certain cases to your attention," and then as in ch. 15 he claims that justice is awry and God has let him down. Hence the discovered response.

As the three responses, and the fourth, are linked with the prayers, so also are the two prefatory sentences, 15:10 and 18:18. These are joined by common matter with the prayers they introduce. Before the petitioner turns in prayer to his God in 15:11 he complains to his mother about his bitter lot. Before he condemns his adversaries and demands justice of God in 18:19–23 he describes in 18:18 their reprehensible behavior, the occasion for his prayer. We therefore join to the prayers, for the exploration to follow, these prefatory verses as well as the responses. When we speak of "confessions," these are what we mean.

The prayers are prayers, and the human component in the dialogue (prayer and divine response) is a prophet, Jeremiah.

The prayers are prayers. A man speaks to God, puts into words his intimate concerns, pleads with his lord and defender, and waits. We find this sense in all six of these prayers. In each confession, at the outset (twice following a prefatory verse), in the opening words of his prayer, the man calls on God by name (with a vocative: "Lord"—יהוה) and continues then to address him with second person pronouns: "you."[5] He tells his story, says in declarative sentences why he needs God's understanding and help: "I have stood before you to speak good on their behalf." "They have dug a pit to take me." He asks God to intervene, addressing him now in the imperative mood or with a rhetorical equivalent: "Give heed to me," "Deal with them," "Is good to be rewarded with evil?" And he voices his confidence in the God to whom he directs his plea: "You are the object of my praise . . . my refuge in a day of distress." Each of the prayers has the form and features of prayer[6]—not of prophecy.

We are assuming that these prayers belong to Jeremiah. Not all scholars agree. We are assuming that they are personal prayers. Not all agree.

As to the first assumption, it is true that prophets rarely address God in prayer or engage him in dialogue. They do so in a prophet's intercessory plea in time of national crisis (Amos 7:1—6), or in a vision narrative, the prophet's claim to authenticity (Isa. 6; Jer. 1), and occasionally besides. As we have mentioned, the place to expect such prayers is the Book of Psalms, and there is a marked resemblance between certain psalms and the prayers of Jeremiah. Since Hermann Gunkel's basic work on psalm typology,[7] scholars have recognized the undeniably close relationship between the prayers of Jeremiah and the "Klagelieder des Einzelnen"[8]—the individual laments among the Psalms. Those prayers and these laments correspond feature by feature, sometimes in language as well as vocabulary, and the question is not whether, but how, they are related. The relationship is not necessarily one of dependency. Neither Jeremiah nor the author of a psalm of this type in the Book of Psalms is clearly imitating the other. In form and language roughly, and in intent undoubtedly, the lament antedates both Jeremiah and the psalmists. The presence of Babylonian equivalents[9] attests to the antiquity of the form, and Ugaritic parallels are evidence for the age of the language.[10] Both Jeremiah and the authors of the Psalms may well have followed ancient patterns—assuming that Jeremiah is the author of the prayers attributed to him in his book.

Gustav Hölscher is a forthright representative of scholars who would deny the confessions to Jeremiah. He collided with Gunkel. Hölscher's work *Die Profeten* appeared in 1914. That was the first year of World War I. Another German scholar, Hans Schmidt, was occupied on the Eastern front, so that Hermann Gunkel "in herzlichen Bereitschaft" wrote the three "Introductions" to Schmidt's *Die Grossen Propheten* to appear in 1915. Gunkel and Hölscher did not agree. Hölscher denied the confessions to Jeremiah: these "psalmartige Dichtungen" were "sekundäre Stücke."[11] Gunkel deplored this recent trend in Jeremiah scholarship: "Ebenso irrig ist es freilich, wenn man neuerdings diese Lieder des Jeremia, die sich so eigentümlich mit den Psalmen berühren, für unecht erklärt hat."[12] In a second edition (1923, LXI) he named names: the recent author of the false opinion was "G. Hölscher."

Against Hölscher, Gunkel held that this most individual of all prophets, Jeremiah, found at hand for his personal need a new literary form, the individual lament.[13] Jeremiah was not the father of this form (common in Psalms and already known to the Babylonians and Egyptians); he merely adopted it. For his prayers he shaped the form to his needs; the prayers are his own.

Scholars before Hölscher had denied not the totality, but parts of these prayers to Jeremiah. B. Duhm had insisted that Jeremiah could not have harbored such thoughts of vengeance as appear in 11:21−23; 17:18 and 18:21−23.[14] These passages (but curiously not 12:3b or 15:15)[15] were supplied by a later reader who did not share the prophet's true spirit. At the same time as Hölscher, Buttenwieser maintained Duhm's less radical view, saying of Jer. 18:21−23: Jeremiah "certainly could not give vent to such implacable and fanatic hatred."[16] Referring to Duhm's position, George Adam Smith[17] observes: "In contrast with its boldness in textual criticism a curious timidity of sentiment has set through recent O. T. scholarship in Germany from which the older German scholars were free." The writings of Knobel,[18] Graf,[19] Keil,[20] and especially Graf suggest that they were somewhat less squeamish, but it is also proper to note that even as Smith was publishing this observation, Hans Schmidt[21] was repeating in a second edition (1923) his earlier observation about prophets: They are passionate men, hating and loving, subject to error and failure. . . They are no saints, but for that very reason they are guides for those who seek. Also Volz, a little later,[22] could not take exception to Jeremiah's "so humanly comprehensible" indignation. Contemporary scholarship is similarly willing to let Jeremiah react in human fashion to the indignities he suffered.

I am glad to find myself in agreement with James Muilenburg who counts the "confessional laments" among the passages which may "with some confidence" be assigned to Jeremiah "unglossed."[23] In the context of this volume I am especially glad to accept J. Philip Hyatt's thought that one factor enabling Jeremiah to maintain his sanity was the circumstance that "he did not hesitate to give vent to his feelings of despair and bitterness."[24]

As a matter of fact, these vindictive cries are so dominantly characteristic of the individual lament[25] that if they were absent from Jeremiah's prayer-laments we would probably insist that some editor had expunged them to clear Jeremiah's character of such "un-Christian" thoughts. Jeremiah was not so free of literary convention that he could ignore the pressure to include in a lament a demand for the humiliation of his adversaries and the vindication of God and his own self.

Moreover, although Jeremiah did not invent the private lamentation, he gave it a distinctive flavor. He did not simply use the form, he personalized it. Far more clearly than in the Psalter, the prayers in Jeremiah partake of the nature of a plaintiff's plea in a court of justice. In quite the same way as a wronged man would approach a human court in Bible times, Jeremiah approaches God as his judge. We do find this concept in the Psalms; there too God is judge of all the earth and the Psalmist calls on him for justice.[26] But the words and phrases with a legal flavor are nowhere so abundant as they are in Jeremiah's confessions.[27] This is one distinctive feature.

Another concerns the identity of the plaintiff and his adversaries. Attempts to identify the "enemy" in the Psalter founder; the language is simply conventional, stereotyped. The enemy there is the "bad guy." So too the psalmist, the speaker, lacks identity and his cause for lamentation is one of a selection of standard complaints.[28] Like all summary statements, these concerning the psalmist and his "enemy" present an oversimplification—but they are right when they are balanced against the Jeremianic confessions.

We should not overstate the case for the Jeremiah material. For his prayers Jeremiah does adopt the inherited form and he freely employs the conventional phrases.[29] And yet he builds himself and his trials into his prayers; his adversaries (unnamed) are more than conventional expressions. When we read the confessions in the context of the considerable biographical information which the book of Jeremiah provides, we can with a degree of assurance identify the speaker, and to some extent the adversaries as well. The interlocutors in the confessions are a person and God, and the person is a prophet, and the prophet is Jeremiah. Gunkel lists in a footnote[30] the most obvious marks of identification: "As God's mouth" (15:19),[31] "to stand before God" (18:20), "Anathoth" (11:21, 23) and "Jeremiah" (18:18). The list could be longer: "You shall not prophesy" (11:21), "We will smite him on the tongue and hear no more of his words" (18:18), "They say to me: 'Where is this word of God? Let it come to pass'" (17:15), "When your words presented themselves I devoured them; your word was a pleasure to me" (15:16), "You filled me with indignation" (15:17), "The word of the Lord has become for me a constant source of shame and disgrace" (20:8), "If I say: 'I will not . . . speak any more in his name' it is in me as a raging fire" (20:9), "I stood before you to speak good on their behalf" (18:20; cf. 15:19), "I have interceded with you" (15:11). The man of the prayers is consistently the injured prophet, the prophet from Anathoth, Jeremiah—consistently, except that being Jeremiah,[32] he also twice refers to himself in his prayers as interceding for his people. He is not faceless.

His enemies, too, are persons, the jeering crowd, the men of Anathoth, the Pashhurs (20:1) and Hananiahs (28:1) and all the other named and unnamed opponents of the prophet in the biographical matter. Attempts[33] to attach each of the confessions to a particular event in the lifetime of the prophet are hazardous, to say the least, yet the confessions are clearly not unrelated to their narrative context and the persona of the prayers are real persons. We cannot agree with the Hölscher school who see in the confessions only misplaced psalms, interpolations in the book of Jeremiah.

Unlike Hölscher, Henning Graf Reventlow[34] has sought not to excise the confessions, in whole or in part, but to convert them. They undergo a sea change and become liturgies. Jeremiah speaks in them but not as a messenger-prophet; he prays, but not on his behalf. Instead, he plays an intercessory role, laying his people's concerns before God. A confession is in fact "eine Klageliturgie, in der ein repräsentativer einzelner, der Prophet, als Vorbeter und Fürbitter die Not des Volkes vor Gott bringt."[35] The erroneously so-called "confessions," he argues, say next to nothing about Jeremiah the prophet, his pain, his love, his indignation—only that as a שליח ציבור he approaches God on behalf of his people.

Now, prophetic literature is not entirely void of occasions where prophets display an intercessory capacity. Twice when Amos sees in visions disaster sweeping over Jacob, he intercedes and averts the catastrophe (7:1–3, 4–6); Ezekiel twice approaches God with a similar plea (9:8; 11:13); on two occasions the king or people of Judah appeal to Jeremiah to exercise his intercessory function in their time of doubt (21:2; 42:2f.); twice Jeremiah mentions the circumstance that God forbade his interceding (7:16; 14:11), implying that otherwise he would speak for the nation; and twice in the confessions themselves he reminds God that, with or without permission, he has interceded for his people (15:11b; 18:20). Intercession was undoubtedly a prophetic function; the only question is whether that is Jeremiah's activity in the confessions. Is he there a cultic functionary representing the community in a public liturgy, as Reventlow would have it? Or is he himself, the prophet, bringing his personal grief to the attention of his God and seeking relief and vindication?

Reventlow deals with four of the six listed confessions[36] and he labels three of these four without question prophetic liturgies. The three are 15:10—21; 17:12—18 and 12:1—5. He is less certain about the fourth: 11:18—20; 12:6; 11:21—23. He does not make his case without effort. Embarrassing terms and phrases[37] confront him, and to make any kind of a case he must frequently resort to a forced exegesis. It takes strenuous mental gymnastics to make of the messenger prophet Jeremiah a cult functionary and to convert his prayers into prophetic liturgies.

Two capable recent works have given Reventlow's proposal the attention it deserves; an essay by John Bright[38] and a book by John M. Berridge.[39] Bright concludes (p. 214) that Reventlow "arrives at his conclusions only by forcing or ignoring evidence." Berridge (p. 210) rejects Reventlow's view that the "I" of the confessions is no more than "the embodiment of the community which the prophet Jeremiah, as the holder of a cultic office, represents." On the contrary, he notes "numerous expressions of a self-conscious individual who bore the name Jeremiah." To this we would add the thought that if the pieces of a chapter which includes a confession do build up to a liturgy as Reventlow contends, the arrangement of the pieces is the work of a liturgist, not of Jeremiah.

Except for the view of Hölscher which, by denying that Jeremiah wrote the confessions, removes them entirely as a source for the understanding of the man Jeremiah, Gerstenberger[40] goes farthest, in his treatment of Jeremiah 15:10—21 and his closing questions there: "Can the other individual complaints in Jer also be explained as compositive elements in some larger textual unit? Can the complaints in Jer thus be shown to be later insertions into an existing collection of prophecies?" (p. 408). Gerstenberger's conclusion goes beyond Reventlow. Their works appeared in the same year (1963), and I have seen no evidence that either was acquainted with the other's views. They go a long way together but Gerstenberger goes farther. Both interpret the confession in Ch. 15 as a prophetic liturgy, but whereas Reventlow holds that Jeremiah is the author and (in his role as cult functionary) the reader of the liturgy, Gerstenberger holds that the whole liturgy is a compilation by a liturgically oriented Deuteronomist (pp. 407f.). Gerstenberger's, too, is a forced interpretation.

I cannot speak for Phil Hyatt but, as for myself, despite Reventlow and Gerstenberger, I am unreconstructed and still see personal prayers and the answers to prayers in the confessions of Jeremiah. These are available as primary literary sources for the understanding of Jeremiah, the messenger prophet.

The problem that I still face is how to account for the presence of these "documents of self-revelation"[41] in their prophetic context. Berridge (who asks the same question) answers: "Each 'confession' has more than merely a private validity" (p. 158), and he refers to von Rad,[42] and also to Stoebe[43] whom he quotes (p. 157) to the effect that the confessions "im Bewusstsein Jeremias eine über die eigene Erfahrung hinausgehende Allgemeingültigkeit gehabt haben müssen." Somewhat earlier Martin Buber asked our question in this form: ". . . why does he make known to us complaints and pleadings, and even resentments and shouts of vengeance?" "Obviously," he continued, "because he thinks all these supra-personally important."[44]

What renders them especially important to a prophet like Jeremiah is the fact that at the end of several of the prayers there came to him what he hears as a divine response, a communication,[45] an oracle. Such communications are, of course, the impulse which sends a prophet on his prophetic way; when he is the recipient of the word, he wearies himself in vain to contain it (Jer. 20:9). At the first God had said to him: "Whatever I command you you shall speak," and had put words in his mouth (1:7, 9; cf. 26:12). Undoubtedly the responses to his prayers, a renewal of the original impulse, were a quantity that lent his confessions significance—more than personal significance. We assume that it was these responses which prompted Jeremiah to share with his people his unshared prayer experience. God's word to him was a word for them. Berridge [46] puts forward "the thesis that Jeremiah's 'confessions' were . . . spoken in public, constituting part of his proclamation"—his "proclamation," the message which he, the prophet, must bring. Whether or not Jeremiah indeed spoke his prayers "in public," which seems improbable, Berridge is right that these answers were what prompted him to somehow get the confessions into the record.

A passage in Jer. 16 is a prime example of a word to the prophet which, though personal, had more than private significance. This passage should now open the way to the theme: prophet as paradigm.[47] Here preparing to make public what he had heard, he says: "The word of the Lord came to me (ויהי דבר יהוה אלי, v. 1)" and then continues with the word: "You shall not marry and have children in this place." It is a private word, having to do with his private life, but as he develops the thought it reeks with shuddering dread. "For so the Lord said of children born in this place and their parents in this land: They shall die diseased and lie unburied like dung on the ground, be ravaged by sword and famine, food for carrion birds and beasts." The private word has implications broad as the land, and Jeremiah, advised not to marry and beget, has become a paradigm for the people. The pattern appears three times within the first nine verses of this chapter: private word and its broad implications, the prophet a paradigm. Here follows the third, a further word to Jeremiah (vv. 8f.): "A house of feasting too you shall not enter, to sit with them to eat or drink." And then its application: "In this place, before your eyes in your own time, I will bring to a close the sounds of joy and mirth, the sounds of bridegroom and bride." With the mention of marriage in the concluding phrases, the thought returns to the beginning of the passage and Jeremiah's private life. He serves as analogy and paradigm, and it is for such a purpose that he makes public what might be regarded as nobody's business.

Jeremiah was not the first prophet to use his marriage (or failure to marry) as an analogy. In an earlier century Hosea, to whom Jeremiah is otherwise kin, starts with similar words: "The Lord said to me" (ויאמר יהוה אלי), and proceeds to publish God's instructions to him in person: "Again go, love a woman, unfaithful and adulterous" (Hos.

3:1), a private matter which he lets stand as a paradigm for the relation between God and Israel.

Jeremiah's contemporary, Ezekiel, quite consciously acts out his analogies, and incidentally supplies a Hebrew equivalent for our word "paradigm." In his marathon lying on public display, first on one side unturned and then on the other, he paradigmatically represents the slow discharge of Israel's guilt, and of Judah's.[48] He does not here vicariously "bear the iniquity of the house of Israel" (ונשאת עון בית ישראל), he makes of himself a paradigm. His performance in 5:1—5, the treatment of his shaven hair, a paradigm for the fate awaiting Jerusalem's inhabitants (זאת ירושלים, "this is Jerusalem," v. 5) is similar; and 12:1—14 is an explicit example which reveals the Hebrew term for his device: In their rebellious mood, the people close out the sights and sounds which might otherwise instruct them (v. 2), and to convey his message the prophet must find a new medium. He enacts in person "before their eyes"[49] the stages of the disaster—the defeat and exile—which he knows to be in store for Jerusalem. He does this publicly, properly expecting his public to demand an explanation. When they do so he is to say: "(I am glad you asked me) אני מופתכם, I am your paradigm. What I have done will be done to them.[50] They will experience captivity and exile" (12:11). In this context the word מופת ("sign," "token," "omen," "portent") seems to have the meaning we here give to the term "paradigm." It has this meaning in Ezek. 24, where again, like Jeremiah and Hosea, Ezekiel involves his public in matters related to his own marriage. At the death of his wife he omits signs and rites of mourning. When he is asked, as was to be expected, to explain the omission, he develops his implicit analogy, equating the death of his wife, the delight of his eyes, with the destruction of the Jerusalem sanctuary, the people's joy. Then God draws the conclusion: "Ezekiel shall serve you as a paradigm (למופת); all that he did you will do" (vv. 15—24). Ezekiel goes a step beyond Hosea and Jeremiah; in these and other presentations he adds a visual element.[51] The people have eyes. If they were willing they could see. Jeremiah is subtler. He only puts on record his confessions. These must suggest the message to such as can read.

Did an event in Jeremiah's life with Baruch dispose Jeremiah to preserve his confessions? Imagine the prophet and his disciple sitting quietly alone. Jeremiah hears the young man sigh. He looks at him and Baruch speaks: "Alas! and Woe! God has added misery to my pain; I am worn out with sighing and find no respite." Jeremiah reflects. The complaint is familiar. Has he himself not given voice to such impatient despair? Repeatedly he had laid his own grief before God in reproachful lamentation. His friend is only mirroring his mood. What comfort now can he bring to Baruch? What comfort indeed had his praying brought him? The distilled essence of what Jeremiah learned in prayer is what he now offers as God's word to Baruch: "What I, myself built I am about to demolish. I am about to uproot what I planted. Would you seek advancement? Desist! I will bring disaster to all flesh, God says, but I will give you your life as reward wherever you go" (Jer. 45). This much Jeremiah says to Baruch. His overtones convey a further query, and a thought: Have you really such good reason, friend, to be so sorry for yourself? Did you suppose it would be easy? We must carry on.

As he replied to Baruch, did Jeremiah open wide his eyes, recognizing a broad truth?

Had he suddenly caught sight of the paradigmatic nature of his own experience with God? He saw meaning in that encounter for Baruch; could it be helpful to his whole people? It is hazardous to weave history with slender threads; we may be writing fiction. Yet the possibility exists that, moved by some such reflections as these, Jeremiah first recorded his meetings with God in prayer, putting his prayers in words, perhaps for Baruch to intersperse among his prophecies, perhaps even communicating them by word of mouth—prayer plus discovered response—to some gathering of persons like the elders of Judah who sat before Ezekiel.[52] This proposal may stand as an alternative to the Hölscher-type interpolation theory,[53] or the confession-as-prophetic-liturgy explanation of Reventlow[54] or Gerstenberger.[55] It is like, but not identical with, the confession-as-proclamation hypothesis of Berridge.[56] It emphasizes the paradigmatic nature of the confessions, comparable with, but more subtle than, the acted-out communication of Ezekiel.[57]

There is no apparent logic in the distribution of these pieces across the chapters of Jeremiah's book—just as there is none for the distribution of the other literary units in chs. 1 to 20. Nor are the six confessions arranged in any meaningful order, except perhaps that the first three, in chs. 11; 12 and 15, are in the form of dialogue: prayers complete with discovered responses, while the second three, in chs. 17; 18 and 20, are monologic. I am not willing to guess at the significance of this observation, if indeed there is any.

Putting on record his confessions, Jeremiah set in motion the process by which he became a paradigm. The theme of prophet as paradigm does not end with Jeremiah and Ezekiel. The writer known as the Second Isaiah and the author of the book of Jonah carried it on, developed it further.

According to what is, in my opinion,[58] the most satisfying interpretation of the "servant" figure, the Servant of God is

> a personification
> of the people Israel,
> as a prophet
> after the manner of Jeremiah.

The servant is not a person, but a personification, a figure of speech. Second Isaiah was a master at the craft of personification. Babylon becomes for him a pampered queen (Isa. 47) and Zion climbs her high hill and raises her voice with glad tidings (40:9). The servant figure is an extended sample of his art.

The servant of God is his people Israel personified, an ethnic community given a corporate personality, a people with assigned work to do, therefore a "servant."

Israel's mission is so like that of a prophet that the servant's features are the features of a prophet: an ear to hear, a mouth to speak and a message to bring to the nations, prophetic תורה to impart to the peoples of the earth. Like certain prophets the servant is exposed as well to all the tribulations of a truth speaker.

The prophet-servant figure so resembles the prophet Jeremiah in one particular after another that without a doubt the Second Isaiah chose, as paradigm for the servant, the life and work of Jeremiah. He obviously had before him the book of Jeremiah, whether in written form or as oral tradition. His source included the confessions along with the third person narratives, and he found just there the model for the figure of his "servant," a man whose life experience matched his people's lot and destiny.[59]

There is so clear a correspondence between the servant and Jeremiah that this conclusion is safe. The implications of the conclusion bear intimately on our theme. Second Isaiah did not overlook the meaning of the confessions among the Jeremianic matter. He sensed their paradigmatic purport. Possibly Ezekiel's way of employing his personal behavior as a paradigm for his people's fate helped Deutero-Isaiah make the connection between prophet and Israel[60]—although it is not Ezekiel but Jeremiah who sits for the portrait of the servant. We cannot say who first perceived why Jeremiah put down for the record his dialogic encounters with God; the reason for his doing so may have been quite obvious to the prophet's disciples, those responsible for the preservation of his words. But it is Second Isaiah, two generations after Jeremiah, who clearly articulated, effectively employed, broadened and transmitted the theme of prophet as paradigm. He was not the last to do so in the Bible.

The author of the book of Jonah put the theme in story form. Jonah, in the title role, is a prophet, like prophets told to go, sent to make proclamation, his destination a distant land, his aim to avert a national calamity. But Jonah demurs; he goes, but in the wrong direction, runs away, putting into action Jeremiah's unacknowledged craving. God counters Jeremiah's craving with a rebuke: "If you come back—," "How will you do in Jordan's dense thicket?" After the truant Jonah he sends a storm and a fish. And Jeremiah sobered, and Jonah redirected, again assume the mantle of prophecy, Jeremiah to be God's mouth and to speak to Jerusalem, Jonah to go and proclaim the doom of Nineveh.

The author of Jonah appears to reach back to the paradigmatic prophet Jeremiah and his dialogic prayers. But to get to Jeremiah he had to look past Second Isaiah, and this has affected his vision: Jonah is as much a "servant" as he is a Jeremiah. Like the עבד, Jonah is a prophet as paradigm. He stands for the generation of Israel whom the author of Jonah knew as contemporaries. And the story calls the people back to their destined mission to the nations, the Ninevehs of the world. Jonah dramatizes the prophet-as-paradigm theme, announced by Jeremiah and incarnated by Second Isaiah.[61]

If one were inclined to ask what place an essay on the prophet as paradigm has in a volume on Old Testament ethics, the key word in the answer might be "responsibility." What Jeremiah learned in his dialogue with God had to do with individual responsibility. It did not relieve him of his duties; it returned him to his task, impressed him with the need to subordinate private peace and comfort to the broader goals. His being chosen as a prophet yielded him a certain assurance of divine concern so that he might well expect to survive and do God's work, but this choice entailed no warrant that the going would be easy. Jeremiah's word of spare comfort to Baruch had the same intent—if anything it is still more direct: "Would you seek advancement? Desist; . . . I will give you your life as reward," but no more. In the chapters in Isaiah God amply reassures his prophet-people Israel—consolation is the prime ingredient in the proclamation of Second Isaiah—but we note, of course, that the people is personified as "servant," chosen to serve, assigned a task and sent on a broad mission. And finally, Jonah is depicted as one who suffers but survives. I have been translating ההיטב חרה לך in Jonah 4:4 and 9: "Are you very angry?" But the NEB gets just the right amount of casual irony into God's voice with its reading: "'Are you so angry?' said the Lord." The point of the paradigm may be just there: "Are you so angry?" Who said it would be easy?

(1) And I would not be writing this paper as tribute to a man (J. Philip Hyatt) for whose insights I am grateful and whose admiration for the man Jeremiah I share.

(2) Meaning specifically: 1) 11:18−23 with 12:6 added after 11:18; 2) 12:1−5; 3) 15:10−11 plus vv. 15−20; 4) 17:14−18; 5) 18:18−23; 6) 20:7−11. I dealt with aspects of this material in a paper entitled "The Confessions of Jeremiah and the Meaning of Prayer," *HUCA*, 21 (1948), 331−354, and then more fully in *Jeremiah Man and Prophet*, 1961.

(3) 15:10 and 18:18.

(4) 11:21−23; 12:5; 15:19−20.

(5) It is only in 20:7b−10 that he adopts the oblique form of meditative prayer.

(6) Not that these features appear in a fixed order; the address does come among the opening words of the prayer, but otherwise the elements freely mingle.

(7) *Einleitung in die Psalmen*, 1966.

(8) Gunkel, *Einleitung*, 172−265.

(9) Literature listed in Gunkel, *Einleitung*, 6f.

(10) Matitiahu Tsevat, *A Study of the Language of Biblical Psalms*, SBL Monograph 9, 1955, 47−51, 57f.

(11) Hölscher, *Profeten*, 394.

(12) Schmidt, *Die Grossen Propheten*, 1915, LXIV.

(13) Schmidt, *Propheten*, 1923, LXI.

(14) Bernhard Duhm, *Das Buch Jeremia*, 1901, 158f.

(15) Duhm, *Jeremia*, 115, 135.

(16) Moses Buttenwieser, *The Prophets of Israel*, 1914, 112.

(17) *Jeremiah*, 1923, 330 n. 2.

(18) August Knobel, *Der Prophetismus der Hebräer*, 2, 1837, 263.

(19) K. H. Graf, *Der Prophet Jeremia*, 1862, 269.

(20) Carl F. Keil, *Bibl. Comm. über den Propheten Jeremia*, 1872, 225.

(21) *Propheten*, 1923, 275; 1915, 269.

(22) Paul Volz, *Der Prophet Jeremia*, 1928, 200f.

(23) "Jeremiah the Prophet" in *IDB* II, 1962, 832, 824.

(24) *IB*, V, 1956, 783.

(25) Cf. Pss. 7:16f. (Eng. 15f); 28:4f.; 35:4−8; 69:23−29 (22−28); 109:7−20 (6−19); et al.

(26) Pss. 9:17(16); 58:12(11); 94:2; 35:1; 109:7(6).

(27) For a detailed development of this observation, see my *Jeremiah*, 112−128, especially 119−121.

(28) Cf. Laurance A. Martin, *A Study of the Individual Psalms of Lament* (Unpublished Dissertation, Hebrew Union College), 1972, 157, 217f.

(29) The uninhibited cursing of one's enemies may have been the routine and conventional thing to do—especially, we may suppose, if one was trying to influence the court.

(30) In Schmidt's, *Die Grossen Propheten* (1923), LXI n. 5.

(31) On the expression כפי תהיה, see n. 37 below.

(32) Who did on occasion "stand before" God to present to him his people's need (21:2; 42:2f.).

33) Like those of Moses Buttenwieser, *The Prophets of Israel*, pp. 89f.

(34) *Liturgie und prophetisches Ich bei Jeremia*, 1963.

(35) Reventlow, *Liturgie*, 225.

(36) Pp. 205−257. He does not analyze the two in chs. 18 and 20.

(37) He finds כפי תהיה in 15:19 troublesome (pp. 226—228).

(38) "Jeremiah's Complaints: Liturgy or Expressions of Personal Distress?" in *Proclamation and Presence, Old Testament Essays in Honour of Gwynne Henton Davies*, ed. by Durham & Porter, 1970, 189—214.

(39) Prophet, People, and the Word of Yahweh, *An Examination of Form and Content in the Proclamation of the Prophet Jeremiah*, 1970. Cf. also Georg Fohrer, *Introduction to the Old Testament*, 1968, 395.

(40) Erhard Gerstenberger, "Jeremiah's Complaints. Observations on Jer. 15:10—21," *JBL*, 82 (1963), 393—408.

(41) S. Blank, *Jeremiah*, 65 ff.

(42) *Theologie* 2, 212 (ff).

(43) Hans Joachim Stoebe, "Seelsorge und Mitleiden bei Jeremia," *WuD* 4, 131.

(44) *The Prophetic Faith*, 1960, 180 (first English edition 1949).

(45) See above, pp. 23f.

(46) *Prophet*, 157.

(47) I had chosen the theme and title of this paper before I came upon the word "paradigmatic" in von Rad, *Theologie*, 2, 216; Gerstenberger ("Complaints," 407); and Berridge (*Prophet*, 148). I am glad for the company.

(48) Ezek. 4:4—6 plus 8.

(49) The phrase לעיניהם occurs here no fewer than 7 times in the compass of 5 vv. (12:3—7).

(50) Note Isa. 8:18, where the prophet and his sons are called מופתים.—The unexpected change from second to third person is in confused recognition of the fact that God is still instructing Ezekiel concerning his reply to "them."

(51) He becomes the very model of a maker of metaphors, a ממשל משלים, 21:5 (20:49).

(52) As in Ezek. 8:1; 20:7; cf. 33:30f.

(53) See above, pp. 25—27.

(54) See above pp. 27f.

(55) See above, p. 28.

(56) See above, pp. 28f.

(57) See above, p. 30.

(58) I have defended the opinion in *Prophetic Faith in Isaiah*, 1958, 49—160.

(59) See Blank, *Ibid.* 77 and 100—104. My observations were anticipated in part by Otto Eissfeldt, *Der Gottesknecht bei Deuterojesaja*, 1933, who lists on pp. 16ff. some of the contacts between the servant and Jer. which I have listed on pp. 101—104 and in the pertinent footnotes 54 to 70 on pp. 218—220. The tenth century Jewish philosopher Saadia reputedly went the whole way and identified the servant as the prophet Jeremiah himself; cf. S. R. Driver and Adolf Neubauer, *The Fifty-third Chapter of Isaiah according to the Jewish Interpreters*, I, 1876, 43 and II, 1877, 19.

(60) At least for certain other insights Second Isaiah was indebted to the writings of Ezekiel; cf. Blank, *Isaiah*, 123—132.

(61) See Blank, *Understanding the Prophets*, 1969, 129—138.

The Dawn of Our Responsibility

Mr. Chairman, Miss Montagu, Mr. President, my rabbinical colleagues, ladies and gentlemen:

Without apology I propose to speak on the Book of Jonah. I shall have something to say also on the intimately related subject of Human Responsibility but I propose to approach that latter subject by way of the Book of Jonah.

The Book of Jonah calls for no apology. Its author lifts prophetic thought to its highest peak. First, then, the Book of Jonah.

If I say "the Book of Jonah" and not "the prophet Jonah", that is because the two are not identical, as some of you will know. It is indeed no disgrace if you do not know it, but they are not the same. There was a real historical prophet Jonah, son of Amittai, from Gath ha-Hepher, about whom no one knows much and most know nothing—and that does not matter, because his significance was ephemeral; he did not write the Book of Jonah.

The Book of Kings refers briefly to that real or historical Jonah of only passing significance. A contemporary of Amos and Hosea, he lived in the eighth pre-Christian century when Jeroboam II was Israel's king, but unlike Amos and Hosea he foretold great victories for Israel's arms, speaking as a willing prophet, a client of his king. When we have said this much we have said all that any of us know about the historical prophet Jonah.

The author of the Book of Jonah adopted him, and about him he spun his deservedly famous yarn. Few remember today that ancient servant of God and king, the willing prophet who promised victory to Jeroboam. The legend swallowed him whole, and the Jonah whom all men know is the surly unheroic hero of the Book of Jonah, associated in most people's minds with a providential whale.

The Book of Jonah—it is of that we speak—uses the forgotten Jonah; it makes of him a man, a Jew, who seeks to elude his destiny in vain and learns about the size of God.

The Book of Jonah may be described as a *mashal*, the kind of *mashal* or "comparison" that was in later centuries to become characteristic of the Jewish midrash. In the midrash, in order to illustrate his point, in order to make concrete his abstract thought, the *darshan* or "preacher" told a story. Not uncommonly he introduced as fictional characters, an ordinary human king, a *melech basar va-dam*, and the king's son or the king's servant, and for his homiletical purpose let them stand for God and Israel. Preparing the way for the later midrash, that is what the preacher did who wrote the Book of Jonah. In his *mashal* God alone is not a metaphor. In his story God is God—but Jonah ben Amittai is no prophet—not in any narrow sense a prophet—he is the people of Israel entrusted with a prophetic task; he is men of any color called to serve; he is any man, "everyman"; he is we. In the *mashal* the city Nineveh is no longer the cruel seat of the ruthless Assyrian Empire. For the preacher's purpose it is simply a foreign place, a

Read at the 12th International Conference of the World Union for Progressive Judaism, London, 1961.

remote place, neither friend nor enemy, a place of men: India, China, Spain, the Congo—anywhere where men are in need. The time of the story is neither the fifth nor the eighth pre-Christian century. Neither the author's time nor the time of Tiglath-Pileser III, Jeroboam II and the historical Jonah ben Amittai; it is the once-upon-a-time time, any time, our time. Tarshish is not a Mediterranean port significant for itself; it is anywhere—anywhere but the right place; it is the opposite direction, the direction a man takes when he turns his back on his destiny, the direction we take when we turn our back on our destiny. The "great fish" is no whale, no known or unidentified, extinct or mythological monster of the sea, it is whatever keeps a people on its course, whatever prevents a man from running quite away, character, history, "fate" to the Greek, to the Jew—God—a manifestation of God's generous will. And, incidentally, the fish did not appear in order to save Jonah from a watery grave: Jonah did not want to be saved from the sea; Jonah wanted to die. He lived because God needed him; the fish was sent to bring him back to land and set him on his purposed way to Nineveh.

That Jonah did not much want to live is a detail sometimes unnoticed but a detail worth noting. The king and men of Nineveh, the sailors on the ship, desire life—Jonah flees life. As the author of the Book of Jonah characterized him by symbol as well as by word, the prophet-people Jonah showed no will to live. On one occasion Jonah offered himself as sacrifice, saying to the desperate sailors: "Hurl me into the sea"; and twice again, in quite un-Jewish words, he asked for death. When he saw that God had justly and mercifully spared the reformed and penitent people of Nineveh he prayed: "Now Lord, take away my life; it is better that I should die than live"; and another time when the sun beat down upon his head and he felt faint "he asked that he might die, saying 'It is better that I should die than live.'" In words again, when God had asked "Are you very angry because of the gourd?" Jonah replied "Angry to the point of death". Quite as striking as the words which the preacher ascribes to Jonah are the symbols: the hold of the ship, and the belly of the fish. For three days and three nights in the belly of the fish Jonah found security, release from his responsibility. It was, indeed, in search of such a place that he had gone to Joppa, found there a vessel, paid the fare and gone below; there as in the fish, while the storm raged without, Jonah had lain "asleep within the belly of the ship." So, by such words and by such symbols, the author of the Book of Jonah made of him a man or people that preferred death to life, valued "peace of mind" above life's demands.

Leave the characterization of Jonah and turn with me to the other persons of the drama. Jonah is a Jew; he says as much: "I am a Hebrew, and worship the Lord, the God of all the world, who made the sea as well as the land." But Jonah is the only Jew in the story. The others, the king, people (and cattle) of Nineveh, and the sailors and captain on the vessel bound for Tarshish—all these are Gentiles, peoples of the other nations. What are they like? What does the author of the Book of Jonah think of the Gentiles?

The author sees them first of all, as simple people—"simple" in the sense of unlearned, religiously naive, not (like ourselves) the favored custodians of ancient wisdom. That is what he means when he describes the Ninevites as a people "who know not their right hand from their left." They have received no *Torah*, no divine instruction. The author knows about them also that these other men worship other gods, gods other than "the

Lord, the God of all the world." In their extremity, he says, the awe-struck sailors loudly prayed "each to his little god." But a most remarkable feature of the book is the fact that its author regards these naive sailors and these same simple Ninevites as both good and generous, sensitive and openminded. To be sure, the Ninevites had done wrong; it was to announce their punishment that Jonah was sent to them. But they attended the prophet's words and they listened. (In an earlier generation the prophet Ezekiel drew an invidious distinction between the stiff-necked Jews and the Gentiles—if the prophet were sent to the nations they would listen, he implied; not so the Jews.) The king and people of Nineveh did not scoff at Jonah; they listened. In the dynamic sense of the word they "listened"; that is to say: they believed the Lord and prayed mightily to God; and they turned every one from his evil way and cleansed his hands of violence. The author of the Book of Jonah found in Nineveh that kind of listening which Amos and Micah, Isaiah, Jeremiah and Ezekiel sought in their people reputedly in vain. But not only the people of Nineveh; the motley crew of the vessel bound for Tarshish—they too, showed themselves reasonable and generous. One dramatic incident in particular reveals the author's estimate of their nature. The sailors have done all they know how: they have prayed aloud, they have jettisoned the cargo; they have aroused the sleeping Jonah and bid him also pray to his God—and all to no avail. They have consulted and cast lots and discovered that Jonah's offence it was which brought the disaster on them. As the seas raged more and more they had asked: What can we do to still the waves? and Jonah, resigned to death, had said: "You must hurl me into the sea; only then will it be calm. I know that I have caused this storm." Here, if anywhere in the book, the nature of the sailors is revealed. They did not do as Jonah said—not for as long as they could last. They pulled hard at their oars to gain the shore, exhausted their strength to save the life of the very cause of their calamity. Only when they could do no more they yielded and did as Jonah had asked. Then when the miracle ensued, and suddenly the waves were stilled, they feared the Lord. "Then in earnest the men feared the Lord and offered him sacrifices and vowed vows." Still more impressive than their conversion, however, is the humanity which makes them spend their whole strength to reach the shore before they consent to abandon the offending prophet. To the healthy-minded author of the Book of Jonah the nations were both reasonable and worthy—and the Jews' service on their behalf was neither a waste nor unrewarding.

Two further relevant details before we put Jonah to work for the World Union.

Jonah was sent to announce the imminent destruction of Nineveh: "Yet forty days!" Why? Why was Nineveh doomed? Not for the people's neglect of hallowed rituals or the improper performance of such rituals. (The author of Jonah did not expect them to behave in accordance with the Priestly Code.) Not for any affront against the nation Israel. (There is no single allusion here to the invasion of Israel's northern borders or to Sargon's capture of Samaria.) The people of Nineveh were condemned and the city was doomed only because of the presence within their society of crimes against persons. When they listened to Jonah and turned each man from his evil ways, when they committed no more *hamas*, no more "acts of violence," God readily forgave them.

Pity—not resentment, a moral sense—not national indignation, motivated the author of Jonah even as these characteristics had moved the prophet Amos centuries before.

And now, this final note on Jonah—a note upon the nature of God according to the Book of Jonah. The God whom Jonah served (though he served him unwillingly) reached far beyond the borders of Israel. He had made the distant city Nineveh and he cared still what went on there. The remote port of Tarshish also was not beyond his reach. After Jonah had identified himself as a Hebrew he had said: "I worship the Lord, the God of all the world who made the sea as well as the land." It is because his God is moral, just and merciful that Jonah must warn the evildoers; it is because his God knows no national boundaries that Jonah is sent to Nineveh; and it is because his God is the Lord, "who made the sea as well as the dry land" that Jonah can not escape his mission even by way of the sea. Jonah's God is beyond geography.

This basic understanding of the nature of the Book and these keys to its meaning will suggest my reasons for choosing to speak of it on this occasion.

The theme of Jonah, like the theme of this Conference, is Human Responsibility. God sent Jonah—not the historical prophet Jonah but Jonah the symbol for Israel in its prophetic role—God sent his people on a responsible mission. Nowhere more clearly than in Jonah and probably nowhere much earlier than in Jonah has the thought become articulate that Israel is responsible for the Ninevehs of this earth. Our sense of human responsibility dawned with the genius of the Book of Jonah.

Do not count it as a serious digression if I stop a moment here to comment on a word that I have just used. I hope you will not quarrel with me because I say that our sense of human responsibility "dawned" with the Book of Jonah—or, stated more precisely, dawned in the time of the Exile in the mind of the Second Isaiah, soon to shine in all its brilliance in the Book of Jonah. Do you feel compelled to remind me that long before that time—as much as a thousand years before that time—in Ur, in the Land between the Two Rivers, the land that was later to become the land of our people's exile—that there and then in that ancient time God had already appeared to our father Abram and commissioned him: Go forth, and be a blessing? Will you say: Surely not that later, but this earlier event was the dawn of Israel's sense of human responsibility?

If you do so argue, I must say in reply: You are asking a question which has lost its significance. For us, in this context, at this distance, for this age, the question is academic—the question whether we shall ascribe to the middle of the second pre-Christian millennium or to the middle of the first (as I do) the tradition of Abraham's call to become "a light to the nations," to "be a blessing." The question belongs among the "battles long ago." When still we were fighting Orthodoxy it had significance; it had meaning while yet we were defending ourselves against the organized hierarchical variety of Orthodoxy. In fact it still had meaning when we were yet engaged in that war within our separate selves, that struggle to come to terms with the less tangible but more menacing variety of orthodoxy which has no outward institutional reality or manifestation but keeps watch deep within our psyches and has something to do with our grandfathers. It still had meaning but it was a personal question. We have come of age now, and we pardon ourselves. That personal question has no significance in the context of our liberal movement and of this body.

The steps can be traced: Ezekiel, the Second Isaiah, Zechariah, Abram's call, the author of Jonah—but nowhere so articulate as in the Book of Jonah: Israel's mission—the dawn of our responsibility.

Yes, Israel's mission, the dawn of our responsibility.

Do we begin to feel uneasy? Through the centuries with the mention of the word "mission" Jews have from time to time felt somehow remiss, unsatisfied, uneasy—and still feel so. Am I unfair to Progressive Judaism if I suggest that in this we resemble Jonah: in our reluctance to set out for Nineveh, in our turning our back on our mission? Or do we still in fact too easily stow away our sense of mission and flee to some Tarshish? We pay our fare no doubt—the first class fare, a generous contribution (and that is important!)—but then we slumber in the belly of the ship.

Our ability to put our sense of mission under wraps and ride off in all directions was notably evident in our discussion of the mission theme at the Conference here in 1949. I had the cherished privilege then of sharing with Leo Baeck, of blessed memory, a day's program on the Mission of Israel. A lively discussion followed on Dr. Baeck's impassioned appeal. Some of the discussants picked up the thought and added their pleas. But others outnumbered these, others who, with this or that personal reservation, directed our sights towards other goals. Several delegates expressed the view, by no means invalid but frankly tangential, that a great deal of work remains to be done within our own ranks. Now, no one will deny that we do have a mission to Jews—to unaffiliated Jews—to secular, uninformed, and lukewarm Jews—to isolated rural families and remote communities of Jews; surely no-one will deny that we have a mission to them, or will be unaware that we are likewise accepting our responsibilities in these areas, and pursuing them with energy and vision.

But when, instead of the mission of Israel, we talk of our "mission *to* the Jews" we are playing the semantic game. We are using the word "mission" in an extended sense, a borrowed and not quite legitimate sense. It is time we chastened our vocabulary, because in fact the "mission of Israel" proper is directed outward. It is a mission to the Gentiles.

And there's the rub. Speak to Jews of a Jewish mission to Gentiles, and they stir in their seats, look over their shoulders, wonder who may be listening. Of course this uneasiness is wholly gratuitous; rightly conceived, our mission is no threat to any group. Pursuing our mission, we would not be seeking members for our synagogues but active acceptance of our values.

We do not think in terms of one big church. We do not conceive of our mission and responsibility as the need to drive all men into one vast, all-inclusive corral, to create a total union of affiliates. On the contrary we see it as our responsibility to publish and make known our distinctive values, to disseminate for the benefit of men—to add to their fund of wisdom—our own unique experience.

For, we have things to say, affirmations to make, truths to spread abroad. We want to say that life is good; it is better than death. We affirm that man is significant, not to be dwarfed by astronomy, capable of nobility. We know that it matters what we do—our behaviour matters. We are convinced that harmony among men is a desirable good and a realizable goal. We possess these and other truths; they are our wisdom. And we do not think that we lose them by sharing them. Admittedly they are not unknown among the races of men, and yet they are not widely held. Admittedly they are not new and untested, and yet they are not broadly accepted. Amazingly many are the persons and groups who will dismiss the implications of these truths or deny their validity. Those men lack without knowing they lack. But we possess these truths; we cherish these robust values; and our wealth is a responsibility. It is our mission to share and to teach. This is no selfish wish; no cause to look about furtively. And yet we hesitate—reluctant Jonahs.

Many reasons might be induced—good reasons for our hesitancy. Without a doubt history has been a major deterrent—times and circumstances did simply not permit. Missionaries *to* Jews have probably also been a deterrent—our distaste for such missionaries combined with our pity for the perplexed among us has held us back. Even our tolerance has been an inhibiting factor; as champions of religious freedom we hesitate to meddle with any man's belief. There are many reasons—and not all of them are excuses.

Perhaps the least acceptable of the reasons is the claim that we do not know enough ourselves to go about teaching others. One may argue that intensive Jewish education must precede any efforts at disseminating Jewish knowledge beyond the borders of Israel. Does this argument have anything to do with Francis Thompson's experience as a book salesman? This British poet *was* a poet—that is to say: he could not earn a living. From the Meynell biography and other gleanings the following tale emerges. Having failed in a whole series of uncongenial ventures Thompson once became "the purveyor of an encyclopedia". But because of a personal circumstance he failed at this undertaking too. So conscientious was this devout Catholic he might have passed for a Jew. He had to give up the agency at the end of two months with no transactions concluded because, you see, he could not start out to sell the encyclopedia until first he had read it through.

Would it be a heresy, would I be betraying my calling, if I were to suggest that learning is not everything? Believe me! I believe in Jewish education. I consider a disgrace and a burden the average Jew's vast ignorance of Judaism. The misconceptions which Jews harbor are frequently as grotesque as those misconceptions of which Jews are the object. I reply with an emphatic "yes" to the question: "Is Jewish education essential?" Education is essential.

Having said which I ask: *Must* we suspend all other activity until we have finished reading the encyclopedia? Does the suspicion arise in no one's mind that reading the encyclopedia is something we do—or prepare to do—in order to avoid doing something else? Could it be a ship bound for Tarshish?

View the problems from another side. Despite much effort and a vast expenditure of funds we are only moderately satisfied with the results of our Jewish child and adult educational programs. We detect an absence of motivation, minimal enthusiasm. Not much caring why and not clearly seeing what they are studying, many students are large-meshed sieves. But suppose for a moment that we were engaged in missionary efforts and were learning in order to teach, who knows what new enthusiasm for our heritage of truth, what warm appreciation for our Jewish values, might not be reborn among us, fathered by our will to give and to teach. We can draw an analogy. What Zionism did for an apathetic Jewry in the first half of this twentieth century an active mission could yet do for the actively goal-less Jews of this second half-century—the wandering Jews of our generation on the move but with no chosen destination.

This reason for postponing our mission: the claim that we ourselves are not Jewishly informed, and all the other avowed reasons might well be detailed and developed and profitably explored and assessed. It is a task that might well be undertaken by a social historian. But I am going now to leave reasons aside and ask you to think with me about two possible explanations for our relucatance to set out for Nineveh. Taken together, these two explanations make up a paradox, for, the first of them is this: that we are not proud enough; and the second is this: that we are not humble enough.

We are not proud enough. We under-value our religious heritage, discount our Judaism. By "Judaism" I mean, of course, our healthy-minded, sane and rational Judaism, its solid walls and vaulted ceilings: I do not mean the playful rococo excrescences. I do not mean the contemplative life.

Judaism for us is not a religion of contemplation. We study, yes; תורה, yes; but we do not withdraw from the world. R. Eleazar did indeed say in the name of R. Haninah תלמידי חכמים מרבים שלום בעולם; and we will not deny this claim that "scholars add to the peace of the world." But we will consider whether it is the תלמוד תורה, "the scholarship," or the שלום בעולם, "the world's peace," on which we set our sights. With all our inherited Jewish respect for "basic research," we yet look beyond this תורה לשמה—look to the applied science; ultimately our concern is for "the world's peace" and not for scholarship as such.

No, our kind of Judaism does not culminate in contemplation—it aims at action. But if we agree to this proposition we have yet to ask: what sort of action? And there may be disagreement. There may be those among us who are willing to stop with means, neglecting ends. For myself I can not believe that Sabbath candles however bright, table cloths however white, *bar mitzvah* collations however extravagant, soaring cathedral synagogues however modern—that any such achievements and agenda, good and necessary in themselves, aids and embellishments of value for ourselves, are in fact the activity we have in mind when we designate our form of Judaism a religion of action and not of contemplation.

We have other activities in mind, and eminent among them is certainly the earnest effort to propagate the values we profess. I am far from suggesting that we have done nothing. We have prepared some excellent tracts, we have held immensely useful institutes on Judaism and Jewish Chatauqua sessions on our university campuses; we have a magnificent program of interfaith fellowhsips at our College-Institute. We have done much; I suggest only that we have not done enough. Were we proud enough we would give such activities a central place in our agenda. We would not leave hidden away any of that light that should shine for the nations. Like Hannukkah menorahs we would display it in our uncurtained windows. This we would do if only we were proud enough.

Or, if you will, you can explain our hesitancy to set out for Nineveh by observing that we are not yet humble enough. Smaller tasks hold no attraction and only what is large is worthy. Our messianic tradition is perhaps to blame. We are still impaled on our ancient massive ideal and can see no goal that falls short of those swords into ploughshares. Our knowledge that God created the vastness of the heavens and the populous earth hypnotically hides from us all little places, the Indian village, the refugee camp, the parched eroded hills of Greece, the migrant workers' caravans, displaced persons, overpopulated cities, and understaffed medical centers. Lacking humility we can not see small useful tasks; we must be doing all or nothing.

Tracts are not enough. It is not enough merely to teach our values to the world. It is our mission also to give body to these distinctive values, to demonstrate our ideals, to act them out. And this I believe is what I most want to say: that we can go about the business of our responsibility to men in small as well as massive ways.

"From our midst must come the participants and the leaders of every great social ideal." If to anyone here today these last words sound like a quotation he has a good memory. They are a quotation: The eminent President of the World Union for Progressive Judaism, Solomon Freehof, who was my teacher at the Hebrew Union College many years ago, and who has never ceased to be my teacher, spoke them here in London at the Liberal Jewish Synagogue just one year ago. "From our midst," he said, "must come the participants and the leaders of every great social idea." I thank him in particular for the word "participants". We need others than leaders, and we need nearer goals than vines and fig trees all over the world. We need to be more humble. It is enough if we diminish by however little the heavy load of human misery. To the extent that the hungry and the homeless, the sick and the lonely, are not words to us but people—to that extent we are implementing our mission. Mission is a social actions committee in America or a social issues committee in England. Mission is a social service committee in Sydney; mission is an Ockenden Venture; mission is a school in South Africa; mission is a Peace Corps. Such activities are not tangential, not peripheral; they are the growing edge of our mission.

Not for the world's sake only—we ourselves need such activities. In a century which threatens so to overwhelm the individual, and as a people which has so recently experienced a tidal wave of hatred, perhaps we in particular need some nearer goals not for the world's sake only—for our sakes too—if merely to help us recover our faith in ourselves. Yes, we should take the lead in social advance, and yes, as participants we should move ahead in achievable stages, gaining confidence as we move.

Have I strayed too far from my starting point? Have I utterly lost the Book of Jonah? I do not think so. Does not one theme run through the exposition of the book and the extended preachment which here follows: the theme of the unfulfilled responsibility of the servant-people Israel? Recognize Jonah clearly for what he is in the book, a personification of a people—of Israel cast in its prophetic role, a symbol for a chosen people destined for a task; conceive the sending of Jonah as the mission, the outward directed mission of that people, and look upon his flight as upon that people's misgivings, reluctance, rationalizations and evasions; consider one by one the details of the story and turn then to the contemporary world—our place within the human scene. The book has no less meaning for us now than for the generation whom its author addressed. Whether that generation heeded his lesson, whether we shall read the lesson, are open questions. How far we have gone on our mission, how far we have yet to carry the light, each of us may estimate for himself.

But one thing is clear: that our responsibility dawned those many centuries ago. The author of the book of Jonah already drew the conclusion: Judaism is not something we *have*, it is something we *do*. And being a Jew is not a condition, it is a program.

The Theology of Jewish Survival According to Biblical Sources

If the theme of this discussion were "the *phenomenon* of Jewish survival" I should have to deal with history and social forces. If the theme of this discussion were "the *strategy* of Jewish survival" I should have to deal with *Realpolitik*. Were the theme phrased as "the *miracle* of Jewish survival" you would expect from me some vaporings and a mystique. I am glad that it is none of these. I find "the *theology* of Jewish survival" a difficult but still congenial subject, especially since, as I understand it, I may limit myself to the relevant biblical material.

For the time being omit the specific and think in general about the theology of anyone's survival. What do we mean when we combine the two concepts "theology" and "survival"? We seem to be asking, do we not, whether God has need for that one's continued existence, an interest in his survival, a stake in his survival, a hand in his survival, or the like. And that, of course, means a God who shapes history—a Providence. However well or poorly we can reconcile this conception with the theology of a scientific age, such a Providence is axiomatic for biblical thought. God acts in history; the experience of mankind is the expression of God's will.

I have noticed that most of the scholars who write a "theology of the Old Testament" simply accept this proposition as common knowledge without documentation. And we can do the same. Any page of the Bible will serve: the God of the Bible is the author of history. The כלל is Providence and miracles are the פרטים. Furthermore since by definition we are only reviewing "the Wisdom of the Past" our method is descriptive and we are not required to defend the proposition as substantially true. It is the frame in which we operate, the unexplored postulate which is our home base.

A related proposition is less obvious but beyond doubt biblical. It too is broad and fundamental and relevant to our study. It is the proposition that God does not simply "make" history but that he also directs it—that the experience of man is an expression not of God's will alone but of his design as well. This, of course, is the area of teleology and even if I thought it necessary for our purposes to explore this area extensively and in depth I could not do so here because I have neither the time nor the philosophical acumen. But again we remember that we are not defending but describing, and illustrations are all we owe.

I ask you to consider with me now three *pesukim*, one from the Priestly account of creation in Genesis 1, and two from the later strata of the book of Isaiah—from Isaiah 45 and Isaiah 19. Out of chaos, empty and dark, תהו ובוהו וחשך (Gen. 1.2) God made this ordered and inhabited world, and he found it good: וירא אלהים את כל אשר עשה והנה טוב מאד (v. 31). On the way to this conclusion, on the way from chaos to order we pass the half of

One among a group of papers on The Theology of Jewish Survival presented at the Convention of the Central Conference of American Rabbis held at Boston, Mass. in 1968.

a verse (v. 28a) that illustrates our proposition. When God had made man in his image, and had distinguished the sexes, then ויברך אתם אלהים ויאמר להם אלהים פרו ורבו ומלאו את הארץ וכבשוה, "God blessed them and God said to them, 'Be fruitful and multiply and fill this earth and control it.'" Does that not sound like a program? Does it not mean a populated planet, orderly and permanent, which God has willed?

There may be more than a surface resemblance between the first *pasuk* and the next. I suspect that the priestly author of the Genesis passage drew his inspiration from the anonymous prophetic author of Isaiah 45.18, whom for convenience we call the Second Isaiah. It is only a fraction of a verse; we might easily overlook it. The prophet throws it in as a kind of aside, in parentheses, a couple of clauses—but it is one of the truly great utterances of biblical man, a towering peak among the peaks. I have forgotten who said it but I read it somewhere: he could forgive whoever robbed him of large parts of the Bible if only they let him hold on to this 45th chapter of Isaiah. That is how I feel too and I am especially attached to this one line there in the middle of a verse, which the author sort of throws away. Here is the whole verse (45.18):

> For thus the Lord has said,
> The creator of the heavens—he is God—
> He who formed the earth and made it
> (Not to be an empty waste did he create it;
> To be inhabited he formed it):
> "I am God and there is no other."

Did you hear the neglected parenthesis? לא תהו בראה לשבת יצרה. He did not create it to be an empty waste—not to revert to תהו. He formed it to be inhabited. The qualifiers stand before the verbs, in the emphatic position: לא תהו—not to revert to chaos, לשבת—to be inhabited. There lies the purpose and there the sure promise. And there in the throw-away line is the inspiration for the priestly author of Genesis 1 and best hope of man in a nuclear age.

The third *pasuk* also from a late chapter in the book of Isaiah is one which, as I remember, brought tears to the eyes of our late colleague Abraham Cronbach ז״ל. It is the last verse of Isaiah 19, or better a pair of verses, verses 24 and 25.

ביום ההוא יהיה ישראל שלישיה למצרים ולאשור ברכה בקרב הארץ: אשר ברכה י׳ צבאות לאמר ברוך עמי מצרים ומעשה ידי אשור ונחלתי ישראל.

The object suffix ה is right in ברכה instead of ו; the pronoun must be feminine to agree with its antecedent הארץ—the earth—צבאות י׳ אשר ברכה בקרב הארץ, "in the midst of the earth which the Lord of hosts blessed"—blessed and populated, if we remember Genesis 1: "And God blessed them and God said to them 'Be fruitful and multiply and fill the earth and control it.'" The allusion is surely intentional and this third *pasuk* takes its place with the other two and rounds out the thought. Here it is then:

> On that day Israel will make a third, along with Egypt and Assyria, a blessing in the midst of the earth which the Lord of hosts blessed, saying:

> "Blessed be my people Egypt, (blessed be) Assyria my handiwork, and (blessed) my possession Israel."

Survival? yes; with God's sure blessing man may survive. That is the sum of these three passages, as they speak to me: mankind may survive.

But you properly remind me that our theme is "the theology of Jewish survival" and that I have been speaking of human survival. Yes, but they are not unrelated; and this last remark cuts both ways. The Isaiah apocalypse notwithstanding (see Isa. 26.20), the end of the human race would by definition mean our end as well, and cutting the other way, according to the same "Wisdom of the Past," Jewish survival might quite well contribute to the survival of the species. This is a thought to which we shall return.

But first some observations in particular about the theology of Jewish survival according to biblical sources. A few years ago I read a paper at a meeting of the Society for Biblical Literature and coined a phrase. The phrase was "irony by way of attribution." (See the essay here following.) The best examples in the prophets of irony by attribution are relevant to the subject of this study, so my mind only seems to be wandering when I talk for a few paragraphs now about this rhetorical device.

You heard me use the trick of attribution just a minute ago. That was when I said "But you remind me that our theme is 'the theology of Jewish survival.'" Of course you hadn't done any such thing, but my saying that you had done so gave me the opening I needed for introducing a supplementary thought. No irony was involved there; it was simply attribution. For attribution with irony I can do no better than to quote my revered teacher Moses Buttenwieser, and his translation of a familiar passage in the first chapter of Isaiah: לכו־נא ונוכחה יאמר י' אם יהיו חטאיכם כשנים כשלג ילבינו . . . In Buttenwieser's vivid language that means: "Come now, let us reason together, says the Lord. 'If your sins be as scarlet they shall become white as snow'—you think so!" Buttenwieser recognized, correctly I think, that in the words כשלג ילבינו, the prophet was not making a statement for God, he was simply repeating a current popular slogan, and doing so only to deny its validity. It is a good trick if you can bring it off. You can disprove the adage that it takes two to make an argument. All by yourself you can engage in heated dialogue, and—more significantly—you can deftly focus on the tension between opposing attitudes or positions.

A passage from Micah 3 will illustrate this method again and it will at the same time bring us nearer to the theme of Jewish survival. Of Zion Micah says that these and these are the faults of her rulers, her judges, her priests and her prophets; and as for the whole populace, he adds ועל י' ישענו לאמר הלוא י' בקרבנו לא תבוא עלינו רעה, "In God they trust, and say: 'Isn't God in our midst? It *can't* happen here.'" To which quoted slogan Micah replies: "(You think so!) for that very reason Zion shall be plowed over like a field, Jerusalem become rubble and the temple mount a wooded height." You heard the dialogue, you felt the tension, and you recognize the relevance. Micah puts words in the mouth of the people only to make them a target for his irony; that is the dialogue. The inhabitants of the holy city trust in God and know themselves safe; but God beholds the urban blight and condemns the city along with its inhabitants. That is the tension. But if

God can, himself, condemn to destruction the very site of his temple and the people that worships him there it follows then that this same God (*mirabile dictu!*) can do without this people—does not depend on Israel. And that is one aspect of the theology of Jewish survival according to biblical sources. According to this grim and relevant prognostication (on which Amos and Micah, Isaiah and, in part, Jeremiah converge) Israel will not survive. God will survive but Israel will perish. Amos agreed: His people must learn the facts of life. He lets God ask הלוא כבני כשיים אתם לי בני ישראל—"Are you not to me even as the Cushites are, O people of Israel?" which Rashi correctly interprets הלוא מן בני נח באתם כשאר העכו״ם? למה אמנע מלהפרע מכם אחרי אשר אינכם שבים אלי?"Are you not descended from Noah even as the other idolators are? Why should I hesitate to divest myself of you, since you refuse to return to me?"

Amos agreed, but he did not at the outset say "positively"; he considered an alternative to disaster and he presented this sort of dialogue-plus-tension-plus-relevance all wrapped up in one verse: דרשו טוב ואל רע למען תחיו ויהי כן י׳ צבאות אתכם כאשר אמרתם—"Only do what is right and avoid the wrong so that then you may live and that the Lord of hosts may be with you כאשר אמרתם, as you like to say." (5.14). Survival is no question, you think. You claim that you have a hold on God; he is with you and you are safe. That could be right, said Amos, but only if your own conduct makes it so. In two subsequent passages the prophet abandons this contingent hope, once (in 6.3) where he speaks of the top brass at ease in Zion and Samaria as men who scoff at the thought of disaster: המנדים ליום רע, and a second time (in 9:10) where he quotes the self-deluding, wish-fulfilling words which he hears his people address to God, לא תגיש ותקדים בעדינו הרעה—his people "who say 'Surely you would not bring on and confront us with the final disaster!'" (You wouldn't do that to *us*!) Amos, of course, believes that he will do that very thing; this prophet sees God's role in the matter of Jewish survival as *negative*.

We can leave this point after citing one clear example more—this time from Jeremiah 7, "the Temple sermon": "Will you steal, kill, commit adultery, bear false witness, sacrifice to Baal, and follow other gods whom you did not know and then come and stand before me in this Temple on which my name is called and say נצלנו, 'We are safe'"? That is the comfortable delusion "We are safe!" But this is the grim fact:

> I will do to this Temple . . . in which you repose your trust אשר אתם בוטחים בו and to the place which I gave to you, and to your fathers, what I did to Shiloh, and I will cast you off as I cast off your brothers, all the spawn of Ephraim (vv. 9f., 14f.).

So much then for the device of "irony by way of attribution." But what of "the theology of Jewish survival"? At this stage in our study we are left in tension. There is on the one hand a prevailing popular sentiment to the effect that under God "there will always be an England," or at any rate an Israel, and on the other hand a strident prophetic challenge to the effect that Israel's doom is near.

As now we move on, I suspect that we shall see the challenge recede, though not without leaving its mark, and the popular confidence rally, though in a significantly modified form.

Ponder with me now the book of Deuteronomy. I mean the shape which the book assumed near the end of its long literary history, during the sixth century, the time of exile, when the facts of life had caught up with the people.

If you wonder why I say this, ask yourselves what the two words mean that conclude the passage which I am about to read (from Deut. 29.23—27)—the two words כיום הזה, "as it is this very day," "as is still the case." Ask, "What day?" Ask, "When is now? What was the time of the author?" This is the passage slightly condensed: ואמרו כל הגוים על מה עשה י׳ ככה לארץ הזאת . . . ואמרו על אשר עזבו את ברית י׳ אלהי אבתם . . . וילכו ויעבדו אלהים אחרים וישתחוו להם . . . ויחר אף י׳ בארץ ההוא . . . ויתשם י׳ מעל האדמה באף ובחמה ובקצף גדול אל ארץ אחרת כיום הזה, "and if all the 'goyyim' ask 'Why did God behave in this manner toward this land?' . . . they shall answer their own question, saying 'Because these did not live up to the covenant demands of the Lord, the God of their fathers . . . but went and served other gods and worshipped them . . . God grew angry with this land . . . and he destroyed them from their land with passionate anger and great rage and he banished them *to another land*—כיום הזה, where still they are (literally, as it is this day)." (Note: In 4.38, however, כיום הזה refers to a time when still, or again, they have their land in possession.)

Whoever wrote this passage in Deuteronomy 29 could no more say, as was said in the time of Amos, "God would not do that to his people," because in simple fact God had already done it. And here we have the perspective we need when we look at the book, *Devarim,* and especially at the frame, the first eleven and the last nine chapters. It is in these sermonic sections of the book, apparently written during the exile or at its end, more so that in the central, probably Josianic, legal kernel, that we find matter relevant to our theme. The tension has not relaxed, the tension of a people chosen yet threatened with extinction. The Deuteronomist says in sounding prose what Amos had said in moving verse. The prophet said (5.14): Only do what is right and avoid the wrong so that then you may live; and as we read year by year on the Day of Atonement, the Deuteronomist wrote (30.19):

העידתי בכם היום את השמים ואת הארץ החיים והמות נתתי לפניך הברכה והקללה ובחרת בחיים למען תחיה אתה וזרעך. I invoke the heavens and the earth as witness against you, I have set a choice before you: life and death, the blessing and the curse. Choose life, that you may live, you and your seed after you.

Survival? yes; it is a human choice.

According to Deuteronomy Israel may choose—but God chose first! Without trying to scrape the bottom of the barrel I listed more than thirty passages in Deuteronomy which in one form or another recall God's free choice of Israel and his free promise of the land. Relax for a while and bask in the choice and the promise—the tension can wait.

Early in the book we find the word נחלה which a late contributor to Isaiah will adopt when he lists עמי מצרים ומעשה ידי אשור ונחלתי ישראל, "my people Egypt, Assyria my handiwork and my possession Israel." This is the passage in Deuteronomy: ואתכם לקח י׳ ויוצא אתכם מכור הברזל ממצרים להיות לו לעם נחלה כיום הזה. It follows on a reference to God's assigning the heavenly bodies as objects of worship to other peoples under the heavens, and it continues here (in 4.20) "But it was you whom the Lord picked and brought from the iron furnace of Egypt to be to him an עם נחלה, a special possession כיום הזה—as still you are," or "as again you are." The verb "picked" לקח in this passage corresponds to "chose" בחר in others, and the expression עם נחלה corresponds to a synonymous עם קדוש and עם סגלה. So in 7.6 (which is repeated verbatim in 14.2): כי עם קדוש אתה לי' אלהיך בך בחר י' אלהיך להיות לו לעם סגלה מכל העמים אשר על פני האדמה. (This was) " . . . because you are עם קדוש, a people holy to the Lord your God; (And) among all the peoples of the earth the Lord your God chose you בחר בם as his own people עם סגלה." And a further variant of this thought brings in God's love for us and for our "fathers": Though God is lord of the heavens and the heaven of heavens, the earth and all it contains, רק באבתיכם חשק י' לאהבה אותם, "the Lord did love your fathers, ויבחר בזרעם אחריהם בכם מכל העמים כיום הזה, and chose their seed after them among all the peoples, even you yourselves alive today"—you, the survivors (10.15). The synonyms may vary, but they all add up to love. Abraham was God's friend, so too his son Isaac and Isaac's son Jacob and all of his family, the tribes of Israel. God declared his love to them and gave his pledge—the land of their sojourning. In Egypt he renewed his promise to the fathers, and again at Sinai, and this book of Deuteronomy glows with the promise. "Because of God's loving you," Moses reminds his generation, "and because of his honoring the pledge which he made to your fathers, God brought you out in his great might and redeemed you from the house of bondage, from the power of Pharaoh, Egypt's king" (7.8). And now says Moses, "Go, take possession of the land which God promised to your fathers . . . awarding it to them and their seed after them" (1.8). The phrase is a formula—the land is always "the promised land" הארץ אשר נשבע י' לאבתיכם—or perhaps better said, if, as it seems, much of the Deuteronomic frame was written during or after the exile "the re-promised land." Even as they are God's possession, the land is their sure "possession," their נחלה (15.4; 20.16; 25.19), and they may confidently hope to live there "in clover" all their long life, as in the frequent refrain Moses suggests: "that you may live long on the land which the Lord your God gives you כל הימים, for all times" (4.40) "while heaven and earth remain," כימי השמים על הארץ (11.21), on the land "that flows with milk and honey" (11.9; cf. 16.20 and 25.15).

What is the theology of the choice and the promise? that God is a free agent and may choose; that all the peoples are his children and he may have his favorite son among them; that all the earth is his and he may dispose of it at will; that he communicates with man and in particular with the family of Abraham; that to the members of that family and most recently to Moses in Egypt and Sinai he renewed his wish to have them as his own, his special possession, and to house them on his own little acre. It is really very simple and abundantly clear, once you have accepted the postulates.

Yes, in the book of Deuteronomy we bask relaxed in the warmth of choice and promise, quite as did the confident contemporaries of Micah who asked "Is not God in our midst?" הלא י' בקרבנו and stubbornly maintained "It cannot happen here" (3.11)—and the equally trustful public of Amos, Isaiah and Jeremiah, as we have seen. So chosen, the beneficiaries of such a promise, the people of Israel in the days of Deuteronomy had no problem of Jewish survival. It was all very simple.

Or was it? Was it all milk and honey? No, the promise was contingent; though God chose Israel, Israel still must choose. We started out with the key passage: "I have set a choice before you, life and death, the blessing and the curse. Choose life." With this demand tension enters the picture again. Exclusive loyalty to the choosing God, obedience to his commands, those are the conditions that Israel must choose to meet if Israel is indeed to survive—and if Israel is to retain its hold on the much promised land. The conditional nature of the choice and promise is evident not only in the just quoted passage: "Choose life in order to live, you and your seed," but everywhere, again and again; the word למען furnishes the key. "And now, O Israel, hearken to the statutes and judgments which I teach you to do למען תחיון, in order to live and enter and possess the land which the Lord, the God of your fathers, is giving you" (4.1),—or למען, "in order to live long on the land . . . (4.40 and often)—or למען, "so that you, and your children may live long on the land" (11.21)—or למען, "so that it may be well with you on the land" (5.16)—or למען, "so that you may bring to a successful conclusion all that you undertake (29.8)—or simply למען תחיה אתה וזרעך, "that you may survive, you and your seed" (30.19).

And then, of course, there is the matter of the ברכה and the קללה, the blessing and the curse—the whole 28th chapter of alternatives, and its satellites: ובאו עליך כל הברכות האלה והשיגוך כי תשמע בקול י' אלהיך: ברוך אתה בעיר וברוך אתה בשדה וגו', "All of these blessings will be yours and fall to your lot if only you are obedient to the Lord your God. Blessed will you be in the city, blessed in the field . . ." and on and on. והיה אם לא תשמע בקול י' אלהיך . . . . . . ובאו עליך כל הקללות האלה והשיגוך: ארור אתה בעיר וארור אתה בשדה, "But if you are not obedient etc. etc. cursed will you be in the city, cursed in the field . . ." and on and on and on (28.2ff. and 51ff.; see also 7.32f., 8.19f. and 30.15ff.). The contingent curses are even more plentiful than the blessings. God's continued acceptance of Israel as his particular people לו לעם קדוש is wholly contingent on such obedience (28.9). They could indeed be left as מתי מעט, "a scant few" (28.62) or in fact be wholly destroyed עד השמדך, 28.45). There is no assurance. The tension and the pattern in the book of Deuteronomy are this contingent promise.

This pattern can also be seen in a different light. As we read it in Deuteronomy, it all sounds very hypothetical: this is how it *may* be when you cross this Jordan and take possession of that land, and you have to watch these things or else—. But we have seen reasons to believe that it is not so theoretical after all. If Israel were not, as represented, in fact listening to Moses in Moab, but were instead hearing a preacher in exile in Babylon, what then would this scheme of things mean? What? Not theory but theodicy—not speculation on what could or could not happen, but an explanation of what had in fact happened. What this scheme of things means to a defeated, decimated, bereaved and impoverished people, uprooted and captive on foreign soil, is an answer to the bewildering question: Why? Why did this happen to us? How could our God let it happen? And the answer adds up to this: that God did not simply "let" it happen, he did it—and for good cause—because his people had made the wrong choice. Do not be misled, it says. Do not suppose that other, more powerful gods gave the victory to Babylonia. You are defeated but your God is not; your present condition bears agonizing witness to the fact that he is in complete control and that his ways are just.

That appears to be a part of the message of the preachers who preached the Deuteronomic sermons to the survivors of the catastrophe of 587—or to the *galut* generations—their sons and their grandsons a few decades later. In a sense the rest of their message is also theology, though not now theodicy. It starts from the fact that these are survivors, a פלטה after Jerusalem's fall. These survivors, pondering the preachers' message while contemplating the חורבן, might just find in it a lesson, and a hope. Although indeed God had freely chosen Israel as his people and had entered into an agreement with them, there still was a fluid quality to the arrangement; it had not congealed to a consistency which denied either God or Israel freedom now. The possibility of survival is neither assured nor denied this people. They had a live option. Defeated, reduced in number, uprooted, they still might choose life. Survival was a human choice—there lay the hope.

Beginning perhaps with the writings of the Second Isaiah the matter of Jewish survival takes on a new dimension. To the vertical, between God and Israel, a horizontal is now added: lines joining Israel and the rest of mankind. And it is here, I believe, that we may find biblical thought impinging on our current concern with Jewish survival. I have said before in other contexts, what I am going to say now, in this final section of this paper, but here it will appear in a new light.

Consider with me the relationship between the problem of Jewish survival and the Deutero-Isaianic concept of the "servant." Even among contemporary Jewish interpreters of the Bible there are differences of opinion on many Isaiah questions, and one has to say what his position is before he starts drawing conclusions about the teachings of the Second Isaiah. It is my view that the author of the sixteen chapters was among the Jewish exiles in Babylonia and that his activity belongs to the years just before and just after the Persian king Cyrus conquered the capital city Babylon. I think too that this third generation of landless Jews on foreign soil were badly in need of his message—and for two reasons. The first reason is that they were a pitiful minority in danger of being engulfed by a dominant culture, and the second that they were desperately poor and deprived of their human rights. They badly needed one to lift them out of those depths. In my opinion also the evidence permits the conclusion that throughout the sixteen chapters when the prophet refers to the עבד י', he means Israel. Repeatedly he speaks of this people Israel as "chosen" and in the same breath he calls the people God's "servant" (41.8, 42.1, 43.10, 44.1).

Take off from this last observation and note: combined with the idea of servant the concept "chosen" has taken on an altogether new value. It has come to mean: commissioned, assigned a task, designated for a purpose. To be chosen is to have a job. We noticed the tension in the time of Amos between the popular notion that God had chosen and would protect and prosper his people Israel and the view of the eighth century prophets that Israel was tragically deluded. In that form the tension is here relaxed. The Second Isaiah now enthusiastically endorses the earlier view that God had chosen Israel. But he has relaxed that tension only to introduce another. To borrow a figure—and I would be glad to name the lender if I could remember who he is—this is now the tension of the arrow in the drawn bow. In the Second Isaiah it is now the tension between the real and the possible, between the actual achievement and the visioned goal.

To a people such as exiled Israel the title "servant" was a cause for dismay, and a tantalizing prospect all in one. "Servant" is what they were, "hewers of wood and drawers of water"—they knew quite enough of that in Babylonia now, as an earlier generation had known too much of it in Egypt. But it was, of course, a different matter to be a servant to God; and they had been hand-picked for the task as well! That lent dignity to the office. And it did more—it gave to a humiliated people a sense of high purpose. It was a broad way from self-hate to pride; purpose rehabilitates a man and builds a nation. It was occupational therapy at its best. It may have been the source of Israel's will to live, the key to Jewish survival then, if indeed it is not even now.

On this last page we have spoken more of men than of God, and you remind me again that our theme is the theology of Jewish survival. Returning then to theology we turn back to the three *pesuḳim* with which we began. Remember their message: God made the earth and man upon it. He found it good and gave it his blessing (Gen. 1.28). He has no intention now of letting it revert to chaos. It shall remain an ordered inhabited world (Isa. 45.18). In his eyes the nations are scarcely distinguishable. Israel his possession, makes a third along with Egypt his people, and Assyria his handiwork (Isa. 19.24f.).

We are moving now within the orbit of the Second Isaiah. Indeed the central passage here is from his pen: לא תהו בראה, "not to be an empty waste did he create it," לשבת יצרה, "to be inhabited he formed it." According to this prophet God had not withdrawn from his creation; the earth and its inhabitants remain his live concern. He wills an ordered world.

The rest is fairly obvious: God's servant Israel has a role in that broad purpose. wgod called this people from Ur, from the edge of the world; freed them from Egypt, from bondage; chose them at Sinai, concluding a pact with them; redeemed his promise, giving them their land; broadened their vision with exile, preparing them for their destined task. Now they have received their assignment. Now they will bring such testimony as only they are qualified to bring that their god is God, he alone, beyond compare, unrivalled. That is the service they owe him, these prophetic witnesses to his sole divinity; this light they bring to the nations; this truth is theirs to bear, until it reaches to the ends of the earth, where the sun rises and where it sets, and reconciles mankind the world over. Israel is the light and the ferment that can preserve the world.

We could go on to illustrate this thought, recalling Jonah, who, if I understand the author's intention, is, like the Servant, a *mashal* for Israel sent to preserve the lives of a distant people; recalling too the much reworked prayer of Solomon at the dedication of his temple and his concern for the stranger from a far off land; and recalling numerous similarly universalistic passages among the prophets, but especially there the twice attested dream of the הר בית י׳, the mountain of the Lord's house. Yes מציון תצא תורה ודבר י׳ מירושלים, "Teaching shall go forth from Zion, and from Jerusalem God's word." But we have seen enough.

Tie these thoughts together and simply ask now: What of the theology of Jewish survival according to these biblical sources? There is no question. Divinely commissioned for such a purpose a people must endure. Called to carry out a task that is far from accomplished a people must persist. Ennobled by a matchless trust a consenting people finds the will to survive.

So much for the biblical sources, the "wisdom of the past." As for ourselves, substantially and significantly, confidence in our message and zeal for our mission might still contribute to our survival as Jews.

I suspect that we who are participating in this Kallah may find ourselves divided into two camps: those whose emphasis is on the messianic and those who, as I do, find our truest hope in our message and our mission.

Irony by Way of Attribution

Preponderantly, prophetic discourse consists of words reputedly spoken by a prophet and God. Although this is obviously true we do not have to read far in the books of the prophets to come upon that occasional word attributed to persons other than God or the prophet—attributed to the people, to the kings or to foreign powers and potentates. The prophet introduces such words for various reasons, most of them rhetorical. Not infrequently, by the device of attributing to others a saying of some sort which he then proceeds to manipulate, the prophet achieves the effect of irony. I propose to look first at a few of the overtly attributed sayings in the prophets, just to get the feel of them—and then to suggest that in some spots we may be overlooking an intended quotation or mistaking it for the word of the prophet, thus missing his point.

I might start anywhere; there are 150 or more of these quotations by count sprinkled among the books of the prophets. Let Ezekiel with his vivid style supply the first examples.

Preparing to deny the validity of a current notion (the notion that prophets are windbags), Ezekiel introduces first a reputedly current saying:

> Why do you people use this proverb concerning the land of Israel, saying: "Time passes and every vision fizzles out"? (12.22).

In another connection he repeats a slanderous charge against himself; people are saying of him that he only talks poetry:

> They say of me: "What is he but a maker of metaphors?" (21.5).

In other circumstances—soon after the fall of Jerusalem—with three separate quotations Ezekiel deftly records the moods of his despairing people:

> Thus you have said: "Our transgressions and our sins have caught up with us and by reason of them we waste away; how can we live?" (33.10).

And again:

> So they say: "Our bones are dry and our hope is lost; we perish all" (37.11, reading כלנו).

And finally:

> Why do you repeat this proverb about the land of Israel, saying: "The fathers ate sour grapes but it is the children's teeth that are on edge?" (18.2).

Quotations of this sort are of inestimable value to the historian; the historian could want no better evidence. In his listening-post the prophet hears what people say and these are his ear-witness reports. They are not his words. These are the non-official voices—an authentic "documentary"—with the prophet reporting. But a prophet-turned-reporter is not always thus admirably factual. When it serves his rhetorical purpose he is quite capable of editorializing. Take Amos for example. Denouncing rapacious merchants, Amos quoted not only what he heard them say, but what he heard them think as well:

> "When will the new moon observance be over
> so that we can offer grain for sale,
> the Sabbath, so that we can open the granaries,
> falsifying the measure and raising the price,
> and cheating with false balances. . .?" (8.5).

Isaiah also reads between the lines and colours quoted words with his own disapproval. What the national security council in Jerusalem was saying about the treaty with Egypt was not quite as he quoted it. The strategists probably said:

"We have confidence in Egypt and find security in Pharaoh's might."

But as Isaiah quoted them they said:

"We have confidence in lies and find security in falsehood" (28.15).

Related to, but not identical with, these last illustrations is the saying which, for example, a Jeremiah wishes into the mouth of his people. A single verse here presents an imagined dialogue between God and Israel:

> "Come back, you wayward sons;
> I will cure you of your waywardness."
> "Here we are; we have come to you
> for you are the Lord our God" (3.22).

The prophet longed to hear the words which he here attributes to his wayward people.

With this last quotation as an example we can now turn to a further observation concerning attributed sayings. Usually they are identified as quotations by some introductory formula: "this proverb", "You have said", "They are saying", "saying", or some such expression. But it is equally possible—in prophetic discourse as in the dramatic style of early ballads—to bring new actors on the scene recognizable only by what they say with no such introductory formula at all:

> "O where hae ye been, Lord Randal, my son?
> O where hae ye been, my handsome young man?"
> "I hae been to the wildwood; mother make my bed soon
> For I'm weary wi' hunting and fain would lie down."

> 3"Come back, you wayward sons;
> I will cure you of your waywardness."
> "Here we are; we have come to you
> for you are the Lord our God."

Now this one last general observation before we turn to the particular: Not all attributed sayings have the form of direct discourse. Consider this passage from Amos:

> Seek good and not evil that you may live
> and that so the Lord God of hosts may be with you as you say (5.14).

"As you say" suggests a quotation, but Amos offers the saying only as indirect discourse: "that so the Lord God of hosts may be with you." The direct form would be "The Lord God of hosts is with us", or simply: "God is with us"—עמנואל, *immanuel.*

But recognize the possibility that in dramatic fashion a saying like this last example, phrased as indirect discourse, might also not be identified as a quotation by any of the usual introductory formulas—and so realize that confusion might well ensue. Amos could have said simply:

> Seek good and not evil that
> you may live
> and that so the Lord God of hosts
> may be with you.

I believe that in several crucial passages in prophetic discourse this does happen, that confusion yields to clarity as soon as we recognize the presence of an attributed saying, and that likewise the prophet's *irony* comes to full expression.

Three or four out of a large number of possible examples will serve to illustrate the device. The passages are familiar and the reader will recognize the words thrown in to fill the ellipses—thrown in unnecessarily because the speaker's voice could as well be made to convey the meaning without the added words. For the most part in these examples I follow the Revised Standard Version and merely fill in the ellipses, with the plus here in italics.

The first is Isaiah 1.18−20:

> Come now, let us reason together, says the Lord:
> though your sins are like scarlet,
> they shall be white as snow, *you say*,
> though they are red like crimson,
> they shall become like wool, *you fondly imagine.*
> *Yes*, if you are willing and obedient,
> you shall eat the good of the land;
> but *not* if you refuse and rebel;
> *if that is your behavior* you shall be eaten—by the sword. . . .

The second is Isaiah 28.20ff.:

> The bed is too short to stretch out in,
> the wraps are too scant to get under.
> The Lord will rise up, *you hope*, as on
>   Mount Perazim,

> he will be wroth, *you imagine,* as in
>   the valley of Gibeon
> to do his deed—*right,* but strange
>   will be his deed,
> and to do his work—*right again,*
>   but alien will be his work.

The third is a little more difficult and a little less certain. It is Isaiah 31.4–6 plus 8, omitting verse 7 as a foreign element and understanding לצבא על in v. 4 to mean not "to fight upon" but "to fight against" (as in 29.7).

> For thus the Lord said to me,
> As a lion or a young lion growls over his prey,
> and when a band of shepherds is called forth
>   against him
> is not terrified by their shouting or daunted
>   by their noise,
> so the Lord of hosts will come down
> to fight against Mount Zion and against its hill.
>
> *But you insist*
> "Like birds hovering, so the Lord of hosts
>   will protect Jerusalem;
>   he will protect and deliver it,
>   he will spare and rescue it."

To this wish-thought of yours I must reply:
Turn to him from whom you have deeply
  revolted, O people of Israel. . . .
And it may then be as you say:
The Assyrian shall fall by a sword
  not of man. . . .

Two final illustrations are separate but linked passages in Amos: 3.2 and 9.7. I understand the first as follows:

> You only have I known
> of all the families of the earth, *you say;*
> *assume this to be so and it follows that*
> therefore I must hold you accountable
> for all your iniquities.

The second passage, the one in chapter 9, has some such meaning as this:

> Are you not like the Ethiopians to me
> O people of Israel, says the Lord.
> Did I not bring Israel up
> from the land of Egypt? *you ask me.*

58

> *Suppose I did; I also* brought
> the Philistines from Caphtor
> and the Syrians from Kir.

These examples illustrate the thought that the prophet not infrequently achieves his purpose by attributing thoughts or sayings to others and then manipulating them for his rhetorical—often ironical—purpose.*

---

*In substantially its present form this study was read before the Society of Biblical Literature at the December 1962 meeting in New York. Professor Edwin M. Good quoted with permission from this as yet unpublished study in his *Irony in the Old Testament*, Philadelphia, 1965. On the subject see also: H. W. Wolff, *Das Zitat im Prophetenspruch*, Munich, 1937; Robert Gordis, "Quotations as a Literary Usage in Biblical, Oriental and Rabbinic Literature", *Hebrew Union College Annual*, Vol. XXII (1949), pp. 157–219; William L. Holladay, "Style, Irony and Authenticity in Jeremiah", *Journal of Biblical Literature*, Vol. LXXXI (March, 1962), pp. 44–54.

"Perish the Day!"
A Misdirected Curse (Job 3:3)

This communication concerns none of the larger critical problems posed by the book of Job but only a curious device which the author of Job employs and its possible significance.[1]

The Job dialogue opens with an elaborate passage, a soliloquy, in which Job curses "his day" (Job 3.3ff.). "His day," which is hardly to be identified with the recurrent anniversary of his birth but must be that one single day in a year long past when he came from his mother's womb—this day—the whole of it, the night time along with the daylight hours—he condemns to extinction with his curse: "Perish the day that I was born, The night that it was said 'It is a boy!'"

An ultimate curse upon a living thing is designed to rob it of its life. Just so this curse upon the lifeless day is designed to render it nonexistent. Job, by his curse, would rub out "his day": "May it not be counted among the days of the year, Nor included in the number of the moons!" Time is governed by the luminaries; the sun rules the day; by night the moon and stars. Their light is the life and soul of the day. So, to extinguish his day, Job damns it to utter darkness. He omits no contrivance; with clouds he would black out the sun and the stars, with shadows eclipse them; like Joshua with his spell halt their heavenly course, hold back the dawn. "May that day be dark . . . May no light shine upon it. May darkness and the shadow of death claim it. May clouds hover over it; May the darkening of daylight affright it. May that night be seized by utter darkness . . . May the stars of its dusk remain dark, May it hope for light in vain; May it not behold the eyelids of the dawn." Since without light the day is not, his curses, if effective, achieve his goal and the day perishes—this day together with its total contents—and he himself is unborn; the door of his mother's womb remains closed and misery is hidden from his eyes.

If we had this one example only of a man cursing his "day," we might be inclined to dismiss it simply as a poetic conceit—a conceit, because, although to us the past is real in the sense that, unlike the unborn future, the past has come to be, yet for us it is no present reality which can be affected by what we now do or destroyed by any available means, least of all by the mere words of a curse. But Job is not the only one to curse his day. In similar distressing circumstances, the prophet Jeremiah reacts in a similarly unexpected manner. In the so-called confession which concludes his twentieth chapter, the harassed prophet gives vent to his anguish with the words: "Cursed be the day on which I was born; The day on which my mother bore me let it not be blessed!" (v. 15). With two examples before us, we may at least suspect that behind the phenomenon there is something more than poetic fantasy.

By way of their identical curses, both men, Job and Jeremiah, express the escapist wish

A Hebrew translation of this essay appeared in the *Bulletin of the Israel Exploration Society*, Vol. XIX, Nos. 1–2, pp. 65–69.

that they had never been born. But also, and quite irrationally, both place the blame for their existence where it does not belong: upon a point in time, upon the *day* of their birth. And, with similar inconsequence, one of them, Jeremiah, continues with a curse upon an innocent bystander, a friend of the family who happened to bring the tidings of his birth to Jeremiah's father: "Cursed be the man who informed my father 'A boy has been born to you,' making him glad." Thus, in addition to their common substance, the two examples have in common this irrational element.

The irrationality lies, of course, in the fact that all of these curses are obviously misdirected. Neither the day nor the bearer of the news was in any way responsible for the existence of Job or of the prophet, nor was either responsible for their present grief, the occasion for their bitterness. Jeremiah displays more logic when, in another confession, in 15.10a, he cries: "Woe unto me, my mother, that thou didst bear me, A man of strife and contention to the whole earth." These latter words are appropriately directed, addressed as they are to the prophet's mother, to one, at least, of the pair in truth responsible for his being. But it is to be noted that Jeremiah reserves for the "day" his curse. When he speaks to his mother, though he utters a bitter cry and more appropriately directs it, his words do not take on the form of a curse: "Woe unto me!"

And this, perhaps, is the key to the understanding of the twice attested curse upon the "day." What is this misdirected curse but an ancient circumlocution, an evasive convention, a form of speech specifically designed to prevent a gross impiety? Probably, indeed, Job and Jeremiah each resorted to a convention and directed wholly irrational curses against the days of their birth simply in order to avoid an impious reference to their parents, the true authors of their being.

Pentateuchal law prohibits curses against God, against the king, and against one's parents: "Whosoever curseth his God shall bear his sin" (Lev. 24.15); "Thou shalt not revile God, nor curse a ruler of thy people" (Ex. 22.27); "He that curseth his father or his mother shall surely be put to death" (Ex. 21.17); "Whatsoever man there be that curseth his father or his mother shall surely be put to death; he hath cursed his father or his mother; his blood shall be upon him" (Lev. 20.9).[2]

It is probable that all of these prohibitions stem from the belief that the very words of a curse have in themselves the power to injure, diminish, or destroy the object accursed. A curse upon God or the king might weaken these and thus do damage to their worshipers or subjects, the speaker of the curse included. Similarly, since a curse works itself out in succeeding generations, a son who curses his parents might thus harm himself—such seems to be the belief.[3] No law explicitly prohibits a curse upon oneself, yet, restrained no doubt by prudence, men seldom took upon themselves a curse—as witness the evasive oath-formula.[4] At any rate, a curse upon oneself presumably affects no others and may be left to one's discretion. Not so, however, a curse upon God or the king which may affect an entire people, or a curse upon parents which may affect all future generations. These are of public concern and are properly subject to legislation.

Yet, it must not be supposed that the fictional Job feared the legal penalty prescribed for one who curses a parent and, for that reason, chose a circumlocution and evaded the letter of the law. It is rather to be assumed, on the basis of the two examples, in Jeremiah and Job, that the prophet employed, and the author of Job poetically developed, a current conventional manner of speaking and that this convention had its origin in the ban against the cursing of parents.

A few further considerations support this conclusion. First, the obvious evasion in the oath of David in I Sam. 25.22, where, according to the present text, in order not to say: "So may God do to David," he says: "So may God do to the enemies of David." Similarly, Nathan, accusing David in 2 Sam. 12.14 says: "Because thou hast greatly blasphemed the enemies of the Lord" in order not to say: "Because thou hast greatly blasphemed the Lord." And Saul's bitter words against Jonathan in 1 Sam. 20.30, where Saul alludes to the rebellious spirit and shamelessness of his son's *mother* to avoid a direct affront to Jonathan. What all of these passages have in common is the element of misdirected blame. Johannes Pedersen in *Der Eid bei den Semiten* quotes similar examples from the Arabic (p. 91f.).[5]

On the same order is the euphemistic substitution of ברך "bless," for ארר "curse" in a number of passages in the received text of the Bible. The root ארר is never employed there with God as its object. It is replaced either by a less offensive synonym or by the euphemism ברך. This euphemism occurs no less than four times in the prologue to Job, in close proximity to the soliloquy in chapter three.[6]

One of the passages in this prologue is of especial significance in this connection. It is the counsel of Job's wife which Job so emphatically rejects. Her advice "Curse God and die" is evidence of the author's awareness of Hebraic notions concerning the curse. It was thought to be so grievous if directed against God, that it might reverse itself and destroy the one who uttered it. This being the context, when a curse against his parents (the authors of his being) is in order, it is not surprising that the writer puts in the mouth of Job, not this gross impiety, but a conventional circumlocution, so that he who has just refused to "curse God, and die" must now find relief in the less hazardous phrase, the misdirected curse: "Perish the day!"

(1) Cf. S.H.Blank: The Curse, Blasphemy, the Spell, and the Oath, in *Hebrew Union College Annual*, XXIII, Part One, Cincinnati, 1950–1951, p. 85, n. 44, where the theme of this communication is very briefly stated. Also, on a related theme, the essay here following.

(2) Further severe warnings against filial impiety occur in Deut. 27.16 and 21.18–21. Cf. also Lev. 19.3, Ex. 21.15 and the Code of Hammurabi, par. 195.

(3) Cf. J. Hempel: Die israelitischen Auschauungen von Segen und Fluch im Lichte altorientalischer Parallelen, ZDMG, n. F. 4, 1925, p. 28.

(4) Cf. Blank, *op. cit.* (The Curse, etc.), p. 89f.

(5) *Op. cit.*, pp. 83–85.

(6) 1.5,11; 2.5,9.

An Effective Literary Device in Job 31

When the speeches of Elihu in Job 32—37 are omitted, the theophany in chapter 38 follows immediately upon chapter 31. Accordingly, chapter 31 is Job's last word before the pronouncing of the divine verdict. It is the climax and conclusion of Job's argument before the heavenly Judge. With it he rests his case. Therefore, we may rightfully expect of this chapter that it will contain the strongest possible statement of the point he regards as most essential.

This essential point is Job's innocence. And he does in fact state this point here, at the conclusion of his argument, in a most convincing fashion. The subject of this note is the method he uses to produce the conviction of his innocence.

To lend conviction to Job's words, the author of the book employs an effective literary device. To be sure, at the very outset, in the prologue where he introduced Job as a man "pious, upright, and god-fearing," who "shunned evil," the author revealed the fact of Job's innocence. But it is yet necessary for us to know that Job himself is convinced of his innocence. If he himself has any doubts about his innocence, he has no problem. He can explain his suffering by the assumption that, as his "friends" maintain, he has some hidden faults, some guilt of which he is only vaguely conscious. We must know that Job knows, without reservation, that he is innocent. We get that knowledge from this chapter.

Moreover, because this is a judgment scene, Job has to convince God that he is innocent. Job has appealed to the divine Judge for His favourable verdict. He has need to clear his name from suspicion—the suspicion which attaches to him as a result of the calamities which he has experienced. He is in the position of an accused man before a human court. He must assert his innocence in a manner well calculated to obtain his acquittal. This, also, he does in chapter 31. He does so by means of an oath.

Formally, his case does not differ from that of the wife accused of adultery who is tried by the ordeal described in the fifth chapter of Numbers, nor from that of the man suspected of theft in Ex. 22: 9 and 10 of whom it is said: "If a man deliver unto his neighbour an ass, or an ox, or a sheep, or any beast to keep, and it die, or be hurt, or driven away, no man seeing it; *the oath of the Lord* shall be between them, to see whether he hath put his hand unto his neighbour's goods; and the owner thereof *shall accept it* (the oath), and he (the oath-taker) shall not make restitution." According to the procedure here described, a man suspected of theft can give proof of his innocence by means of an oath, which oath the injured party must accept as proof.

Job 31 is such an oath, or, better, a whole series of such oaths. The text of the chapter may be in some disorder, but even as we have it, the chapter contains at least four unmistakable examples of the oath. That, in itself, is not remarkable; it is the form the oath takes in this chapter which is worthy of note.

The Bible contains many examples of the oath. The oath is a curse which a man accepts upon himself conditionally; that is to say, *if* he has done what he denies or has failed to do what he asserts. In taking an oath, a man says: "Let such and such a calamity befall me if I have done, or if I have not done, so and so." But the peculiar thing about the oath in the Bible is this: that almost without exception, when an oath is quoted, a part of it is suppressed. For example, David swears: "God do so to me, and more also, if I taste bread, or aught else, till the sun be down" (2 Sam. 3:35); these are the words he uses; he leaves unspecified the ominous contents of the "so" and the "more also." This is the invariable form of the eleven Biblical examples of this oath-formula. But that is not all. Far more frequently in the Biblical oath, even the evasive words "God do so to me, and more also" are entirely omitted and all that remains is a truncated conditional sentence with nothing but the protasis or condition—"If I do (or did) so and so". . .or "If I do not (or did not) do so and so. . ."—only this and no more; the conclusion containing the dire consequences is entirely suppressed.

Why? There is abundant Biblical evidence to suggest that fear, and fear alone, dictated the form of the evasive formula and caused the suppression of the condition. What is evaded and suppressed is the conditional curse. What is avoided is the naming of the calamity to befall the oath-taker if he is committing perjury. With an overpowering fear, one feared to name a calamity, convinced that if once it were put into words it would possess reality.

One of the visions of the prophet Zechariah (Zech. 5:1–4) enables us to recover the fantasy associated with the oath in the mind of Biblical man. In this vision the prophet beholds what his angelic guide identifies as a "curse" (אלה) going forth over the face of the whole land. He sees it as a giant scroll, fifteen feet high and twice as long, flying through space. This curse goes, the prophet learns, and enters unerringly into the home of the thief and the perjurer; it abides in the midst of the house and consumes it, even its timbers and its stones.

Also in the description of the trial by ordeal of a wife suspected of adultery (Num. 5:19–27) this fantasy is revealed. The essential ingredient of the potion she must drink is the curse written on a scroll and rinsed with water. Like the curse in the prophet's vision, which enters the house and consumes it as rot, this curse, too, enters the guilty body and fills it with corruption.

If Biblical man surrounded the oath-curse with such disturbing fantasy, as indeed he seems to have done, there is little wonder that ordinarily he refused to take upon himself the curse of an oath, even in its conditional form. Convention, the fruit of fear, prevented him from speaking the words which named the curse. From the belief in the effective power of the spoken word, a rigorous word-taboo arose—a word-taboo that is hardly ever violated; only three times in the entire Bible.

A complete oath with nothing suppressed occurs in Psalm 7, another in Psalm 137. The third example is this thirty-first chapter of Job. It is the classic Biblical example of an oath in the form of a complete conditional curse upon one's self. The received text of this chapter contains at least four clear instances of the complete oath: (1) verses 5, 7, and 8; (2) verses 9 and 10; (3) verses 13, 16–17, 19–22; and (4) verses 38–40. In each of the four complete oaths in this chapter, the final verse contains the apodosis, the curse which is to befall Job, the speaker, if he has been guilty of committing any of the offences or omitting any of the acts of piety and righteousness listed in the foregoing conditional clauses. These grim curses (in verses 8, 10, 22, and 40) are as follows: (If I have at all failed in my duty) "let me sow and another eat, let the produce of my soil be uprooted" or "let thistles grow up instead of wheat and weeds instead of barley"; (and if I have been guilty of any offence) "let my wife grind for another, let others bow down to embrace her" or "let my shoulder blade drop from my shoulder and my arm be rent from the socket."

The notable feature of this remarkable chapter is that Job says things here which are customarily left unsaid, or, at the most, concealed in the evasive oath-formula. We can appreciate the dramatic effect of this climax in the Job dialogue only if we recognize it as practically unique in this respect. Job boldly defies all convention, violates a word-taboo, and, without restraint, puts into words what is hardly ever spoken. Daringly he invites such disasters as the failure of his crops, the loss of his possessions, the alienation of his wife, the horrible crippling or maiming of his own body. No Biblical audience could have heard Job speak in this fashion without shudders and astonishment, and nothing was better calculated to produce in his hearers the conviction of Job's innocence than these curses pronounced by Job upon himself, this audacious breach of the word-taboo.

When the author of Job put into the mouth of Job this whole series of complete oaths, he was undoubtedly conscious of the effect he produced. After this there could be no question either that Job was innocent or that Job himself knew himself innocent.

The Nearness of God and Psalm Seventy-Three

It is a pleasure to offer for publication, in honor of a good friend, Charles Lynn Pyatt, a suggestion for the improvement of a great psalm and a brief discussion of its central theme.

The crux to be considered is the last three words of the 24th verse of Psalm 73: ואחר כבוד תקחני. The forced rendering of these words in the King James version, retained in the RSV, represents the traditional interpretation: "and afterward receive me to glory." But the traditional interpretation, implying as it does, reward after death, is unacceptable in the context. The idea of reward after death does not belong in the book of Psalms. The Revised Version margin: "and afterward receive me *with* glory," is only a little better. It, also, is forced out of the awkward Hebrew of the original and is unsuitable both in its broader and in its narrower context. So, nearly all modern scholars have recognized that the text of this half verse is faulty and various improvements have been proposed. The following suggestion results from an attempt to find the reading which best suits the thought structure as well as the literary form of the composition.

Psalm 73 is usually classed with the "didactic" psalms and if we are able to escape the somewhat unpleasant overtones of the word "didactic," we may so designate this psalm. Its author has had an experience which he wants to share with others for the benefit of their souls. And he does so here in what has become one of the best known and best loved psalms in the psalter.

The experience can be briefly told. A paraphrase of the psalmist's narrative would read as follows:

> Once I envied transgressors. Sleek, smug and successful, they arrogantly deny God's providence. To my shame be it said, I almost copied them. My own ascetic piety, I asked myself, what good has it done me? But now I see that I was passing through a crisis of faith. Fortunately for me, I learned in time to contrast the ultimate earthly fate of transgressors with my condition. I realized that eventually and suddenly God punishes the wicked and that I, on the contrary, even now enjoy God's presence continually. That is enough. I find complete joy in the nearness of God.

Despite a number of stubborn obscurities in the text, the thought structure of the psalm, as a whole, is relatively clear. The narrative moves in a direct line to the affirmation which serves as its climax and conclusion, the theme and point of the psalm: I find complete joy in the nearness of God; I know no higher good than the nearness of God. The problem text is a part of the climax and conclusion of the psalmist's narrative and an acceptable solution of the difficulty must fit into his argument at this high point.

The literary form of Psalm 73 is simple. The psalm is made up of couplets—of verses paired, each pair expressing a single idea. Admitting that verse 10 is not to be understood and that that the meaning of 17a escapes us; despite these uncertainties, we are yet certain that the psalm is composed of couplets. Twenty-six of the twenty-eight and one-half lines of the psalm fit into this pattern. The first line (v. 1) is a one line announcement of the conclusion, effectively placed at the very beginning:

> "Yes, God is good to the upright
> The Lord to the pure of heart."[1]

The twelfth line (v. 12), which also effectively stands alone, states the conclusion of the first major argument:

> "Lo! so it is with the wicked
> And the smug have achieved success."[2]

And the last half-line of the psalm (v. 28c) is a gloss. All the rest, the remaining twenty-six lines, fit together as couplets. And each couplet is composed of four predominantly synonymous cola. Verses 21 and 22 are a misplaced couplet; they should precede v. 17.[3]

A few examples will make the pattern clear and, at the same time, reveal a part of the thought. Verses 4 and 5, a couplet composed of four synonymous cola, speak of the wicked:

> "They experience no pangs,
> Unimpaired and stout is their strength,[4]
> Of human misery they have no share,
> They do not suffer as men do."

The next four cola (verses 6 and 7) have the same structure. It is still the wicked of whom they speak:

> "Consequently, arrogance is their neckpiece,
> Violence clothes them as a garment,
> Covetousness (?) proceeds from them,
> Excessive are their hearts' desires."[5]

Verses 8 and 9 are similarly paired:

> "From the depths they speak evilly,
> Frowardly they speak from the heights,[6]
> They circulate in the heavens their talk,
> Their speech goes about on the earth."

Beginning with verse 13, speaking now of himself and his ascetic piety, the psalmist still employs units of four cola each. The first of these couplets (v. 13f.) well illustrates the form:

> "To no avail whatever have I kept my heart pure
> And washed in innocence my hands
> And suffered daily
> And tormented myself morning by morning."[7]

The recognition of this pattern does two things. It makes more obvious the unsatisfactory character of the problem text. And it suggests what thought must originally have been expressed in this place.

The problem text comes at the end of the eleventh couplet (verses 23 and 24). The first three cola in the couplet lead naturally to a thought other than that expressed by the fourth, according to the received text. They say:

> "But I am with thee always
> Thou holdest my right hand
> Guiding me by thy counsel. . ."

The common denominator of these three-fourths of the couplet prescribes the limits for the fourth. The common denominator is the nearness of God—or, in the bold metaphor of the psalm, God's physical presence: "I am with thee," "thou holdest my right hand," "guiding me." And this, according to the literary form and the thought structure of the psalm, must be the import also of the final clause in the couplet.

We assume, then, that originally the final clause continued the metaphor of the physical nearness of God and we observe, further, that the immediate parallel to the problem text is the first half of v. 24: בעצתך תנחני, "guiding me by thy counsel."[8]

If now we turn to the received text, looking for what, according to this parallel, could have completed the 24th verse, we find there the required sense without radical emendation. In all probability, the original text read:

> בעצתך תנחני ואחריך תדביקני,
> "Guiding me by thy counsel, keeping me near."

If we write the present consonant text beneath the proposed consonant text, omitting spaces, vowel letters and final forms, the two appear as follows:

> Proposed text: ואחרכתדבקני,
> Present text: ואחרכבדתקחני.

Only one consonant occurs in the present text which is not in the proposed text, and the position of only two others is different. The present text is probably the result of the accidental transposition of the two letters *taw* and *bet* and a subsequent attempt to make sense out of the resulting confusion.

The proposal ואחריך תדביקני, literally: "and behind thee thou makest me to cleave," is good idiomatic Hebrew. Psalm 63:9 shows how natural the language is. There we read: דבקה נפשי אחריך בי תמכה ימינך, "My soul followeth hard after thee, thy right hand upholdeth me" (RV). Not only is the root דבק here also used pregnantly with the preposition אחרי (cf. Jer. 42:16; I Chr. 10:2) to describe the relationship between the psalmist and God, but here too in the parallel member, God holds the speaker by the hand. The correspondence is very close and Psalm 63:9 lends strong support to the reading proposed for 73:24.

The *hiph'il* form of the verb דבק occurs in a similar, similarly anthropomorphic context in Jer. 13:11: "as the girdle cleaveth to the loins of a man (הדבקתי אלי את כל בית ישראל)—

so have I caused to cleave unto me the whole house of Israel and the whole house of Judah," saith the Lord (RV.—Cf. also Ezek. 3:26; Deut. 28:21 *et al.*).[9]

If the proposed solution of the difficulty in v. 24 is correct, the three final couplets of Psalm 73 originally brought the psalm to a triumphant close.

23. But I am with thee always
    Thou holdest my right hand;
24. By thy counsel thou leadest me
    Keeping me near.
25. Whom have I in heaven but thee
    And having thee I want nothing on earth.
26. Though in body and mind I waste away
    My portion forever is God.
27. Lo, such as are far from thee perish;
    Thou destroyest whoever wanders from thee.
28. But my greatest good is the nearness of God;
    I put my trust in the Lord. . . [10]

So much for the critical note to verse 24 of Psalm 73. Instead of an irrelevant allusion to a future reward, the verse is part of the psalmist's description of the joy of God's nearness. And this emerges as the theme of the psalm, as the thought which its author shares with us.

A study of the concept "the nearness of God" could include the whole of biblical theology and religion. Of the many observations which might be made on the connotations of the concept, three are of interest here for the light they shed on Psalm 73.

The first observation is this: *The nearness of God was sometimes meant in a real sense, sometimes in a figurative sense.* It can hardly be doubted that biblical myth conceived of the nearness of God as something quite real. God could be far away in space or he could be nearby. He could go away and he could approach, coming from a distance. So in the narrative of the building of Babel (Gen. 11.5), he comes "down" to see the tower which the men have built and, in the song of Deborah (Ju. 5:4, cf. v. 23), he comes from Seir, from the fields of Edom to fight the kings of Canaan. Some contemporaries of Ezekiel (Ezek. 8:12; 9:9) express the thought that he has forsaken the land and gone away, and in Ezekiel's vision of the restored community (Ezek. 43:2ff.) God comes from the East through the eastern gate into the rebuilt temple. Descriptions of this sort—and there are many—are myth or they are vestiges of myth and in them God's "nearness" is real: God approaches physically through space.

In other contexts, however, as in Psalm 73, God's "nearness" is a figure of speech and the reality it possesses is poetic reality. Metaphorically, here, the psalmist speaks of his intimacy with God in terms of God's nearness. Only the language of mythology remains. The conclusion of Psalm 73 is mythological in the sense that the 23rd Psalm is a myth (cf. v. 4 of Ps. 23).

The second observation we may make is this: *They whom God approaches may regard his nearness as a threat or as a boon.* To return to examples already cited, when

God came down to view the doings of the builders of Babel, it was only to discomfit and disperse them. When he came from Seir to give a welcome victory to Deborah's forces, he struck with terror their Canaanite foes. Ezekiel's contemporaries in Jerusalem before 586 found comfort in the thought that their pagan rites in the Temple were not observed. They said: "The Lord seeth us not, the Lord hath forsaken the land." In like manner, the scoffers of whom the author of Psalm 73 complains persist in wickedness, trusting in the remoteness of God. They say (v. 11): "How does God know? Does the Most High take heed?"[11]

When, on the other hand, according to Ezekiel, God takes up his residence again in the restored temple, the thought of his nearness is surely to be a source of confidence for the regathered inhabitants of Jerusalem. And so with God's nearness, which the scoffers must fear; it is for the pious author of Psalm 73 a rich and rewarding experience.

In other words, the nearness of God is retributive in nature; God approaches for judgment, to punish or to reward. Thus, exultantly, according to the words of Deutero-Isaiah (Isa. 50:8), Israel exclaims: "Near at hand is my vindicator" (i.e., the divine judge who will give to Israel the favorable verdict).[12]

Reduced to a formula, the difference between those who regard God's nearness as a boon and those whom it strikes with terror is simply this: they treasure God's nearness who are conscious of his favor; they fear it who might expect him to be hostile. It is possible that Isa. 58:2 presupposes such a formulation: In part it reads: כגוי אשר צדקה עשה ... קרבת אלהים יחפצון, and this might be translated with a touch of irony: "as though they were a people who have done righteousness . . . they desire the nearness of God."

By and large, there are three categories of persons who, like the author of Psalm 73, may without fear legitimately "desire the nearness of God"—and this is the third of the observations concerning this concept.

The first category, which appears also to be the earliest, is God's people, Israel. The idea that God's nearness is no threat, but a benefit to Israel, is pre-prophetic. It is the uncritical view that God and Israel are so bound up, the one with the other, that God approaches only to aid his people and defeat its enemies. It is uncritical also in the sense that the people appears not as an aggregate of individuals but as an undifferentiated community enjoying divine favor. It goes without saying that this notion was among those most violently disputed by the pre-exilic prophets. During the exile, however, a Deutero-Isaiah could espouse it anew (Isa. 41:10, 13; 50:8; 55:6; cf. Ps. 148:14; Deut. 4:7; Zech. 13:9).

Unlike the first, the second category is composed of individuals, of single persons who, like Moses, Gideon, or Jeremiah, may be called the elect of God. It is said of them that God is "with" them and his nearness endows them with more than ordinary powers. When Moses asks, "Who am I to stand before Pharaoh and deliver Israel?" God replies, "I will be with you and this will prove to you that I have sent you" (Ex. 3:12). When Gideon is summoned to leadership, he demurs with self-deprecation, and God says to him, "I will be with you, and you shall destroy Midian to a man" (Ju. 6:11ff.). The pattern is repeated in the inaugural vision of Jeremiah (Jer. 1:6–8) for whom the nearness of God is a shield against his adversaries (Jer. 1:19; 15:20; 20:11).

This category of charismatic persons, of whom Moses, Gideon and Jeremiah are merely examples, stands midway between the first and the third of the categories. The third category, like the second, is made up of individuals—in this instance, individuals like Job and the author of Psalm 73, who by reason of some virtue seem to *deserve* God's nearness. Although the thought is expressed here and there (Lam. 3:57; Deut. 4:7; Isa. 55:6) that whenever God is called, he is near, this thought is qualified in Jer. 29:12–14 and Ps. 145:18: he is near to all who call upon him earnestly, בכל לבבכם, באמת ("If with all your hearts ye truly seek him...").[13] Perhaps the qualifying idea was interpreted by some as involving fasts and castigation of the soul because, in Isa. 58:3, persons are quoted who ask: למה צמנו ולא ראית עניגו נפשנו ולא תדע. These persons who, according to the preceding verse, "desire the nearness of God," complain that despite their fasting and self-affliction, God has not seen or given heed.

The idea that, by mortification, one might invite God's presence, may well have existed at one time for, not only this passage but another in Trito-Isaiah and one in Psalm 34 suggest the idea. Specifically named there as persons who enjoy the nearness of God are "the crushed": דכאי רוח, נדכאים, דכא, "the lowly": שפל רוח, (Isa. 57:15; Ps. 34:19) and "the broken-hearted": נשברי לב (Ps. 34:19).[14]

Certainly the idea of mortification is not common in the literature of the Old Testament. But it does appear here in connection with the concept of the nearness of God. And it seems to lurk also in the 73rd Psalm which, more than any other, deals with this concept, the nearness of God. Why does the psalmist here refer to his ascetic piety if not to tie it in with the theme of the psalm? Speaking of the crisis through which he passed, in the couplet verses 13 and 14, he describes his unwelcome thoughts:

> "To no avail whatever have I kept my heart pure
> And washed in innocence my hands
> And suffered daily
> And tormented myself morning by morning."[15]

And in the conclusion (v. 26), he reverts to this theme:

> "Though in body and mind I waste away," he says
> My portion forever is God."[16]

Possibly the idea of renunciation occurs also in the famous lines (v. 25) which are paired with these:

> "Whom have I in heaven but thee?
> And having thee I want nothing on earth."

The crushed, the lowly, it seems, the broken-hearted, who suffer in body and mind: in short, the "Jobs" of the Bible are they who appear to enjoy most specially the nearness of God.

Nevertheless, true to the dominant ethical spirit of the Old Testament, the author of Psalm 73 puts the emphasis where it belongs. At the very beginning of the psalm, he states his considered conclusion: "Yes," he says, all evidence to the contrary notwithstanding,

"God is good to the upright,
The Lord is good to the pure of heart."

אך טוב לישר אל אלהים לברי לבב.¹⁷

(1) This essay deals with only one of the several difficulties presented by the Hebrew text of this psalm, that contained in v. 24b. Several proposals for the improvement of the text in other places are accepted in what follows without detailed discussion. Most of these proposals are to be found in one or more of the published commentaries. (The suggestion offered very tentatively in note 5, below, may be new.) Here, in v. 1, MT לישראל is read as two words אל לישר, a reading proposed by H. Graetz (*Kritischer Commentar zu den Psalmen*, Breslau, 1882), who cites Ewald and Schorr and is cited in many recent commentaries.

(2) Reading ושלוים for ושלוי עולם.

(3) As suggested among others by R. Kittel in *Komm. zum A.T., Die Psalmen*, Leipzig, 1929, p. 245.

(4) Reading למותם as two words: למו תם.

(5) Reading לבבם for לבב (haplography). Although MT חלב is almost certainly wrong, it is hard to say what word it replaces. The above translation supposes that it was מחמד (cf. the phrase מחמד עין in I Ki. 20:6; Ezek. 24:16, 21, 25) or even מחמל (cf. מחמל נפש in Ezek. 24:21). The whole of v. 7 is obscure and the translation at this point hardly more than a guess.

(6) Reading ימיקו for יעמיקו and עשק for עתק.

(7) Reading והוכחתי (a *hoph'al*) for the noun ותוכחתי.

(8) The meaning of the verb נחה is clear from its use in Ps. 78:14, for example: וינחם בענן יומם, "he led them in a cloud by day." The position of one who "leads" or "guides" is in front of the one who is led—but not too far in front.

(9) The reading proposed here is better Hebrew than the admittedly simpler emendation proposed by H. Graetz, *op. cit.*, quoted by Buhl in the third edition of Kittel's *Biblia Hebraica* and adopted by J. M. P. Smith in the University of Chicago *American Translation*. With a proper feeling for the requirements of the context, Graetz divided the words differently, substituted a *yod* for a *vav*, and proposed the reading: ואחריך ביד תקחני, which Smith translated "and by the hand thou dost take me after thee." Although this is distinctly better than the present text and fits quite well into the context, it is not wholly satisfactory. In the first place, the repetition of "by the hand" here is improbable after ביד ימינך in the first line of the couplet and, in the second place, the combination תקחני אחריך to "take" someone "*after*" one is not biblical idiom. For this meaning, the verb לקח is construed with the preposition עם (Ju. 4:6; Gen. 48:1) or את (Ex. 17:5).

(10) Reading ביהוה for באדני יהוה.

(11) Biblical skepticism is always "practical." It is a denial not of God's existence but of his presence and, indeed, of his concern.

(12) Similarly Job 31:35.

(13) Among those who call upon God and desire his nearness are persons who, in Ps. 10:1; 22:12, 20; 35:22; 38:22 and 71:12, speak such words as למה יהוה תעמד ברחוק or אלהי אל תרחק ממני.

(14) Cf., also, Isa. 61:1; 66:2; Ps. 51:19; 101:5; 138:6.

(15) See above, note 7.

(16) Omitting צור לבבי.

(17) Conversely, according to Prov. 15:29: רחוק יהוה מרשעים, God is far from the wicked; cf. Ps. 119:155.

Some Observations Concerning Biblical Prayer

I

ברוך הבא בשם יהוה

The expression ברוך הבא בשם י׳ does not mean: "Blessed be he that cometh in the name of the Lord."[1] Current liturgical usage is contrary to the biblical idiom. The reference in the Bible is not to a "coming in the name of the Lord."

Quite apart from the original intention of the Hebrew expression—which shall yet be considered—one must ask what indeed the English rendering is intended to mean. What does the modern officiant intend to say when, for example, he refers to a bride and groom, to a father presenting his son for circumcision, when he refers ceremoniously to any persons, as "they that come in the name of the Lord"? "To come in the Lord's name" is not an English idiom of transparent meaning. The officiant probably intends to say that the couple, the father, or other persons so designated are engaging in a ritual honoring God, that they are showing themselves submissive to a divine command, that their presence in the cultic situation is for the sake of God. The officiant probably intends to commend the persons thus addressed for their evident piety. But the English idiom is not adequate for his intention. If this is his intention why does he not say: "Blessed be he that cometh for the sake of God's name" or "in accordance with God's will" or "in loyalty to God"? Or why does he not use a different biblical idiom?

A different idiom, more suitable for his purpose, indeed occurs. It is the combination ללכת בשם י׳, not "to come" but "to walk in the name of the Lord," and this idiom is liturgical. It occurs in Mic. 4:5. The verse which contains it is a liturgical supplement to the paragraph which it concludes. This paragraph, Mic. 4:1–5, is practically identical with Isa. 2:2–5, though the version in Micah is one verse longer. It is the sunburst of messianic promise that begins with the words: "It shall come to pass at the end of days that the mountain of the Lord's house will be established as the highest mountain . . ." Both versions, the one in Isaiah 2 and the one in Micah 4, have liturgical supplements and these are very like each other. The one in Isaiah reads: לכו ונלכה באור י׳, "O house of Jacob, come (לכו), and let us walk in the light of the Lord." The one in Micah, though differently phrased has similar import: כי כל העמים ילכו איש בשם אלהיו ואנחנו נלך בשם י׳ אלהינו לעולם ועד

All the nations may walk each in the name of its god,
But we will walk in the name of the Lord our God forever and ever.

The verbs in the two passages, in Isaiah and Micah, are forms of the one verb הלך, "to walk." However adequate the English idiom "to walk in the name of the Lord" may be for the intended sense, the meaning of the Hebrew original is clear enough. Both liturgical supplements (the one in the form of an exhortation, the other a pledge) express Israel's desire to be associated with the Lord, its God. The one uses the formula "to walk in the light of," the other "to walk in the name of"; both express loyalty and dedication. This is probably the sense which the officiant today wants to find in the combination "to come in the name of the Lord"—but without justification.

What the Hebrew expression בוא בשם י׳ means in the Bible is surely not what the officiant today intends. This latter combination occurs twice, and its meaning is not suitable for liturgical use. It has quite a different sense. It occurs first in David's response to Goliath's challenge and it means "armed with God's potent name as with a weapon." David says to the challenger: "You come (בא) against me armed with sword, spear and lance, and I come against you armed (only) with the name of the Lord of hosts (ואנכי בא־אליך בשם י׳ צבאות), the God of the armies of Israel whom you have taunted" (I Sam. 17:45). "Armed with" is a quite suitable rendering here of the Hebrew preposition בְּ־, the preposition translated "in" where in other contexts it appears in the phrase "in the name of the Lord."

When today the officiant exclaims: "Blessed be he that cometh in the name of the Lord" surely he does not mean: "he that cometh armed with the potent name of the Lord," but that is quite as surely the meaning of the preposition here; the parallel "with sword, spear and lance" and the continuation of the narrative, both point undeniably to this meaning. This is the meaning of the preposition also in the one remaining biblical passage which contains the combination בא בשם י׳. Here, in II Chron. 14:10, in the stress of battle, the King Asa prays: עזרנו י׳ אלהינו כי־עליך נשענו ובשמך באנו על־ההמון הזה, "Help us, O Lord our God, for we leaned on Thee and came against this multitude armed with Thy name."

The idea of the potent name of God is familiar; God's name goes to war on the side of his elect. So, with confidence a psalmist can exclaim: "By Thee we fell our enemies, by Thy name we trample our foes" (Ps. 44:6). Another can plead: "O God, save me by Thy name, vindicate me by Thy power" (54:3), thus equating "name" and "power" (שם and גבורה). Surrounded by enemies like swarming insects, burning thorns, yet another can repeatedly boast: בשם י׳ כי אמילם, "by the name of the Lord I cut them off (?)" (118:10–12; cf. Zeph. 3:12). It is similar with Ps. 33:20 f.; 89:24 f.; 124:7 f. and especially 20:2, 6 and 8. The last cited verse is reminiscent of David's words to Goliath; the verb is uncertain[2] but the idea is clear: God's name is mightier than chariots and horses. It is not strange therefore to find David coming against Goliath and Asa coming against a multitude armed with the name of the Lord.

It is these that properly "come in the name of the Lord," not the persons referred to liturgically in the formula: ברוך הבא בשם י׳. The customary translation of the formula is faulty. The phrase "in the name of the Lord" which appears in this formula is erroneously attached in translation to the words "he that cometh." The phrase בשם י׳ does not modify the subject הבא; it modifies the predicate ברוך, "blessed." The subject here does not like David "come in the name of the Lord"; in the name of the Lord he is blessed. The elements combined in the formula are blessing and the name. These two elements are frequently thus combined. For, the name of the Lord was potent, according to biblical thought, not in battle only, but to bless as well.

The combination of blessing and name appears in II Sam. 6:18 (and in the almost identical passage I Chron. 16:2): When David had done with offering the burnt offerings and the peace offerings "he blessed the people in the name of the Lord of hosts."[3] The unquoted words of his blessing may well have been: ברוכים אתם בשם י׳, "Blessed be ye in the name of the Lord." (The equivalent formula ברוכים אתם לי׳ appears in fact in I Sam. 23:21; II Sam. 2:5 and Ps. 115:15.)

The significance of the mention of the "name" in this context is clear: it introduces the agent of blessing; it draws the blessing into the orbit of religion. A blessing, like a curse,[4] can be self-sufficient, effective by reason of the energy inherent in the words of blessing. "Blessings on thee!" is alone a benediction requiring no fulfilling agent other than itself. A blessing is self-fulfilling—this according to biblical thought. But, already in biblical times, the "profane" blessing (like the curse) was drawn into the religious sphere and associated with Israel's God. One of the ways by which this was done was by adding to the bare formula of blessing (ברוך) the phrase בשם י׳. When a friend approached one could greet him simply ברוך הבא, "Blessed be he that cometh." Or one could add piety to the sentiment, and convert a wish into a prayer by pronouncing him "blessed in the name of the Lord."

There were persons whose privilege it was "to bless in the name of the Lord," and there were places favorable for blessing. The privileged persons are mentioned in Chronicles and in Numbers but most frequently in Deuteronomy. These were Levitic or priestly groups. "Then the Lord divided off the tribe of Levi," one passage says, "to bear the ark of the Covenant of the Lord, to serve before the Lord, to minister to Him and to bless in His name until this day" (Deut. 10:8; cf. 18:5, 7; 21:5). "And Aaron was divided off..," another says, "he and his sons forever, to make burnt offerings before the Lord, to minister to Him and to bless in His name forever" (I Chron. 23:13). The frame which encloses the priestly blessing at the end of Num. 6 is explicit: "The Lord said to Moses: Say to Aaron and his sons: So shall you bless the children of Israel; say to them: 'May the Lord bless you and keep you . . .' And they shall place My name on the children of Israel and I will bless them" (22—27).

The place as well as the person had bearing on the form of the blessing. According to the passages just cited, a Levite or a priest in particular, blessed in the name of the Lord, placing God's name on the children of Israel. These, naturally, gave the blessing a religious color. Naturally too, if the place was a house of God the blessing assumed a religious aspect. The blessing under consideration, the blessing in God's name which occurs in Ps. 118:26 is a prime example. In this context "he that cometh" is a worshiper approaching the temple, and they who speak are doubtless the priestly officiants within. In the name of the Lord they bless "him that cometh" and they also say ברכנוכם מבית י׳, "We bless you from the house of the Lord." The expression מבית י׳, "from the house of the Lord," is like the phrase מציון, "from Zion," in Ps. 128:5 and 134:3, both of which read "May God bless you from Zion."

But it was not alone the temple personnel who used the pious form of blessing, and the blessing in this form was not spoken only in the precincts of the temple. It percolated among the people, so that even passers-by could greet one another with blessing shaped with similar religious intent. Thus the words of the psalm:

> "The blessing of the Lord upon you.
> We bless you in the name of the Lord" (Ps. 129:8).

This last cited greeting, incidentally, is the most striking evidence that in the blessing ברוך הבא בשם י׳, the phrase בשם י׳ modifies the predicate ברוך and not the subject הבא. No one here is "coming." The blessing is simply ברכנו אתכם בשם י׳, "We bless you in the name of the Lord."

The result of these observations is this: that the officiant today and modern translators of the Bible would do well to abandon the meaningless reference to him "that cometh in the name of the Lord" and translate correctly according to the biblical idiom:

> Blessed be he that cometh,
> Blessed in the name of the Lord

This essay appeared in the in the 1961 volume (XXXII) of the *Hebrew Union College Annual*, nine years before the publication (in 1970) of the *New English Bible* translation of the Old Testament. In the same sense now this NEB reads

> Blessed in the name of the Lord
> Are all who come . . .

II

אבי

When a man says piously: "O Lord!" or "Father!" he has spoken a prayer; whether he continues or not, he has said something already. He has addressed himself to God, become involved, expressed his sense of relationship with God. Invoking God—"calling on his name" is the biblical term—*is* prayer. Just as, when the officiant blesses "in the name of the Lord" it is his intention to associate God with the blessing, so when the worshiper calls on God's name he hopes to awaken a response in God, in order that they 'two may be related.

The invocation or address is a formal element usual in biblical prayer—usual to such an extent that it appears almost essential there. The first or the second word in a biblical prayer is likely to be the name of God or its equivalent, in the vocative construction. Attributes may follow or not, and the address may or may not be repeated in the body of the prayer, but at least it stands at the beginning and serves an important purpose. It directs the prayer to its proper object and, too, the mind of him who prays. It provides the focus. But not this only; naming God is itself and alone an act of worship.

Prayers throughout the Bible confirm these observations. A few of them, all cited from the book of Jeremiah, may serve as illustrations:

Thou art right, O Lord, if I argue with Thee . . . (Jer. 12:1).

O Lord, my strength and my fortress,
And my refuge in a time of distress,
To Thee . . . (Jer. 16:19).

Heal me, O Lord, and I shall be healed,
Save me . . . (Jer. 17:14).

Thou hast enthralled me, O Lord . . . (20:7).

Listen, O Lord, to me,
And hear the speech of my adversaries (18:19).

In this last cited prayer after four verses the address is resumed:

But Thou, O Lord, knowest . . . (18:23).[5]

So right and regular is this feature in these prayers that where it may seem to be missing a conjectural restoration is sometimes admissible. In Jer. 11:18 as it stands, Jeremiah appears to be speaking about God in the few words which make up the first half of the verse, although in the three words which form the second half-verse, and indeed in the remainder of this prayer, he is addressing himself to God. It is tempting, therefore, to find a vocative in the first word of the prayer, just where according to the usual pattern we expect to find it, and then to read the verb which follows as a second person form, thus: הודעתני י׳, "O Lord, Thou didst inform me," continuing: "and I knew; then didst Thou show me their doings." The address is resumed in v. 20. Similarly, in Jer. 15:11; although the opening words of the verse are now אמר י׳, "God said," clearly here the prophet is speaking. He is speaking to God; and God is not speaking either to people or prophet. For this and other reasons it is tempting again to construe י׳ as a vocative and for אמר to read אמן as in the Septuagint, that is: "Indeed, O Lord . . . "[6] with God immediately addressed.

Prayer in Jeremiah, then, normally begins in this fashion; only one other word, or at most a phrase, precedes the vocative, which may otherwise be the very first word of the prayer. It is established at the outset that the speaker is addressing himself to God. He calls on God's name.

Jeremiah's prayers illustrate the principle. Illustrations abound. For the most part in the book of Psalms, those psalms that are prayers, and the prayer portions of composite psalms, those prayers too that are scattered in the other biblical books, begin in this fashion, calling on the name of God. (So Amos 7:2 and 5; Ezek. 9:8; Isa. 38:3; Dan. 9:4; Ezra 9:6, and many more.)

Two prophetic passages, one in Jeremiah and one in Hosea, throw further light on the significance of the invocation. In both of these passages God is speaking to Israel, his people, his bride. In the passage in Jeremiah God hopefully showers his people with gifts: "I said . . . I will give you a land of delight . . . And I thought: You will call Me 'Father' (אבי) and turn from Me no more" (3:19). God wanted Israel to say "Father!" to call Him "Father." The mere address would be a sign of devotion; this is what the continuation implies: "and turn from Me no more." It is the same as if they said what only a few verses later Jeremiah imagines them saying: "Here we are. We have come to You, for You are the Lord our God" (v. 22). It is the same as if they said what, earlier in this same chapter Jeremiah imagines them saying: "You are the companion of my youth," for there in the fourth verse this declaration follows on the invocation "Father!" quite as, in v. 19, "and turn from Me no more" follows on the same address. In the preceding chapter Jeremiah cites an aberration. He chides the erring masses who "say to the wooden thing: 'You are my father!' and to the thing of stone: 'You gave birth to me!'" (2:27). There is nothing wrong with the prayer; what is said is right. It is merely misdirected. Saying "My Father!" is good; addressing the words to a wooden image is an offense.[7] Also this illustration is otherwise instructive. The parallel exclamations permit the inference that "Father!" can mean this too: the confession of dependency, of creatureliness—"You gave birth to me."

Thus a cluster of passages in Jer. 2 and 3 suggests some of the things that a mere vocative can imply: devotion, affection, dependency. The invocation "Father!" can itself be a prayer.

Not only may a prayer be misdirected, as when, in Jeremiah's words, men say to "the wooden thing: 'You are my father!'" According to a passage in Hosea one can also employ the wrong form of address; properly addressing God one can call Him by the wrong name. God will see to it, Hosea says in 2:16–18, that His people call Him by a suitable name. In the desert God will woo His unfaithful wife, will give her presents of vineyards and hope, and she will respond again to Him there as she did in her youth. When that occurs, God says, "you will call Me 'Husband!' (אישי) and no more call Me 'Baal!' (בעלי)." Although the word *ba'al* can likewise mean "husband" and another prophet can call the land of Israel *be'ulah* ("espoused"), employing a cognate of *ba'al* (Isa. 62:4), this designation was too intimately associated with the Canaanite god to be acceptable to Hosea. It mattered, according to him, what name one used when one addressed God in prayer. The passage in Hosea continues with the words: "And I shall remove the names of the Baals from her mouth and they shall be mentioned no more" (Hos. 2:19; and cf. Josh. 23:7).

In biblical prayer certainly the most usual address is God's proper name יהוה, which conventionally we translate "O Lord!" *'El* and *'Elohim* are frequent; "Lord of hosts!" is also common (I Sam. 1:11; Isa. 37:16, and often). And there are others: "Husband!" as in Hosea 2, is not usual, "Father!" as in Jeremiah 3 is hardly more so, in biblical times.[8] "O King!" occurs, as in Ps. 145:1 and 20:10 (cf. Jer. 10:7); and "Judge!" (שופט), as in Jer. 11:20 (cf. Ps. 94:2).

Since different images of God are present in the mind of man, and God may be any of these: father, friend or husband; king, judge or master; shepherd, warrior or even "Santa Claus," but when one prays He may not be an impersonal or philosophical abstraction, the first cause, the life force, the wholly other, the superego, or even the moral law, a man will choose, when he prays, to address himself according to his circumstances to one or another of his images of God. And that too is an important function of the invocation with which still, following the model of biblical prayer, we begin our prayers. The address not only provides the focus, it sharpens the image. And it is, itself and alone, an acceptable prayer. אבי, "Father!" is a prayer.

I had completed this section of this paper before I noticed the relevance of a New Testament passage: "When we cry 'Abba! Father!' it is the Spirit himself bearing witness with our spirit that we are children of God..." (Rom. 8:15–17).[9]

III

לקרוא בשם יהוה

Exod. 20:24b is the charter of the synagogue. This is not at all how students of the Bible have understood the verse, but a plausible interpretation leads to this conclusion. The synagogue owes its existence to the thought which in its original form this half-verse expressed.

This section of this study is related to the two which have preceded. It is a matter of where one mentions God's name.

The verse from Ps. 118: ברוך הבא בשם י' ברכנוכם מבית י', considered in section I, leaves the impression that the effective blessing is the one which the temple personnel pronounce in the house of God in the Lord's name. Passages which assign to the Levites or the Aaronic temple priests the privilege of blessing in the name of the Lord (as above) strengthen this impression. The location of such passages—in Deuteronomy, Numbers and Chronicles—points to the source of this assumption: it emanated from the Jerusalem temple. Along with the elevation of the Jerusalem priesthood, Deuteronomy celebrated Jerusalem as the place which God chose "for his name to dwell there" (לשכן שמו שם). Deuteronomy does not refer to Jerusalem by name, but only because the book is attributed to Moses, too far in advance of Solomon's building activity for a specific reference. In due course, when the Deuteronomic historian told of the dedication of the temple, he did not hesitate to identify it. Then God said of Solomon's temple: "I have consecrated this house which you built, to place there My name forever, and My eyes and My thoughts shall be there continually" (I Kings 9:3). Enjoying such repute Jerusalem was naturally the place where effective blessings "in the name of the Lord" might originate.

But the primacy of Jerusalem was repeatedly challenged.[10] It was not long after the Josianic reform that Jeremiah announced the doom of the "house." It would fare like the former "house" at Shiloh (Jer. 7:1–15). And only a few years later, while yet the temple stood, Jeremiah denied its claim to unique authority. To Judeans exiled with Jehoiachin to Babylonia he wrote urging patience, and for God he said to them "Call Me (וקראתם אתי) ... and pray to Me, and I will hear you" (29:12). The prophet did not count as a hindrance the distance separating Babylon from Jerusalem but asked his people on foreign soil to invoke God there, confident that God would hear. Although allegedly God's name was "dwelling" in Jerusalem, Jeremiah summoned his people to "call" God in Babylonia.

A generation later, some decades after 587 and the deportation under Zedekiah, the temple lying in ruins, another prophet, the Second Isaiah, still saw no hindrance in the way. With or without a Jerusalem temple the exiles still might confidently invoke their God. "Seek the Lord while He may be found," this prophet said, "call Him (קראוהו) while He is near" (Isa. 55:6a). Incidentally, this latter passage is suffused with the spirit of its author, with the characteristic elation of the Second Isaiah. He means what the words say: that the time is uniquely propitious, that God is presently responsive and at hand, and that God's people have only to snatch the golden moment. It is, nevertheless, significant in the context of this study that this invitation comes to a people exiled far from the site of a ruined temple.

Not these two prophets alone, a chorus of voices among the passing generations disputed the claims of the rebuilt temple, its cult and its personnel.[11] Speaking for God by Nathan to David, one of them asked: "In all My going about among all the people of Israel did I ever say . . . . : 'Why have you built Me no house of cedar?'" (II Sam. 7:7). And another said for God: "The heavens are My throne, the earth is My footstool. What house that you might build for Me or what sanctuary (מקום) could serve as My resting place?" (Isa. 66:1).

The spirit of Psalm 145 is notably universalistic; here God's enduring concern is for His whole creation. It is not surprising then to find in this psalm the broadest sort of declaration of God's availability: קרוב י' לכל קוראיו, "The Lord is near to all that call Him"—with only this qualification: "to all that call Him in truth" (v. 18). The psalmist here phrases poetically another of the thoughts which Jeremiah communicated to his fellows in Babylonia. כי תדרשוני בכל לבבכם ונמצאתי לכם נאם י' . . ., "'If you seek Me with your whole heart, I will be responsive to you' God says" according to Jeremiah (Jer. 29:13b—14a). But the psalmist says more than the prophet. The word "all" in the phrase "to all that call Him," repeated in the parallel "to all that call Him in truth," has a breadth which Jeremiah, writing only to the Judeans in exile, had no reason to express.

The foregoing section of this study considered what it means to "call" God, to address Him, to mention His name. Addressing God the worshiper expresses his devotion, his affection, and his dependency. But he also initiates a relationship with the God whom he invokes. He invites a response from Him whose name he mentions. It is of course possible, and in biblical times it was apparently not unusual, for a person to address himself to a "strange" God, to mention a wrong name. Hos. 2:19, cited above,[12] expressed God's determination that the names of the Baals be mentioned no more. The passage in Joshua is to the same effect: ". . . That you come not among these peoples left with you and mention not the name of their gods (ובשם אלהיהם לא־תזכירו) and swear not by, nor serve, nor worship them" (Josh. 23:7). להזכיר בשם, "to mention by name," is the new term here in these two passages. It means the same as לקרוא, "to call' or address or invoke—with perhaps the added sense "to specify." It is the term that appears in Exod. 20:24b.

The text of this half-verse is not above suspicion. According to the massoretic tradition it reads: בכל המקום אשר אזכיר את־שמי אבוא אליך וברכתיך, which seems to mean "In that whole place where I shall mention My name I will come to you and bless you." According to this massoretic tradition the statement begins with the words בכל המקום, "in that whole place." The Samaritan Pentateuch here reads simply במקום, with the article but without כל, i. e., "in the place." The Syriac version has כל but does not render the article. It either read בכל מקום (without the article), or understood the received text to mean not בכל המקום "in that whole place" but בכל מקום, "in every place."[13] The Syriac version had a different tradition also for אזכיר את שמי, instead of which it appears to have read תזכיר את שמי—not "where I shall mention My name" but "where you mention My name."

I suggest that the Syriac has somehow preserved the original text and that it read בכל מקום אשר תזכיר את שמי אבוא אליך וברכתיך, "In every place where you mention My name I will come to you and bless you."

If this was indeed the original text, no wonder it suffered change! The words בכל מקום אשר תזכיר את שמי, "in *every* place where *you* mention My name," are so manifestly at odds with the recurrent Deuteronomic formula, במקום אשר יבחר י' לשכן שמו שם, "in *that* place which *God* will choose for His name to dwell there" (Deut. 16:2 and often), that the two principles were openly at war with each other. This may be what happened: that a rival recension of the original text put in its appearance, which new recension, in the spirit of Deuteronomy, gave the victory to Jerusalem. According to this recension the text may have read במקום אשר אזכיר את שמי אבוא אליך וברכתיך, "In *that* place where *I* shall mention My name I will come to you and bless you."[14] "That place" is of course the Deuteronomic place which God will choose for His name to dwell there, and thus the heterodoxy of the presumed original of the Exodus verse is expunged.

What then of the text as it has come down to us? This form is a compromise. It preserves in part both the original and the recension. It rejects the original תזכיר in favor of the "correction" אזכיר, but it combines the original בכל מקום with במקום to produce the meaningless conflation בכל המקום, "in that whole place."

Whether this is a true or a fanciful description of the process by which the Hebrew text of this half-verse attained its present form, the presumed original form (as it now appears in the Peshitta) has great interest in the context of this study. Here, again, is that presumed original: "In every place where you mention My name I will come to you and bless you." What does it say? Not that the Jerusalem temple alone is the source of blessing and that God can be found there alone, but that wherever men make mention of His name, call, invoke, address Him, He comes in response to their call and He blesses.[15] The statement is openly polemical. It denies the validity of a contrary proposition. It disputes the claim of the Jerusalem temple and priesthood to unique authority. The passage was not written before but after the Josianic reform, and written to take issue specifically with its intent. It was the Deuteronomic principle which it set out to deny (and if the process described in the foregoing paragraph is right the author of the first recension well knew what he was doing when in defense of the principle he removed the opposition by radical surgery). Before the Josianic reform there was no reason for such a statement. When sanctuaries were scattered throughout the land there was no point in stating the natural and the obvious. There was no need then to say "in every place where you invoke Me I respond"; that was taken for granted. It was only after Jerusalem had challenged the right of the local cult centers that anyone would find it necessary to defend their authenticity. But then it became essential. The author of Exod. 20:24b is to be counted among the champions of the local centers. He was one of many dissidents who defended local autonomy against the encroaching authority of the Jerusalem priesthood, after the Exile, in the days of the second temple.[16] Into an ancient code of laws, in a not illogical position,[17] he inserted this half-verse.[18] Wherever, God had said, in Babylonia or Egypt, in the villages or capital of restored Judea, temple or no temple—wherever men called on

Him in truth, He would be near, He would respond with blessing. Such is the import of Exod. 20:24b. It is the charter of the synagogue.[19]

IV

ברוך אתה יהוה . . .

The force of the blessing . . . ברוך אתה י׳ is attenuated if instead of "Blessed be Thou, O Lord" we translate "Praised be Thou, O Lord." Blessing has a quality that praise does not share. A blessing is a giving, a gift, an offering. To "bless" the Lord is to bring Him an offering. It is right to say we "offer" a blessing.

Can we then benefit God? Perhaps today's theology must deny that we can, but the less sophisticated religion of biblical man took it for granted. That a blessing is a giving is a compelling corollary of the belief in the potency of words, their inherent substantiality. If words have reality, an evil word is an evil thing and a good word is a good thing. A man can bring to God an offering of words, bring benefit to Him with words.

The seal ברוך אתה י׳, characteristic of the Jewish liturgy, is as rare in biblical literature as it is common in post-biblical prayer. It occurs in Psalm 119:12 and in I Chron. 29:10, and not otherwise. The Chronicles passage is in a chapter with no parallel in Samuel-Kings but with features characteristic of the Chronicler. And the time of the 119th psalm may well approach the time of the Chronicler. The evidence suggests that the formula obtained currency no earlier, say, than the fourth century, however common it became in later times.

Other biblical blessings with God as their object are indeed more usual. As the Concordance will show, the expression ברוך י׳ appears no less than 24 times, and related expressions a further 7 times (ברוך אדני, ברוך אלהים, ברוך צורי and ברוך י׳ יהי).Three times in Hebrew and once in Aramaic a form of this blessing occurs by which a man blesses "the name of the Lord": להוא שמה די אלהא מבורך and ברוך שם כבודו (twice), יהי שם י׳ מבורך. The difference between this frequent form: ברוך י׳ with these variants, and the other: ברוך אתה י׳ is that the former refers to God in the third person instead of addressing Him as "Thou": "Blessed be the Lord" instead of "Blessed be Thou, O Lord." There is this formal difference—no difference in substance. Biblical man blesses God.

Roughly two out of three times when a man blesses God in the Bible he intends thus to express his gratitude to God for a favor God has done him. He means to "return" thanks, to "offer" thanks. The proportion may be still higher, exceptions may be rare, but in approximately two-thirds of the examples of such blessings their nature is obvious. They are a return for a favor experienced. The following examples are typical and suffice for the demonstration: "Blessed be the Lord, the God of Israel, who has today granted me one to sit on my throne, my own eyes seeing it" (I Kings 1:48; cf. 10:9); "Blessed be the Lord who has delivered you from the power of Egypt" (Exod. 18:10); "Blessed be the Lord God, the God of Israel, who alone does wonders" (Ps. 72:18); "Blessed be the Lord because He has been marvelously merciful to me . . . " (Ps. 31:22); "Blessed be the Lord because He has heard my supplication" (Ps. 28:6). David, Jethro, this psalmist or that one, many persons named and others unnamed, conscious of divine favor experienced, express their gratitude in the form of a blessing. They render as bullocks the words of their mouth.

This last quoted simile, which likens human speech to sacrificial animals is taken from a verse in Hosea (14:3) the text of which is not above suspicion. The Hebrew reads: ונשלמה פרים שפתינו. For "bulls" (פרים) the Septuagint appears to have read פרי, "fruit." There is not indeed a great difference—fruits served as well as animals for offerings—and in either case the sense is guaranteed by the verb. The verb שלם means "to make payment," and the common term *shelem* "sacrifice" is a cognate. Whether, therefore, the comparison be to bulls or to fruit the lips make payment, bring an offering. The thought here in the second half of this verse continues Hosea's thought earlier in this same verse: קחו עמכם דברים ושובו אל-י', "Take with you words and return to the Lord." Words themselves are the offering brought.

This was the thought likewise of the author of Ps. 69, who wrote:

> I will praise the name of God with a song,
> I will magnify Him with thanksgiving.
> And that will please the Lord more than an ox,
> A bull with horns and cloven hoofs (31 f.).

With an artful play on words he compared a *shīr* and a *shōr*, a song and an ox, and said that the thanksgiving hymn is more pleasing to God than the feast. What the author of another psalm expresses is only a variant of this same thought. Imploring God to hear him, the author of Ps. 141 asks:

> Let (the words of) my prayer count as incense before Thee.
> The lifting of my hands as the evening offering (v. 2).

In this manner he too ascribes reality to the words and gestures of prayer.

According to the psychology of biblical man it means nothing to say of speech: it is "mere" words. The words of a blessing are material and ponderable like incense and animals. These passages from Hosea and the Psalms are not simply figures of speech; there is matter in their poetry.

The way the writers use the word *berakhah* "blessing," is evidence to that effect. They let it mean sheep and parched grain, cakes of figs and springs of water, as well as a spoken formula. Jacob urges Esau to accept his *berakhah* because God has favored him and he has everything, so Esau accepts the munificent gift of goats and sheep, camels, cows and asses, which Jacob has set apart (Gen. 33:11).[20] Achsah asks a "blessing" of her father Caleb because she dwells in the dry Negeb, and he gives her springs of water (Josh. 15:19; Judg. 1:15). Fearing David's anger, Abigail hurries to meet him, bringing as a peace offering ass-loads of loaves and wine, dressed sheep and parched grain, raisins and figs (I Sam. 25:18), and she calls the sum of them a *berakhah* (v. 27). David accepts the present and makes peace with Abigail and her house (v. 35). David sends spoil of war as a *berakhah* to the elders of Judah (I Sam. 30:26). And Naaman, grateful for his cure, urges Elisha to accept a *berakhah* but the man of God refuses to take anything (II Kings 5:15 f.).[21]

If such tangible gifts, payments or offerings as these that men gave or urged upon one another went by the name of "blessing," a blessing indeed had substance; it could enrich, benefit, increase the recipient. It is even so with the gift of words which a man brings to God as a blessing. And that is why "Blessed be Thou, O Lord" is a proper translation of the recurrent liturgical formula ברוך אתה י׳. Speaking so, a man makes a return to God for the good that God has given. When he offers his blessing to God המוציא לחם מן הארץ, "who bringeth forth food from the earth" he is making a thank offering of words for sustenance granted. When he offers the blessing to God "whose world is thus," שככה לו בעולמו, he is bringing a thank offering for beauty experienced.

When with such words the creature addresses his Creator, it does not seem to him at all that he is "appearing before the Lord empty handed." He is bearing a gift, a reward, a return which will increase and benefit his God.

So it is also, and finally, with the blessing which one man speaks to another. The giver gives and the recipient receives and the blessing has substance. A benediction is a benefaction.

---

(1) This despite the translation of the half-verse from Ps. 118:26 in LXX and Vulg. and in the English translations including the RSV.

(2) As it stands it may be an allusion to Exod. 20:24b; cf. n. 15, below.

(3) The Chronicles passage omits "of hosts."

(4) See Blank, "The Curse, Blasphemy, the Spell and the Oath," HUCA XXIII—Part I (1950—51), pp. 73—95.

(5) See also 32:17 and 14:7 (resumed in v. 9 and then in v. 20).

(6) See Blank, *Jeremiah, Man and Prophet*, Cincinnati, 1961, Chap. VIII, n. 9.

(7) Cf. Hos. 14:4 "And to the work of our hands we will no more say: 'Our God!'"

(8) But cf. Isa. 63:16; 64:7.

(9) Cf. also Mark 14:36 and Gal. 4:6.

(10) What follows repeats in part a suggestion which I made in 1945 in an article entitled "The Dissident Laity in Early Judaism," HUCA XIX, pp. 13f. I offer it here again in a different setting with more assurance.

(11) See the article cited in the preceding note.

(12) P. 82.

(13) Despite the note by G. Quell in the critical apparatus to the third edition of Kittel's *Biblia Hebraica*, to the effect that the Syriac version read בכל מקום (without the article), I confess to some uneasiness about this conclusion. To be sure the Syriac has only בכל אתר די; but may this not be merely a matter of idiom? In view of the word כל which precedes and the relative pronoun which follows the noun, does the Syriac idiom want the article? Do כל and די not determine the noun—even without the article? I took this question to my colleague, Dr. William Hallo, and he was inclined to agree that they do. He noticed the variants which appear in the Aramaic Targums. The Berliner edition of the Targum Onkelos, like the Syriac, reads simply בכל אתר די, whereas the Targum Pseudo-Jonathan (ed. M. Ginsburger) reads בכל אתרא די. He suggested the possibility that the former is idiomatic, while the latter rendered literally, and used the definite article because it stood in the Hebrew text. If this is so, the Syriac, along with Onkelos would lend no support to the view that the article was originally lacking in the Hebrew; and the Targum Pseudo-Jonathan on the contrary would suggest the presence of the article in the original.

Whether or not the Syriac, with the Targum Onkelos, points to a Hebrew original without the definite article, the present Hebrew text בכל המקום, "in that whole place," is meaningless, and the English versions correctly translate "in every place"—thus silently adopting the proposed correction בכל מקום.

Incidentally, the Targum Jerushalmi of the rabbinic Bibles, the "fragment targum," approximates another variant in the Syriac (which is to be noted immediately). It renders the clause: אשר אזכיר את שמי in the *second* person instead of the first, reading בכל אתר דתדכרון ית שמי קדישא, "in every place where *you* (pl.) call to mind My holy name."

(14) This is essentially the Samaritan text. The differences are not substantial. The verb appears in the conflate form אזכרתי and an idiomatic שמה follows on שמי, thus: . . . במקום אשר אזכרתי את שמי שמה. (Incidentally, this Samaritan text suggests that the idiomatic שם may once have followed on שמי in the original and have been lost by haplography.)

(15) See n. 2, above. Ps. 20:8, as it stands, may allude to Exod. 20:24b in its presumed original form. The psalmist's words: בשם י׳ . . . נזכיר are a logical reaction to the promise contained in the Exodus verse: בכל מקום אשר תזכיר את שמי . . . , and may lend support to the view that this was their original form.

(16) See the evidence presented in the paper cited in n. 10.

(17) *Op. cit.*, p. 13.

(18) President Morgenstern recognized the half-verse as an addition a number of years ago. See his "The Oldest Document of the Hexateuch" HUCA IV (1927), p. 93.

(19) At the end of my essay several times mentioned here, "The Dissident Laity in Early Judaism," I referred to the essay as "a chapter in the 'pre-history' of . . . *the Synagogue.*" It is gratifying and significant that President Morgenstern reached essentially the same conclusions as I did there, but largely on the basis of other evidence. He presented his conclusions in an essay entitled "The Origin of the Synagogue" which appeared in Vol. II of the *Studi Orientalistici in onore di Giorgio Levi Della Vida*, (Rome, 1956). I believe we agree that (as I suggested on p. 2 of "The Dissident Laity") the Deuteronomic reform was "only an incident in a struggle between Jerusalem and powerful centrifugal tendencies, with which the Second Temple had continually to contend—a struggle which was settled only when the Romans destroyed the Temple leaving the synagogues in undisputed control."

(20) In 32:14, 19, 21, 22 and 33:10 he calls the "blessing" an "offering" or "present," a מנחה.

(21) Cf. also Isa. 65:8 (the wine in the cluster is a *berakhah*) and Joel 2:14.

Men Against God
The Promethean Element in Biblical Prayer

Men who pray figure prominently in Hebrew Scriptures and Jewish tradition. But these men do not all pray alike. Some of them pray in a mood of submissive penitence—this is the commoner, the approved way. Others, strange though it sounds, stand up to God in prayer and demand their due. In distress and danger, they defend their rights, the rights of men, against the encroachments of an arbitrary or tyrannical God. We may call these others "Promethean." In the modern romanticized sense of the term, these men and the spirit of their prayer are Promethean.

Also, these men and the spirit of their prayer do not agree with the prevalent mood of Protestant theology and its doctrine of man. Nevertheless, or for that very reason, these men and their spirit may have some meaning for our times.

This study is a descriptive review of such Old Testament material as may be termed "Promethean."

The sources for this study are of two kinds. First, there are the narratives—the tales of colorful personalities who figure in the Bible story and play the Promethean role. And secondly, there are the Promethean prayers, the motifs of which form the subject proper of this study. The characters boldly drawn illuminate the manuscript on which the words of prayer are written.

Not all of the biblical personages, real or mythical, who challenge divine authority, illustrate our theme. "The infernal serpent" and "all his host of rebel angels" (the Lucifers of the Bible) who rivalled or sought to supplant God or share his prerogatives—these form a separate category.

The Promethean personalities do not, for example, include that mythical figure "Helal, son of the morning"[1] nor his fellow who "walked up and down in the midst of the stones of fire" in the "mountain of God"[2] nor yet those "sons of God" whose forbidden commerce with "daughters of men" failed to lift the veil of man's mortality, instead of which they themselves were doomed to "die like men."[3]

Nor do they include those paler shadows of the stars, the men who questioned God's primacy and sought to frustrate his decrees, not "our grand parents" who, had they only eaten of the right tree, might have compelled God to share his immortality, not the ill-fated builders of the "tower," not, in later generations, that boastful axe the stout-hearted king of Assyria,[4] nor his successor the king of Babylon who made the earth tremble and kingdoms quake,[5] nor yet the "virgin daughter of Babylon" who said in her heart "I am and there is none else,"[6] and not the prince of Tyre, proud because of his beauty, who said "I am a god."[7] Fascinating though they are themselves, these are not the Promethean figures associated with biblical prayer.

The Presidential Address delivered at the annual meeting of the Society of Biblical Literature and Exegesis on December 29, 1952, at the Union Theological Seminary in New York.

It is not, indeed, among the rebels that we find them, but among the faithful. They hold fast to God even while they question his decrees. Though they defy, they do not deny him.

It is seldom, too, that we find them in physical contest with God. Isolated are the obscure narratives of Jacob who struggled through a dark night with God and prevailed, and Moses the "bridegroom of blood," whom also God proved at Massah, with whom God strove at the waters of Meribah.[8]

But we do find them among the numerous accounts of men wrestling with God in prayer; it is these which illustrate our theme.

Two biblical passages list persons apparently credited with more than ordinary influence, persons whose prayers God cannot lightly ignore. In the one,[9] speaking to Jeremiah, God denies that either Moses or Samuel, much less the prophet himself, could sway him now towards the faithless nation and, in the other,[10] similarly, God reveals to Ezekiel his intransigeance: In a time of retributive calamity, Noah, Daniel, and Job would intercede with him in vain; though for their own righteousness the three might themselves escape, they could not rescue any others. But both passages imply that if the prayers of any mortals could avail, it would be the prayers of these named heroes of virtue: Moses, Samuel, Jeremiah, Noah, Daniel, and Job.

Properly the name of Moses leads all the rest; for he more often than others and more successfully takes issue with God. When, after they had made the golden calf, God decided to destroy the stiff-necked people, Moses produced two reasons why he should not do so. And, whether because of the cogency of his argument or because it was Moses who presented it, God acceded to his request.[11] And when the people, alarmed at the majority opinion of the spies, determined to return to Egypt and God lost patience, again it was Moses who intervened and again "the Lord said: סלחתי כדברך, 'I have pardoned according to your word.'"[12]

Probably it was the record of these incidents which, in later centuries, created the rabbinic legends of a Promethean Moses. Two such legends refer, in fact, to the scene at Sinai:

An authority in the Babylonian Talmud comments on the somewhat remarkable words spoken by God to Moses in Exodus 32: "Now therefore let me alone." This teacher exclaims: "Were it not written in the Bible, it could not have been said. Moses held on to God as a man his friend by the garment and said, 'Lord of the world, I will not let you go until you forgive and pardon them.'"[13]

And an aggada in the Palestinian Talmud, less restrained than the Bible, permits Moses on this occasion in fact to prevail over God in physical contest. When God was about to hand the two tablets of stone to Moses, God still grasping them above and Moses below, the people sinned with the golden calf and God resolved to withhold the gift. Indeed, the precious Ten Commandments would never have come into man's possession had not Moses then, at the last moment, with sheer physical strength, wrested the tablets from the hands of God.[14]

The reference to Samuel as an intercessor comparable to Moses may be related to the passage in the first book of Samuel where his persuasiveness is concisely noted: ויזעק

שמואל אל ה׳ בעד ישראל ויענהו ה׳ "And Samuel cried unto the Lord for Israel and the Lord answered him."[15] In its present form, this narrative makes him responsible for a military victory; but originally Samuel may here have prayed successfully for rain—here as in the 12th chapter where there can be no doubt of it. There Samuel calls for rain and it falls on that same day.[16]

A latter-day Samuel went by the name of "Onias the circle drawer." According to a familiar tradition, he received his byname as a result of an heroic deed. By means of prayer he ended a drought of two years' standing, but only because, in the course of his prayer, he drew a circle in the dust around him and vowed not to step outside until God gave the needed rain. Nor was he satisfied with drizzle or with cloudburst; he stood his ground until he got a rain of suitable proportions.[17] Simeon ben Shetaḥ was the rabbinic authority in the time of Onias, the first pre-Christian century. According to the Mishnah, Simeon was displeased at the manner and tone of his prayer. He said were this not Onias, he would in fact excommunicate him. But what can Simeon do? Onias speaks petulantly to God and God does his bidding, even as a father whose son speaks so.[18]

At the time of the drought to which Jeremiah's list pertains, however, so great was the offense that neither a Moses nor a Samuel would have done any good. Nor yet a Jeremiah. The prophet Jeremiah, too, deserves his place among these bolder spirits; repeatedly in times of trouble he prayed for the people[19] and repeatedly God denied him this high privilege.[20]

If we ask why—Why was Jeremiah forbidden to pray? Could God not merely turn a deaf ear to his prayers?—we may be left with the surmise that God did indeed find it hard to wave aside his prayers and the prayers of men like him. And if we ask further why this is so, why God cannot simply refuse their petitions, we are reminded of Abraham of whom it is said: והאמין בה׳ ויחשבה לו צדקה, "he believed in the Lord and he accounted it to him for righteousness,"[21] even as it is said of Moses that he found favor in God's eyes[22]— and of Noah.

Noah heads Ezekiel's list of potential mediators. If, at such a time, any mortal could persuade God to spare his fellows, Ezekiel implies, it could be such a one as Noah. Of him it is said: "Noah had found favor in the eyes of the Lord";[23] and it is also said: "Noah in his generations was a righteous man and blameless."[24]

Along with Noah, Ezekiel names Daniel and Job. But, since the biblical books which celebrate these two heroes of the spirit are most certainly later than Ezekiel's reference and are, therefore, no sure guide to his meaning, all we may confidently say about Daniel and Job is that already in Ezekiel's day (if not before),[25] they enjoyed a reputation like that of Noah, whose virtue had set a limit to God's freedom and prevented the extinction of mankind.

Noah became the pattern for other heroes, too—those who on the "last day" will survive the cosmic catastrophe, those in the Isaiah apocalypse instructed, like Noah, to enter their chambers, to close the doors behind them, and to hide "until the indignation be overpast."[26]

Although the intimacy between God and Israel prevented the development in Old Testament times of the idea of intermediaries between them, the author of Isaiah 63 toys with the idea even while rejecting it: "... Abraham knows us not," he lets the people say,

> "And Israel does not acknowledge us;
> You, O Lord, are our Father,
> Our Redeemer from everlasting is your name."[27]

Nevertheless Abraham ranks with Moses and with Noah among the biblical personages whose persuasive powers God had to acknowledge. Abraham would surely have snatched Sodom from destruction if only those few—ten, even—had been worthy of his prayer.[28]

The mention of two later personalities, one almost modern, concludes the first part of this study:

Day after day, day after day, in sackcloth and ashes, a legend relates, Rabbi Eleazar of Modi'im prayed aloud: "O Master of the World, let not this be the day on which you enter into judgment with your people"; and so compelling was his prayer that the Romans could not conquer Bethar, last stronghold of Bar Kochba, until a means was found to silence this pious man. Ironically, it was Bar Kochba himself who caused the death of his protector, and then Bethar fell. This was in the second Christian century.[29]

In 18th century Volhynia there lived a ḥassidic rabbi, Levi Isaac of Berditshev, whose prayer out of the depths has become a Yiddish classic. He addresses God familiarly in this prayer and some might think that he makes impudent demands. He says, in part:

> "Good morning to you, Lord of the world!
>   I, Levi Isaac, son of Sarah of Berditshev, am come to you in a legal matter concerning your people Israel.
>   What do you want of Israel?
>
> It is always: Command the children of Israel!
> It is always: Speak unto the children of Israel! . . .
> I, Levi Isaac, son of Sarah of Berditshev, say:
> I shall not go hence, nor budge from my place until there be a finish
> Until there be an end of exile. . ."[30]

It is reported that Rabbi Naḥman (a fifth generation Amora) said: חוצפא אפילו כלפי שמיא מהני[31] which Marcus Jastrow rather tamely translates: "Boldness will carry its point even against heaven."[32]

Now, our sources afford glimpses not only of the persons who strove with God in prayer but also of the strife itself. And for news of the strife, we can turn to other persons than those who are mentioned by name—others in addition to Abraham, Moses, Samuel, and Jeremiah. The Promethean figures include many an unnamed psalmist and advocate whose personalities are preserved only in the daring words they spoke. The words of these named and unnamed heroes reveal a number of recurrent themes, propositions with which a man armed himself when he approached God in unequal contest. These propositions are not the more common expressions of submissive piety and humble petition. Like the figures in the narratives, these are the compelling reasons, the cogent postulates, the barbed weapons in the arsenal of prayer.

Prominent among these arguments is the appeal to God's self-interest. If unwilling to act on behalf of the individual or the nation in distress, God is advised then to act for his own sake, for his name's sake.[33] This is the first of the two arguments with which Moses persuades God not to destroy the nation worshipping the calf. "What will people say?" Moses asks. "Egypt, for example. That you delivered the Israelites from bondage only to slay them in the wilderness."[34] In the incident of the spies, he repeats this argument more pointedly still: "What will they say? That it was for want of ability to fulfill your promise that your slew them in the desert."[35]

In a spirit of independence, the one who uses the argument "for thy name's sake" renounces any claim for special treatment. "I am not," he seems to be saying, "asking any favors. I merely call your attention to the fact that in your own interest you must act in such and such a manner."

> "Arise, O God, plead thine own cause;
> Remember thy reproach all the day at the hand of base men . . ."[36]

As a matter of fact, the argument "for thy name's sake" is theologically respectable. It is not, as it may sound, an appeal to God's vanity. It is an aspect of the larger concept of universal salvation, which has to wait until God's sovereignty is universally accepted. In this context God is expected to be jealous for his good name with an altruistic jealousy.[37]

But the theme of God's own interest is given a special twist, somewhat less respectable, in three of the Psalms (the sixth, the thirtieth, and the eighty-eighth). Assuming as they do, that human adulation is pleasing to God, the authors of these psalms remind him, with what amounts to blackmail, that none but the living render him praise—and it is not to his interest to surrender his worshipers to death.

> "For in death there is no remembrance of thee;
> "In the nether-world who will give thee thanks?"[38]

> "What profit is there in my blood when I go down to the pit?
> Will the dust praise thee? Will it declare thy truth?"[39]

> ". . . Do the shades arise and give thee thanks?
> Is thy mercy declared in the grave?
> . . . Are thy wonders known in the dark?
> Thy righteous deeds in the land of forgetfulness?"[40]

The second decisive argument with which Moses confronts God in the molten calf affair is the reminder that God himself has, so to speak, restricted his own freedom. Once in the past, when he chose Abraham and the seed of Abraham forever, God exercised his freedom—and in doing so limited that same freedom henceforth. His choice then became a commitment for the future. "Remember," Moses says, "Remember Abraham, Isaac, and Israel, thy servants to whom thou didst swear by thine own self and saidst unto them: I will multiply your seed as the stars of heaven, and all this land that I have spoken of will I give unto your seed, and they shall inherit it forever."[41] Again and again, as in this argument of Moses, men refer to God's commitment not only to Israel in general[42] but also specifically to the house of the kings of Judah by way of their founder, David.[43]

They had what amounts to a technical term for the divine commitment; they called it a חסד. To designate God's alleged commitment to the patriarchs, they used this term along with the words ברית ("covenant") and שבועה ("promise"),[44] but to designate his commitment to the line of David, they definitely preferred the term חסד.[45] Having the tradition of these divine commitments, it is perhaps understandable if the presumed beneficiaries sought the presumed benefits. They could, by the way (and this is a significant aside)— they could have respect only for a God whose word was sure.

At times this second argument appears disguised as a hymn. Here the recital of God's former mercies is not a mere mentioning for gratitude. Since to the faithful it is axiomatic that God is consistent, his past conduct is also a warranty for the future. Having not only pledged his word (the חסד) but also embarked upon a matching course of action, God is not now at liberty to depart from that course, for in him caprice would be intolerable. Therefore, if God has acted as, in a lament, his worshippers claim, the mention of past favors, so different from his recent inexplicable conduct, is not praise but a reproach and the hymn not wholly innocent.[46]

"I remember" is the common introduction, and the recollection is clamorous rather than nostalgic. Remembered for the most part is the deliverance from Egypt with the attendant wonders and subsequent care,[47] or—evidence not only of God's good will but of his unlimited power as well—the epic of the world's creation.[48]

How, indeed, can a friendly and powerful Lord betray his servants whom he has, so to speak, trained to put their trust in him?

We should, of course, not overlook the fact that the atmosphere of complacency in which the argument thrives is the same as that which evoked the heated polemic of the eighth and seventh century prophets. Repeatedly subsequent centuries saw reaffirmed, as here, the notions those prophets opposed.

The third argument is one which Abraham proposes, which God accepts as valid, and which all but saves Sodom. It is the demand that God remain true to his moral nature. "Wilt thou indeed sweep away the righteous with the wicked? . . . Shall not the Judge of all the earth do justice?" השפט כל הארץ לא יעשה משפט.[49] All biblical writers bear witness to this basic concept, notably, among them, Jeremiah and the author of Job. The "confessions" of Jeremiah are one persistent demand that, by repudiating Jeremiah's detractors and upholding the prophet himself, God should give evidence of his just nature.[50] And what does Job require of God but that he be merely just?[51]

There are two courses open to the afflicted: they may confess, repent and seek atonement—that is the usual course; or they may regard themselves as victims of injustice and adopt the attitude of aggrieved innocence, disclaiming guilt and insisting upon a rectification of the wrongs they have suffered. It is the bolder spirits who take this latter course, the Jobs and Jeremiahs who claim that the fault is God's, not theirs.

Their disclaiming of guilt takes a variety of forms. They say: though our fathers sinned, *we* are innocent and with manifest injustice we suffer for *their* sins. These are the authors of the "sour grapes" proverb repudiated by Jeremiah and Ezekiel.[52] In the sense that the youth is father to the man, one psalmist expresses a variant of this same thought when he pleads: "Remember not the sins of my youth."[53] Sometimes the denial of guilt takes the form: If we have sinned, we are indeed not aware of it; and what kind of a God would exact a penalty for an unrecognized offense?[54] And now and then it is said: God's standards are simply too high. Men cannot be expected to attain perfection. "There *is* no man that sinneth not."[55]

The author of Psalm 143 betrays ambivalence: he both wants and does not want God to judge him. Although he appeals to the righteousness of God: עֲנֵנִי בְצִדְקָתֶךָ, "Answer me in thy righteousness,"[56] without transition he continues: "Enter *not* into judgment with thy servant; For in thy sight shall no man living be justified."[57] Perhaps it is untempered justice, which in the latter verse he fears, whereas the divine righteousness, which in the former he invokes, recognizes and discounts the common frailty of mortals. Let God judge, he seems to say; let him judge indeed, but let him not be petty, let him not be unreasonable.

Similar is the denial—not of all guilt, but of guilt commensurate with the penalty. The thought is that a quantitative relationship must prevail between them. According to Deutero-Isaiah, even God accepts this principle. This is the prophet's meaning when he says of Jerusalem: "She has received of the Lord's hand double for all her sins." The penalty has been excessive and Zion may now claim reparations.[58] Zechariah agrees: the agents of God's anger, turned loose against Israel, exacted a disproportionate penalty— "for I was only a little angry and they wrought excessive evil."[59] The seventy shepherds in Enoch are guilty of the same excess and, according to that apocalyptic parable, they are treated accordingly on the Judgment Day.[60]

Finally, the denial of guilt may be only that and nothing more. The author of Psalm 44 does not mince words. He bluntly declares:

> "All this has come upon us although we did not forget you—
> Although we were not false to your covenant.
> Our heart did not turn back
> Neither did our steps decline from your path...
> If we had forgotten the name of our God
> Or spread forth our hands to a strange god
> Would not God search this out?
> For he knows the secrets of the heart."[61]

And boldly the author of the great lament in Isaiah 63 and 64[62] calls the people's guilt an illusion. No fault of theirs invited this disaster; quite the contrary! the disaster produced the guilt—no, it produced only the appearance of guilt.

> "Behold you were wroth with the result that we appear guilty;
> [You were angry] and we are accounted transgressors.
> Yea, we are all become like an unclean thing
> And all our virtues like a polluted garment."[63]

So much, then, for the compelling arguments. Not these alone but also the manner of the praying was counted on to insure the prayer's effectiveness. The psalmist applied to his own situation the mocking words which Elijah addressed to the prophets of Baal: "he is musing, or he is gone aside, or he is on a journey, or peradventure he sleeps and must be awakened";[64] and, thinking thus, the psalmist also called him "louder" and louder, and louder still, until, in spirit, his prayer resembled the tempestuous clamor of the Baal prophets in the oratorio.

The psalmist is sometimes overwhelmed by the thought, not that God is being unusually severe with him or his people, but that God is doing something much, much worse, that he is looking the other way, indifferent to their fate, that, in biblical terminology, he is "hiding his face." This phrase denotes various degrees of estrangement, from a passive forgetting or not heeding[65] to an active rejecting and leaving unprotected.[66] When the terrifying thought arises that God is indeed hiding his face, at such a time unimpassioned, temperate speech gives way to an insistent, importunate demand bordering on panic.

The arguments are the same, but there is an added urgency. This urgency is expressed in three different ways. It is expressed as an accusation—an accusation addressed to God bluntly and directly: "You have enticed me,"[67] "You have been to me like a deceitful stream."[68]

Or it has the form of an impatient demand, a variant of the imperative; "Look at me!"[69] or its companion "Awake! Why sleepest thou, O Lord?"[70]

This demand, "Awake! Why sleepest thou, O Lord?" is cited in the Talmud. In a list of the reforms of the High Priest John Hyrcanus, the Mishnah says: "He abolished the מעוררים, the awakeners."[71] And in the Babylonian Talmud[72] someone fortunately asks: "Who were these awakeners?" They were the levites, he learns, who were assigned the special duty, day by day, to ascend a platform and to cry aloud: עורה למה תישן אדני, "Awake! Why sleepest thou, O Lord? Awake! Why sleepest thou, O Lord?"

And last among the forms which give expression to this unbridled urgency is the desperate question. The question is a variant of "How long, O Lord?"[73] or "My God, my God, why hast thou forsaken me?"[74] The question "How much longer?" occurs apparently as a conventional formula in Babylonian ritual laments[75] and its use in our psalm literature seems at times to be similarly conventional. Indeed, a liturgy adopts and repeats bold phrases which were no mere phrases when a crisis begot them. And, certainly, not every occurrence in this literature of the accusation, the question and the demand, is equally earnest. The psalms will contain the borrowed conventional phrase as well as the fresh hot demand.

The sixty-second chapter of Isaiah is one of the finest compositions in the minor anthology that goes by the name of Trito-Isaiah; it is also the best biblical expression of this fresh urgency; and it is this striking chapter which suggested to me this theme. Its author is the true Prometheus among the psalmists. His opening words reveal his spirit:

למען ציון לא אחשה   ולמען ירושלם לא אשקוט

"For Zion's sake I will not hold my peace,
And for Jerusalem's sake I will not rest,

> Until her triumph go forth as brightness
> And her salvation as a torch that burneth."[76]

We miss the whole point of the chapter if we fail to recognize the speaker of these lines. It is not God but the psalmist who vows to hold not his peace nor rest. And it is still the psalmist who is speaking in verses 6 and 7:

> "Upon your walls, O Jerusalem
> I have stationed watchmen.
> Neither by day nor by night—
> Never shall they hold their peace.
> You remembrancers of God
> Allow yourselves no quiet (אל דמי לכם);
> Yea, and allow him no quiet (ואל תתנו דמי לו)
> Until he establish it
> Until he make Jerusalem
> An object of praise in the earth."[77]

As, in verse 1, the speaker denies himself peace until he sees salvation dawn for Jerusalem, so precisely, in verse 6, he denies his watchmen peace until that day. And these appointed שומרים are men like him—men who pray, who pray urgently and ceaselessly ever the same prayer for the salvation of Jerusalem.[78] It is their business, his business and theirs, to remind God of his commitment to Jerusalem. Their function as "remembrancers" is very like what God requires of Israel in Isaiah 43:[79]

> "Put me in remembrance; let us argue together;
> State your case that you may be justified,"
> הזכירני נשפטה יחד   ספר אתה למען תצדק

As in that passage, so here, the מזכירים are "stating their case" and stating it with all the power they can muster and with unwearying persistence. So sure of himself and the right of his cause is the author of Isaiah 62 that he leads a protesting chorus in uninterrupted prayer designed to force the hand of God.

Which is more striking, this man's audacity, or the simple faith by which he knows men's prayers disturb God's peace?

And with this thought we may conclude, pausing only to say one special word to those members of this Society whose major interest is the New Testament rather than the Hebrew Bible. If, in thinking of this presidential address, you feel the need to characterize it briefly for filing in your memory, may I suggest you think of it as a Jewish commentary on a saying of Jesus preserved by Luke. I refer, of course, to the words:

> "Ask, and it will be given to you;
> Seek, and you will find;
> Knock, and it will be opened to you."[80]

(1) Isa 14: 12 ff.
(2) Ezek 28: 11–19.
(3) Gen 6:2f.; cf. Isa 25:7f., Ps 82:7.
(4) Isa 10:12, 15; cf. 37:23–25.
(5) Isa 14:4, 16.
(6) Isa 47:1, 7, 10.
(7) Ezek 28:2, 17.
(8) Deut 33:8.
(9) Jer 15:1, cf. 14:11.
(10) Ezek 14:12 ff.
(11) Exod 32:9–14; cf. Deut 9:25–28; Ps 106:23.
(12) Num 14:11–20. Cf., also, Exod 5:22 f. and Num 11:11–15 where Moses is quite out of patience with God.
(13) *TB Berakot* 32a.—Here and often (see below) rabbinic fantasy sharpens the point of the biblical phrase.
(14) *TP Ta'anit* IV.8, 68c.
(15) I Sam 7:5–10.
(16) I Sam 12:16–18.
(17) *Mishnah Ta'anit* III.8.
(18) *Loc. cit.*; cf. Judith 8:31.
(19) Jer. 42:4; 18:20; 15:11; cf. 32:16.
(20) Jer 7:16; 11:14; 14:11.
(21) Gen 15:6; cf. Neh 9:8; Ps 105:42 and Ps 106:30 f.
(22) Exod 33:17.
(23) Gen 6:8.
(24) Gen 6:9.
(25) Cf. the Daniel who figures in the Ugaritic "Tale of Aqhat" V 4–8, etc. to be found in translation in Pritchard, *Ancient Near Eastern Texts*, Princeton, 1950, p. 149ff. Before he became the hero of the biblical book, Job, too, may have been celebrated in tradition as one who possessed intercessory powers (cf. Job 42:8 ff.). Job and Prometheus are frequently compared; see E. Bussler, *Hiob und Prometheus, zwei Vorkämpfer der göttlichen Gerechtigkeit*, Hamburg, 1897; W. A. Irwin, "Job and Prometheus," *Journal of Religion*, XXX (1950) pp. 90–108; H. G. May, "Prometheus and Job," *Anglican Theological Review*, XXXIV (1952).
(26) Isa 26:20.
(27) Isa 63:16; cf. 51:1 f.; Jer 31:15.
(28) Gen 18:22 ff.; cf. 20:7, 17.
(29) *TP Ta'anit* IV.8, 68d.
(30) The complete prayer, the "Kaddish of Levi Isaac of Berditshev," may be found in the "Jewish Reader": *In Time and Eternity*, Schocken, New York, 1946, p. 94 f.
(31) *TB Sanhedrin* 105a.
(32) In a *Dictionary of the Targumim, Talmud, etc.*, s.v. חוצפא.
(33) Jer 14:7; Ps 25:11; 79:9f. and often.
(34) Exod 32:12.
(35) Num 14:15 f.; cf. Isa 59:1 f.
(36) Ps 74:22; cf. 74:10, 18.
(37) I Kings 8:41–43; Isa 45:6; Ps 98.
(38) Ps 6:6.
(39) Ps 30:10.
(40) Ps 88:11–13.
(41) Exod 32:13.
(42) Deut 9:5; II Kings 13:23; Jer 32:22; Mic 7:20; Neh 9:8 and often.

(43) II Sam 7:13b, 15f.; I Chron 17:12b—14; Ps 89:29 f., 34—38; Jer 33:17, 20—21a; II Chron 6:42; Isa 55:3. Cf. Blank, "The Dissident Laity in Early Judaism," *Hebrew Union College Annual* XIX (1946), pp. 11 f., 33ff.

(44) Cf. the references in n. 42; also Deut 7:8 f.

(46) E. g., Ps 22:4—7; Ps 44:1—10; Ps 80:9—13; Isa 63:7—15. In each of these examples note the reproachful tone of the final verse.

(47) Pss 44:4; 80:9; Isa 51:9 f.; 63:12; Dan 9:15 *et al.*

(48) Pss 74:12—17; 77:12 ff.; 102:26; 143:5 *et al.*

(49) Gen 18:25.

(50) Jer 11:20; 12:1; 18:19 f., etc.; cf. Blank "The Confessions of Jeremiah and the Meaning of Prayer" in *Hebrew Union College Annual*, XXI (1948).

(51) Job 13:15, 18; 23:3 f.; 27:2, etc.

(52) Jer 31:28; Ezek 18:2.

(53) Ps 25:7.

(54) Job 13:23.

(55) I Kings 8:46; cf. Job 4:17; Ps 130:3.

(56) Ps 143:1.

(57) Ps 143:2; cf. 130:3.

(58) Isa 40:2.

(59) Zech 1:15 (though the last phrase is awkward Hebrew this seems to be the meaning). Cf., also, Isa 10:5—7; 47:6; 61:7.

(60) Enoch 89 f., especially 89:62, 69; 90:22, 25.

(61) Ps 44:18—22.

(62) Isa 63:7—64:11.

(63) Isa 64:4b—5a; cf. Blank, "'And All Our Virtues'—An Interpretation of Isaiah 64:4b—5a" in *JBL* LXXI (1952), p. 149 ff.

(64) I Kings 18:27.

(65) Pss 10:11; 13:2; 44:25; 22:25; 69:18; 102:3; Isa 59:2; Micah 3:4; cf. the "iron plate" of Ezek 4:3, *et al.*

(66) Pss 27:8; 88:15; Deut 31:17 f.; 32:19 f.; Jer 33:5; Ezek 39:23 f.; Isa 54:8; 57:17; Pss 89:47; 30:8; 104:29, *et al.*

(67) Jer 20:7; cf. Blank "The Confessions of Jeremiah, etc.," p. 344.

(68) Jer 15:18.

(69) Ps 13:4; cf. Isa 64:8; Pss 25:16, 18 f.; 59:5; 80:15; Lam 1:9, 11; 5:1 *et al.*

(70) Ps 44:24; cf. Pss 35:22 f.; 59:2—6; 80:2—4; Isa 51:9, *et al.*

(71) *Mishnah Sota* IX.10.

(72) *TB Sota* 48a.

(73) Ps 13:2 f.; cf. Pss 74:10; 79:5; 89:47; 90:13; 85:6; Hab 1:2, *et al.*

(74) Ps 22:2; cf. Pss 10:1; 42:10; 43:2; 74:1; 88:15; Lam 5:20; Jer 14:8, 19, *et al.*

(75) H. Zimmern, *Babylonische Hymnen u. Gebete* in *der Alte Orient* VII, Leipzig, 1905, p. 8; M. Jastrow, *Die Religion Babyloniens u. Assyriens* II^1, Giessen, 1912, pp. 16, 43, 109.

(76) Isa 62:1.

(77) Isa 62:6 f.—Note that God is referred to in the third person.

(78) Compare the Sumerian "Lamentation over the Destruction of Ur" translated and annotated by S. N. Kramer in Pritchard, *op. cit.*, p. 455 ff., especially line 80 ff. and note 25.—Cf., also, I Kings 8:59 and Ps 55:18.

(79) V. 26.

(80) Luke 11:9.

Addresses

Starting from Where You Are
Sermon for Service of Ordination, 1959

Dr. Morgenstern, Dr. Glueck, Dr. Eisendrath, Mr. Goldman, colleagues academic and rabbinical, friends and honored guests, members of the class of 1959: Like those fantastic beasts in the vision of the prophet Ezekiel, I find myself, in this place on this occasion, looking at once in more than one direction. I must decide which way to think. In this place on this occasion quite easily I might be led to think back and to speak of times long past. My memory does not reach back to 1883, back to the first of the ordination services held in this place, nor does it reach indeed to any of the twenty-two graduations which followed here. And yet it goes back far enough to inspire the backward thought. It goes back at least to the joyous day when Blank "made the team." In view of a certain circumstance, a certain president of the Hebrew Union College, now its cherished president *emeritus*, was practically forced to give me my big chance. When he came to ordain my class, you see, he was quite unable to resist the circumstance that in that year we who were to graduate numbered eleven. That he should send us forth as a team to spiritual victory was therefore plainly inevitable.

Yes, I well might be inclined to the backward thought, and yet, having you before me, my friends of the class of 1959, without hesitation I make a different choice. I choose to think forward, to think of your to-day and your tomorrow. And, if yesterday at all invades these moments it must be your yesterday—for you are one, and your yesterday is a part of your today and your tomorrow.

I trust that all these people here assembled will not judge me impolite, if in a certain sense I turn my back on them and speak to you, and about you, and about your feelings to-day and your way into the future. Because today is your day, even at the risk of seeming discourteous I propose to talk with you; and who else are here are welcome to listen over your shoulders.

The most of you in this year's class are married. Your wives should be sitting there with you, for today is their day as well as yours. They helped to make it (which was no small task) and they deserve to share it with you. I speak to them as I speak to you.

About this day I feel that we may without embarrassment be moderately sentimental—sentimental not merely because your parents are here and your families, thankful parents and justifiably proud—sentimental for that reason, to be sure; but also because this a moment of parting.

There have been occasions when you sat on the edge of your narrow desk chairs, notebooks half closed, and waited for a bell to ring. Somehow I do not think of you poised in that fashion at this moment. Somehow I am without cynicism. If I read this moment right you feel as I feel, a bit sad at the parting—you feel as I felt when I sat where you sit: not impatient, not desolate either, because I cherished the prospect of new adventures, and yet sentimental about the parting—sentimental and perhaps apprehensive a little. If it is so and you feel that way, my friends, you have a right to your feelings. Well may you flavor this moment with a twinge of sadness and a measure of apprehension. For, to leave the sheltering hearth and plunge into the jungle of a new strange Jordan, is no simple matter.

Here you have put down roots, and here you have made some friends. Cincinnati has been a home—temporary but a home—and you are about to leave home. The College has been a shelter, a place of nourishment and companionship. As members of one class you have grown together in shared endeavor and achievement, in tension and in celebration; you have played together and prayed together, and now you are going each his way.

You have established some ties with your teachers, too. You have proved that Faculty and students are not natural enemies, and that a class struggle is not inevitable. Some friendships have been formed which will not end with your departure. You and I (and speaking for others on this Faculty, I can safely say: you and we) have been through much together, and intending no ambiguity I can say: we will miss you.

With honest sentiment you may feel sad at leaving, and we may feel sad at your going. Sad, perhaps—but not sorry; we are not sorry for you. Adventures lie before you. In new soil you will put down roots and will flourish. New friends, new experiences are there. Your tomorrow is there.

But while today lingers I am privileged still to say a word to you; I may say a word about yourselves and about your people. This is the word I would give you, each for his tomorrow: Be what you are, be simply so; respect yourself and your people and go on to brave accomplishment, starting from where you are. It is a modest formula but I offer it as a key to your future: Respect yourself and your people; be what you are; start from where you are.

You are not likely to mistake my meaning. You will not confuse being what you are with being easily satisfied. You will not suppose that starting from where you are means stopping where you are. It is far from my purpose to provide you with rationalizations for conceit and leisure. Do not hurry out to join the Lotus Diners Country Club. No—I am commending the harder not the easier course. If a time ever comes in any man's life when he may say to himself: "I have learned enough; I have done enough" this for you is not that time. It is not that time for any of us and surely not for you. A self-satisfied, self-congratulating, complacent clergy is an abomination of abominations and a betrayal. Being what you are means something quite different. It means accepting yourself as you presently are with no reproach, and going on from here.

That you are not as yet a finished scholar (and you are not) is no cause for reproach. You have gone far enough for a start. Now, day by day and year by year, alert and sensitive, freshly motivated by new challenges and learning by teaching, gaining by spending you will go on from where you are, broadening your knowledge, deepening your understanding, mellowing to maturity.

That you have as yet done nothing spectacular (if, indeed, you have not) to mend the woes of the world, that also is no cause for reproach. Though possibly other generations of students have been more active in social endeavor—for, with rare exceptions, students today are distressingly docile—even here you have been touched at least by the crusading spirit and surely ahead lies the time of your accomplishment, when you will give body and substance to the social ideals which you profess.

That you are not Orthodox (and as I know you, you are not) either in belief or in practice, either in knowledge of folkways or in ability to quote the sources with ready fluency, is no cause for reproach. You need not apologize because you do not stand today where your fathers stood. There would be cause for wonder if you were *not* different. We are children of our age. Unashamed and without regret we face up to the fact that we have changed and that time past is irretrievable. We are Reform Jews, and theoretically we have no regrets that times and we have changed—theoretically no regrets, but in practice there are many among us who are confused and timid, apologetic reformers with feelings of guilt towards our fathers. In a modern Judaism which claims kinship with prophetic thought this is unfortunate—unsuitable, indeed, among the heirs, be they liberal or conservative, of a people which tolerated the prophets—unfortunate and unsuitable.

Here too you will not mistake what I have said. I am not asking you to despise your past—that would be despising yourself. Willing to be what you are, you will not apologize for thinking forward; but neither will you cut yourself off from the house of your fathers. Your people, your family, your youth—all these are your earlier self. You are organically one with them. Self-respect in any man includes respect for his own former self. A self-respecting man will not despise, but neither will he make an idol of his past. He will accept himself both individually and corporately and prepare to move on from where he is.

Now it is good that you should know where you are. Nevertheless, if you have not yet defined your religious position (as probably you have not)—not yet defined it precisely and finally—even that is no cause for reproach. In to-day's world you would need rather to apologize if you had adopted a rigid and ordered theological system. Swiftly our thought ways are changing. Daily, science alters our perspective, pushes back yesterday's horizons; and only closed minds can now be content with closed creeds. We can no more think, for example, in terms of a one-planet, earth-bound, man-centered God, much less in terms of a comfortable patron God, a Jewish family God. New theologies are surely in the making and we need to be phrasing questions instead of answers in our day, asking instead of dogmatizing. So, do not be alarmed if you don't have all the answers. But if you don't have any questions, my friends—feel your pulse.

It is not the first time that Jews have faced new questions. You will remember their experience long ago, in the days of the prophets. You and I have studied together the thought of the prophets. May I remind you to-day, though the last of our class-bells has rung, of an observation which we made during one of our final sessions? This we observed about the fate of the prophets: that the people, in the end, adopted the prophets whom they had spurned. Each prophet in his day, gifted with a vision deeper than his people's, saw what as yet they could not see, and the people were constrained to ridicule the prophet and reject his undevout questioning. Marvellously, nevertheless, they preserved his words, and a later generation proudly owned them. So buds came to flower, and there was fruit, and Judaism lived and it grew. The prophets were the feelers; with the reach of their vision they felt out the course and as a people, following, we moved forward. Now to stop reaching out would be a cowardly repudiation of our Jewish way, a travesty of Reform, unpardonable smugness. If at all we need apologize it is for the timidity, for the apprehensive backward glance.

You will be called to this place when I have finished and will receive rabbinic ordination. It is as rabbis that you will leave this sanctuary. Let no one then reproach himself that he has not here been consecrated prophet. Neither in Cincinnati nor in New York or Los Angeles are we conducting a preparatory school for prophets. Authority is not vested in the president of the College-Institute to consecrate prophets nor is any vested in the president of the Union of American Hebrew Congregations to confirm the award of such a title. So let no one reproach himself tomorrow that he was not today appointed prophet; let him rather go from here content to be what he is and impressed by the weight of the one only charge that he has received. Let him as rabbi serve his people.

Let him, then, go forth to serve quite as he is and simply so—perhaps not a finished scholar, possibly without a notable record of achievement, in all likelihood, according to prevailing notions of Jewish piety, a less pious Jew than his fathers, conceivably a bit confused in matters theological, and not at all a consecrated prophet—a little short of perfection, that is (though one might have to argue this point with his mother)—yet as balance to his imperfection, a man unwilling to stop where he is, resolved still to grow in knowledge and in understanding, determined now to pursue his visioned goals with maturer wisdom and with creative patience, devoted always in the exercise and deepening of his own honest personal piety, steadfast ever in the ongoing search for the good and the true, content but not satisfied, at peace with himself but not apathetic, a rabbi and rightfully conscious of his worth.

Thus far, my friends, I have been speaking of you each in relation to yourself; let me now address another, a much briefer word to the subject of yourself in relation to your people. It is to be their friend that you go to your people and to guide them in their quest for the good and the true—to be friend and guide. Consider with me these two undertakings, and in each case start with yourself.

You go from here to be a friend; you leave this place, this temporary home, for a new place, to find among strangers a new home. As a stranger you go to them to be their friend. It is conceivable, of course, that you will feel lonely among them; you may be prompted to wonder who is to be friend to whom. Accept your loneliness if you do; the feeling may serve a purpose in your life, may prove not a foe but a confederate. It can sharpen your awareness of the human state, alert you to the symptoms, involve you with the lonely others.

For, loneliness is a common thing, and crowds are like mountains. You have seen mountains, towering walls of granite, played on by the changing light of night and day and the shadows of passing clouds, played on by rain and ice and snow, but the mountains unchanging, and perhaps you have been impressed as I have been impressed by their menacing indifference. Perhaps you have seen equally indifferent crowds, insensitive, made up of scurrying units, each unit preoccupied, each apprehensive, each already late for something; for a crowd is a wall, as coldly indifferent as the hills, and a man can be most fearsomely alone.

It is the role of a friend to lighten such loneliness, and to be such a friend is the role of a rabbi. This is your calling: to be a friend to your people, in that fashion to deliver them from being statistics, to help them to significance. And the undertaking holds intrinsic rewards. In the very process of being a friend you will yourself dispel your loneliness and yourself acquire significance.

Finally then, and with equal brevity, the question: How will you guide your people in their search? It is a question we have often pondered together. When we have seen what agonized failures the prophets were, in their generations, we have wondered what might save us, if anything could, from their experience of frustration. It is your question now. Although, indeed, you do not set out wholly to emulate the prophets, a part of your program is not unlike theirs, and you will want to guide your people towards some of their goals; therefore you are asking: how?

I offer you this thought: that if you would guide your people you must have them with you. A guide must be in contact, in sight of his company; he must be able to communicate with his people and they be able to hear him. A rabbi who would guide his people must speak their language.

This also is a point at which misunderstanding could easily enter. You could think that I am warning you not to "talk over the heads" of your people. If you did not know me you could think that here I distinguish levels of worth and intelligence and that I mean to say: you must first "stoop" to the level of your people before you can raise them up to where you stand. But no, I do not see you standing bored on a higher plane, looking back down and tapping an impatient foot. That is not my attitude; neither am I here making a value judgment. When I say that a rabbi who would guide his people must be able to communicate with them I am not asking you to talk down to the congregation; I am merely making a practical observation. There is no greater barrier to communication than an attitude of condescension; and the key which will open to you the minds of others is your respect for their integrity.

Look within and see that this is so. When do you hear what another man says? When, respecting your integrity, he allows you to be yourself; when, accepting you on your own terms, he excites you to go on from where you are; when, if you take to yourself only as much of his thought as can serve you, he still is content. Looking within, you find that you set limits to your hospitality; the house of your mind is occupied, and when new ideas seek entrance you first consider those housed within. You cherish your identity and you hear only him who honors it. So it is if one would speak with you.

So it is if you speak with others. Not condescension but respect will open to you the minds of your people. Combine respect for your people in generous measure with the respect you owe to yourself. Be then their guide, their friend and guide, perhaps their leader.

Not impossibly you are called to leadership. If you cultivate that living sympathy which makes you a friend to people—a friend from within yourself outward to them; if with self-awareness you respect the persons of your people—a people that looks to you as their guide—and they hear you because you care; and again, if resolutely you go on from where you are, seeking new goals and pursuing them, combining with widening vision creative will, you are indeed destined to lead as well as to guide your people.

Let it be so. I trust you each one, my friends, starting from where you are, to go on to rich fulfillment. May the sense of God's nearness attend you! May he bless you as you go each his way! Amen.

A Foundation Is to Build
Founders' Day Address, 1963

In recent days a new foundation has been laid and history made. In the week when on our Cincinnati campus we observe this Founders' Day in memory of builders, we have with ceremony and prayerful earnest festively opened the Biblical and Archaeological School of the Hebrew Union College in Jerusalem, Israel. Packed with memories and hopes, these days are days of prospect and of retrospect. We remember, and we prepare.

To the earlier founders a new founder has been added today. Happily we do not memorialize this latest builder; we salute him. We salute Nelson Glueck, a man alive with a vision and a persistent will, who first dreamed his dream and then, with daring and determination, pushed and wangled, joked and swore, borrowed and begged, prayed and "politicked," until at last his dream rose from the earth and settled down on its firm foundation: the Hebrew Union College Biblical and Archaeological School in Jerusalem, Israel—complete with book, spade and chapel. We salute the man and his dream, our dream!

When we think, as we do at this season, of the presidents, and the chairmen, the professors and the students, of the rabbis and lay leaders, of all the men and the women whose vision founded and built and sustained this College-Institute here on American soil, this year we think gratefully too of those who at the side of Nelson Glueck, turned a dream into a building and set in motion in Israel the forces that this new foundation inevitably generates.

I want to speak of three things: of a foundation, a problematic, and a two part program.

I

First, a foundation. Thinking of Founders' Day I found myself thinking of foundations—foundations and their meaning. What is the function of a foundation, I asked, and quickly the thought came: "A foundation is to build." "Colloquial," I told myself, "but expressive; a thought to expand and apply."

A founder does in fact not build a house; he merely begins the work. He lays his foundation so that on his foundation others may raise the building—on a good foundation a good building. No, a foundation does not simply sit there: "A foundation is to build."

And Reform Judaism does not simply sit there. When Reform Judaism looks like a pyramid, sitting plump on its broad base, weatherbeaten, pressing heavily downward, it is not being Reform. The essence of Reform is in its reach; Reform is most true to itself in its changing, growing, reaching, fighting.

The founding of a school in Jerusalem by the one great Reform seminary of the century, is not a return to a homeland, not a settling back on an ancient foundation; and certainly we have not gone to Israel to be absorbed there. The founding of this school denotes a fresh exploring of the recorded past for new values, a continued reaching beyond the frontiers of written history for new knowledge, a determined winning through to new truths in the clash of ideas.

Yes, in the clash of ideas. Opposition is the food of Reform. Where Reform goes unchallenged it slackens, weakens and fades; it thrives on controversy. If now, together with the Union of American Hebrew Congregations and the World Union for Progressive Judaism, the new Hebrew Union College Biblical and Archaeological School in Jerusalem with its modern chapel represents, as it must, a new outpost of Reform, it may expect continued opposition. Good! The resistance to Reform Judaism in the state of Israel may prove to be the very irritant our world-wide movement needs for its continued growth and vigor. If being exposed to the religious ferment in Israel stirs us to awareness—that is very good. We have been sitting too long. We should not be worried by—we should welcome the challenge.

If to meet the challenge Reform resumed its role as a fighting faith, as a militant movement in Judaism, that would be no disaster but a benefit. Ideally Reform is a fighting faith, Judaism militant. Ideally, Reform is to Judaism now what in the eighth, seventh, sixth, pre-Christian centuries the Hebrew prophets were to the ancient religion of Israel. That is what those prophets were: the outstretched arms, the fingers groping their way to new understanding. If life may be seen as a mold proliferating on this culture medium, this planet Earth, and if man may be seen as the advancing rim of that most admirable mold, those prophets were in their day the growing edge of the spirit of man. And though as Reform Jews we know that we fall humiliatingly short of the ideal, somehow we still are conscious that ideally—ideally and essentially, today—Reform Judaism is that same growing edge, that outreach of the human spirit. It was and yet shall be a militant movement—and the challenge which may come in Israel can only further, not impede, the return of Reform to its essential original nature.

II

Next, a problematic. If this is our role then our responsibilities are heavy indeed. We cannot rest on assumptions—not normally, and especially not today when a whole new problematic has arisen. Dramatically stated: the problem does not now center on life after death, immortality, heavenly reward; it centers on life itself, on the possibility of continued life on earth, on the here and now. Is there to be, we wonder, one vast population explosion—one—not here but in heaven, and then, through unnumbered geological ages, a long, long pause?

Someone reminded me recently—it came as a voice from the past—of a sentiment I expressed at our ordination exercises here a few years ago. "Do not be alarmed," he said I said—"do not be alarmed if you don't have all the answers. But if you don't have any questions—feel your pulse" (unquote). Bless him for remembering; I could say the same today. We are alive and alert and we have no dearth of questions.

It is not a matter of atheism. We are not asking: Is God a figment or reality? We live in a believing world. Our questions have to do with man's place in God's world—man's future (if any), man's role and God's role.

In a letter to an editor in a recent number of a national magazine I found a word I had not known, the word "biocide." Taking one's own life is "suicide"; our generation witnessed, and some survived, an attempt to destroy a whole ethnic group and coined the word "genocide"; and now we can conceive—we may be tragically coming to terms with—the possibility of the extinction of life on earth—at least we admit the concept to our consciousness with a word: "biocide."

It may be too large a word for the prospect. If certain research on the effects of radiation is trustworthy insects could survive a cataclysm which would destroy all other life. (Blessed are the bugs for they may inherit the earth.) But there is small comfort in that thought and the problem of the future of life on earth clamors insistently.

"Social service" is not effete. The needs and claims of the victims of disease, of deprivation, of injustice, are as real as ever they were, and we are called as always we have been to comfort the sorrowing, relieve the sufferers, give rest to the weary. Charity is still in style, and, far from being outmoded, love has taken on a new dimension. Alongside the claims of the individual now are arrayed the claims of life itself—and the religious problematic raised by man's new potential for self-destruction.

We are not in competition. We are not in competition with atomic physicists exploring the structure of matter, seeing galaxies and constellations in the minute particles far beneath the threshold of our vision. We are not in competition with astronomers discovering worlds and distances and shapes beyond the reach of our widest imaginings. We are awed and excited by their revelations but we are not in competition with them—our questions are not theirs.

The questions we ask are the questions men ask not of astronomers and physicists but of religion. This is the shape of our questions:

What is man, and what his destiny?

Is there meaning in history; does purpose move the world? Does anything mean anything?

Is it man's fate to become a drifting dust on a lifeless planet? Who will prevent it? God? Ourselves? No one?

Are these gloomy thoughts unfounded? Shall man achieve yet undreamt messianic Utopias? How, then?

Where does God belong in this process, if process it be? Is God just? Why did six million Jobs breathe suffocation at the whim of a maniac? Does God reward virtue? Where? Does he hear prayer? My prayers? What is prayer?

Where does man belong—where do I belong in all of this space? Am I a "statistic"? Does it matter what I do?

Does human conduct matter? Are human rights a religious concern? Is human survival a concern of religion?

These are among our questions, not new perhaps but newly urgent today. Well, are we ready with today's answers to yesterday's questions asked now with a fresh urgency? Are we ready? I am afraid that we are not, not ready with today's answers, and not willing either, simply to dust off old answers and serve them up for today's needs. So we have work to do; we have answers to seek. And we must be prepared, the while we seek, to tolerate a measure of uncertainty. We are not untrue to our calling if we so do. As Reform Jews that is indeed our way of life.

III

Lastly, a two part program.

Where is our wisdom to be found? In our past, and in our prayers. Here is a program worthy of a great foundation: to explore the past, and to search in prayer.

Yes, in our past there is wisdom. Human experience is a mine of wisdom. Even among the rubble of old answers we may indeed find well cut quarried stones to build into the structure of a faith for today.

A lot of years ago when Israel still was Palestine I spent some weeks not far from Jerusalem observing the excavation of a *tel*. You will know that a *tel* is a mound, a configuration sought out by archaeologists because they know in general from its contours what they will find beneath the surface. The shape is evidence that layers of occupation are buried there one above the other, each succeeding city built on the debris of its predecessor. "Debris" is not quite the proper word—on the "material," or the "stuff," the "substance" of its predecessor. Foundations were left. The new age built on the old foundations. Not that alone—the new age used the stuff of the old. When the *tel* is excavated and buildings are uncovered a trained archaeologist, watching the size, the shape, the finish of the building material, will now and then observe, firmly fixed in the courses of a more recent wall, a finely hewn stone, massive and solid, obviously saved from an earlier pile, extracted from the stuff of the past, built into the new-built structure. The prophet Zechariah may have had such a practice in mind when, speaking of Zerubbabel rebuilding the destroyed Temple, he said of him: "He shall bring forth the top stone with shoutings of 'Grace, Grace', unto it" (והוציא את־האבן הראשה תשואת חן חן לה).

Biblical and archaeological studies are comparable to the practice one sees here at work. The student of the Bible and the archaeologist search the past. Page by page they turn the layers of the past to read what is written there. They read in context what they find, and no study of the record except in context is worthy of the name of science. Preachers may use the Bible in skillful rhetoric; that is an ancient and honorable occupation and it is legitimate and proper. They know what they are doing. They are aware, when thus employed, that they are not interpreting the Bible but using it. As scholars these same preachers would act otherwise. They would read the record as the scholar does, the written and the excavated record, the Bible along with the potsherd, the stone, the mosaic and inscription, in its historical context only, and according to the *peshat*, according to the plain and literal meaning, seeking thus to recover the past—the past and its values.

We who have more than the antiquarian's interest in the past, we who have human concerns, are not content simply to recover what we may of the past; we would have it yield up for us its values as well. We follow the unmarked way to wisdom, in search of the hidden treasures. We ask what fine hewn stones lie buried there, stones to be saved from the past, held aloft with shoutings of חן חן, "Grace, Grace"! and built into our new defenses.

It is not possible to think of the Jerusalem school without remembering that it contains a chapel. A Biblical and Archaeological School it clearly is, but when you have said A for Archaeology and B for Bible you will also go on to say C for Chapel. The Jerusalem school is no seminary. The Hebrew Union College-Jewish Institute of Religion located in Cincinnati, New York and Los Angeles is a seminary; that is its essence. All other activities are tangential here, and the education of rabbis in the Reform tradition is our business. Not so the school in Jerusalem. Nevertheless, the presence of a Chapel in that school is greatly significant. It is a symbol, the symbol of our quest.

A chapel is a place of prayer. And prayer is the other source, along with the past, to which we look for wisdom. Prayer is a seeking, a search, a quest. Surely that is how we think of prayer, as a quest, a reaching. At times we fall prey to confusion and, false to our essential nature, try to make something else of our prayer. There is a trend toward the reverse of outreaching prayer, a wave of traditionalism even in Reform, escape into ceremony. Hear what Reform Jews are saying; listen to their rabbis—to some of their rabbis; observe the doings in our temples, the debates in our Conference, and you may think that prayer has become something different for us. Cradled in the warmth and comfort of the familiar, linked with the dead and reassured by the generations, there are those among us who would make of prayer a tranquilizer, a placebo. Prayer has that virtue; who would deny that prayer brings peace? But that is neither its only nor its highest virtue. At its best prayer is a seeking.

And prayer at its best is what we need now. To our questions today Shabbos candles, the Seder, Jewish music and more Hebrew are not the answers. These presumed answers are of a different magnitude. They belong in a different compartment of our human nature. They do not talk the same language as the questions. I like Shabbos candles, the Seder, Jewish music, more Hebrew. They are a bonus which I enjoy as a Jew. I might have said they help me preserve my Jewish identity, but I do not think that I need such aids. I am a Jew and these things come to me as a welcome bonus. They are not themselves the answer to man's real question, how he can preserve life—*his life*, maintain his identity as man. For Jewish identity is not enough; and being a Jew is not a goal, not an end, but an opportunity. When will we begin to realize and prepare to admit that the questions are far too large for mere symbols however pleasant and warming? Will the challenge in Israel teach us to pray?

It is too bad if men who should be leading our congregations in prayer (that is the expression: to "lead" in prayer)—it is unfortunate if men sent out by the congregation (that too is used of us: the שליח צבור, the one "sent on" ahead); if they do not lead whose business is to lead, do not strain forward, but are themselves dragged along, or only float, riding the waves as it were—that is unfortunate. Such surfboarding may be exhilarating, but when the sport is over where has the rabbi taken his congregation? Or for that matter where has he got to himself?

But prayer as a quest, outreaching prayer—a Biblical and Archaeological School would not be whole without a chapel, a place where such prayer will be spoken—and where if not in such a place? Nothing less could lend completion to the goals of that school. For, the study of Bible is rounded out by the prayerful search, and the study of archaeology is crowned by the prayerful search. The student of the Bible is not through with his work until he has sought and found the meaning behind the meaning of the Bible, nor is the archaeologist through until he has asked and learned what may be learned of the life force that decreed the artifact. The chapel, the place of questing prayer, perfects and unifies and lends a character to each separate part of this great College, here in America, there in Israel.

It may be that you, my hearers, are not wholly satisfied with the open-ended creed of a liberal religion, not tolerant of doctrinal suspense. If that is so and if you say to me: "we cannot build a faith out of denials and uncertainties, out of doubts and unknowns; a hod full of questions does not start a wall." I shall agree with you readily and completely. Questions are not the stuff and substance of our faith. The questions only send us in search of the substance which we will build into a vital faith. We will build that faith not of reeds and straw but of tested stones, not of drifting words but of cherished values.

And the cornerstone of the structure is the steadfast Jewish affirmation, the ancient biblical demand: *choose life*—ובחרת בחיים—*choose life!* The rest is commentary.

Today we celebrate the essence of this institution, the very nature of our movement. As apostles of Reform we know ourselves true to our essence only when we show the way—the way not backward but onward—they way onward to continued life, when with life our constant focus we build towards a future for mankind here on this good earth.

Coming of Age in America
Opening Day Address, 1966

Allow for three or four absences over the years since 1914, Mr. President, and I believe that these are the forty eighth Opening Day exercises that I have attended in this chapel. That is slightly more than half of all of the Opening Day exercises in the 92-year history of this College. It should be some kind of a record. For forty-seven of those exercises I sat where you are sitting, ladies and gentlemen, colleagues, students new and old. But today—well this is my "big chance."

I have seldom seen Nelson Glueck flustered. I do remember one time. He had just married Dr. Glueck, and her mother was holding a reception for them at her home. I offered my congratulations and good wishes, quite naturally on that occasion, and the future President of the Hebrew Union College-Jewish Institute of Religion was that flustered when he shook my hand that I heard him say: "Thank you, Nelson." I was there and I heard it with my own ears, so I am qualified to testify that the tale is genuinely apocryphal. "Thank you, Nelson," *I* heard him say. One of us was flustered, anyway.

Matters being thus, it is quite appropriate that Sheldon Blank (I almost said "Sheldon Glueck")—that Sheldon Blank should be the Nelson Glueck Professor of Bible at the Hebrew Union College. Also it is a dignity and a satisfaction which I greatly cherish. This is my first opportunity to express my appreciation in public, as here and now I do, at this service which officially opens the ninety-second academic year of this potentially great institution.

Observing, as a good Jew will (for, why should one take chances?) the רקיע or division that closes off this academy from the one above, I mention also a man out of our common past. Just about the time when Nelson Glueck and the young man destined in time to become the Nelstn Glueck Professor of Bible were awarded the Bachelor of Hebrew degree—it was not B.H.L. in those days; it was simply B.H.—at that time, fifty years ago, a book was published which I have on my shelf. It is called *The Philosophy of the Bible*. I mention it because its author, were he still living, would be celebrating his one hundredth birthday this year at this time. I am speaking of David Neumark, עליו השלום, Professor of Jewish Philosophy here for a number of years, a colorful person with a short reddish beard, affectionately known as "Pat." If I did not learn from him very much in the way of formal philosophy it was not his fault but mine, and with some warmth of feeling I think of him now as a peace-loving and equable man. Yes, he was peace-loving. Students asked him once in class (during the football season, that was) whether he owned a revolver. When he said no, should he? they asked again "But what if a burglar breaks into your house?" and he answered with a reply that ended the game: "He should bring his own revolver."

Incidentally, "Pat" Neumark was also a master of the English language—"master" in the sense that he was not to be intimidated by anything like a dictionary. If the word that he wanted did not exist, he made it. I am especially fond of his "divine dispensal" and his "unoverbridgeable chasm." I still puzzle over a word in a sentence which I want to quote from his *Philosophy of the Bible* (p. 282). I am not certain about the phrase "to hang after delusions." My guess is that it means "to hang onto delusions." At any rate, for my purpose that is what *I* want it to mean and I amend it accordingly. The sentence concerns Koheleth of whom we naturally think on this Sabbath of Sukkot. Of that man's philosophy Neumark wrote: "The best philosophy of life, according to Koheleth, is not to hang after (rd. hang onto)—not to hang onto delusions, to enjoy everything within one's reach, but with temperance and judgment under the guidance of certain practical rules of life." I believe that Pat Neumark had a "philosophy of life" and I suspect that it was not unlike his description here of Koheleth's philosophy: not to hang onto delusions, to enjoy what is within one's reach, with temperance and judgment.

Latch on now to that phrase about delusions. A story is told of another Jewish philosopher—and this also may be a genuinely apocryphal story but at any rate it is genuinely relevant. You may have read it, as I did this summer, in a column by John Ciardi. Professor Morris Cohen of City College New York had, in the words of Ciardi, reached the "end of the introduction-to-philosophy course when a coed arose in the role of intellectually ravished virtue and declared, 'Professor Cohen, you have knocked a hole in everything I ever believed in, and you have given me nothing to take its place!'" But Professor Cohen, Ciardi continues, "had a mind well poised against the slangs and narrows of outrageous virtue."

"'Young Lady,' he replied, 'you will recall that among the labors of Hercules, he was required to clean out the Augean stables. He was not, let me point out, required to refill them.'" End of quotation, end of anecdotes.

A student has a tough time at the Hebrew Union College. We confuse him, and we rob him right and left.

Yes, we confuse him. We throw the whole book at him. In the beginning, as at the first beginning, there is chaos. The student views a *tohuvabohu* made all of paradigms and vocabularies, new idioms and strange thought patterns, dates and facts and disturbingly consequent reasoning—a chaos with darkness spread over its vast expanse. The beginner must confront this stubborn matter and master it. *It* must learn who is in the driver's seat. *Now* I say "in the driver's seat"—expressions change with the years. When I myself was a beginner I might have said, it must learn who is "in the saddle," but now, of course, with two cars in every stable, I say: the material must learn who is in the driver's seat. And that requires discipline—self-discipline. One has to be mean to be master.

The student also has to learn. He has to learn to be robbed and to like it. Normally a person does not like being robbed and becomes resentful. But a student has to learn that all is being done for his own good, and enjoy it. He has probably brought a lot of things from home (overcoat and galoshes, yearbooks, chocolate bars—just in case), a lot of possessions. That is not good; really he needs the help of his teachers and his fellow students to dig out from under all his gear. Before he can discover himself beneath them he has to be helped out of some of those protective wraps. To learn to go it on his own he has to loose his clutch on that security blanket. He has our sympathy, of course; we know that all of this is shocking and painful, and that his sense of injury is real—but the process is an essential part of his education. It is a big, big world out there.

Abandon the metaphor. What we steal from the student is his notions—those he treasures most, those he brought with him to help him become a good rabbi. If he is listening he should hear things about these notions. He may go into a class in Bible and hear a professor say (without claiming originality for the thought) that the more one reads the prophets the more the impression grows that God does not much care for religion. Or he may be persuaded that all in all, over the centuries, religion has done more harm than good. Or a careful analysis may suggest that the efficacy of prayer depends on what happens in the worshiper while he prays and even that its full meaning abides in that happening. He may hear with initial disbelief that his *tallis* is his "comforter"; he may come to wonder how much of his Jewishness is homesickness, and how much of his resistance to historical method is his justified or self-imposed fear of offending an esteemed and venerable grandparent. He may hear (or fail to hear) that historical and significant are not the same thing and that the injunction: "A stranger shalt thou not oppress; for ye know the heart of a stranger, seeing ye were strangers in the land of Egypt" has monumental significance as a perfect paradigm of empathy quite apart from the historical question whether, or how many of, the tribes of Israel were enslaved in Egypt. He may want to say in a chapel sermon: "God and Israel are united by an eternal covenant" and then be encouraged (though not required) to say instead: "Israel has drawn unending comfort from the faith that she and God are joined one to another as by a covenant" or (viewed from a different angle): "Our Jewish sense of responsibility is a direct descendant of the tradition that a two-way covenant unites us and our God." In other words, he may be urged to nourish his integrity and so to state as fact no more than he can without self deception believe and in plain language defend. He may indeed be yet more cruelly challenged. If he learns he suffers, as one suffers who is fallen among thieves.

He may, of course, not learn. He may leave as he enters, with all his treasured notions still about him. If so, he has squandered his years; he has not found himself.

What is the best that may happen to a man during his years at this College? Optimally this may happen: he will lose to the robber-band whom (whatever he says under his breath) he addresses as "Doctor" and "Professor" and to their apprentices who go by the name of "Juniors" and "Seniors" and such—lose to them, worn down by their mental cruelty, sundry treasured notions—and in the process discover himself.

The possible and desirable end to the way of discovery which a man travels at the College is that indeed he discovers his true self. The self encased in disbelieved "beliefs" is shifty, evasive, surly, humdrum. A man must hate himself who professes to believe what in fact he can not believe, and he can not but like better his unencumbered self. There may, ts course, be a further increment; for the freshly opened mind may find new values to replace the discarded delusions. But with or without this possible plus, the acceptable self is the authentic self.

Is not this the all-important unavowed goal of all education: that a man discover his authentic self, and live with it in peace?

A person who has accepted himself has gone a far way on the road to compassion, for a man can not learn to accept other men until first he has learned to accept himself. wour literature knows of a man who, when he had abandoned his delusions, found compassion. The mellow author of the book Koheleth, a relaxed and charitable man, appears to have gone this road. Through free inquiry, by a process of testing and inexorably discarding time-encrusted comforting "truths" he arrived at negations which became an affirmation. He excels even Job and all the Prophets in his challenge of the pious maxims that then passed as currency; but he does so without apparent guilt and surely without apology.

Marvellously then his acceptance of the self that he finds at the end of his search becomes the source and impulse of his vast pity for the human state. We have just read as *haftarah* the passage in which Koheleth puts into words that pity. About him he sees a competitive society, every man for himself, every man alone and lonely.

> Lo the tears of the oppressed
>   and none to show them compassion,
> Power on the side of their oppressors
>   but none to show them compassion.   (4:1 b)
>
> And I beheld all toil
>   and all profitable labor;
> It is nothing but one man's envy of another.   (4:4a)
>
> A man is alone without a second,
>   no son or brother
> And no end to all his toil.   (4:8a)

So far the sickness; the remedy follows, such as it is. Koheleth can see one only remedy; with all his wisdom he knows of no remedy superior to this: that the helpless band together for strength, that the enstranged huddle together for warmth.

> Better two than the one;
>   they may profit better from their toil.
> Indeed if they fall
>   the one can lift his comrade,
> But if he be alone that falls
>   there is no second to lift him up.
>
> Moreover if two lie together
>   they are warm,
> But how can one alone be warm?   (4:9−11)

There is not much of this in Koheleth but it is unmistakably present. The author of this little book—this moment of truth—does not stop with questions and denials. Like the prophets, along with his doubts he brings a program.

A program, yes; but it is the way of Koheleth to teach by indirection. He shuns "thou shalts" and "thou shalt nots." He clears away rubbish and leaves the doors open. He makes visible the light out there and the moving air. But his voice is without authoritarian tones, his language is only suggestive and permissive. If we tried to rephrase what he says in this passage and recast it in the form of precepts, though aware that Koheleth seldom employs such forms, we might find him saying: "Look about you and learn pity. See the pain in your brother's eyes, feel his hurt. Draw near to him to help, do not turn aside. Share with him your warmth, relieve his loneliness, so may you both survive."

These are the words of Koheleth by implication only, and they are as close as he comes to the formulation of a moral code. His repeated advice to the young to enjoy their life while they can is wistfully beautiful, but not so much an expression of a moral principle as a reflection of mellowed age.

> The good and proper way, as I myself have seen, he says, is that a man should eat and drink and enjoy the whole yield of the work he does under the sun, all the days of the life that God gives him, for that is his due.
> So far Koheleth.

Now please to step outside with me, out from this little red schoolhouse, our microcosm. As we speak of persons we can speak of peoples. We can speak of American Jewry—its Opening Day. American Jewry too is entering on a period of self-study leading to authenticity. None are better prepared for such a search than the liberal Jews of America, no institution is better qualified than the Hebrew Union College to lead in the search, and no time is more appropriate than the present.

Look about you. A whole generation of homeborn Jews is coming of age in America. In the indexes of the *American Jewish Yearbooks* to date the word "immigration" appears for the last time in the volume of 1957. We are neither a colony of Jewish settlers from western or from eastern Europe, nor a random segment of a diaspora. We can be ourselves, aware and purposeful, and without debt and without apology.

The state of Israel is a valued resource but it is only that. We shall still import ideas from Israel but we shall be selective. Not all notions "made in Israel" are well conceived and executed. Some indeed look good in an American Jewish home, others clash with our deco/ and can not be readily incorporated into our spiritual economy. And we must be the arbiters, choosing to enrich our lives with all that has meaning, but choosing.

A yet more obvious resource is our Jewish tradition but on the same terms. Tradition is a valued resource and we have to master it, a treasure and a prized possession. But observe: it shall not possess and master us. We are, again, the arbiters.

This thought is not of course new to Jewish experience, nor is it alien to Reform. The deepest roots of Reform draw nourishment and strength from the Bible, and in the Bible from the prophets in particular. Our prophets asked questions and fearlessly proclaimed the answers that they found. And doing so they gave to Judaism a new and lastingly valid shape. But Reform is most like the author of Job in his willingness to freely question even the axioms. Of any who would say to us: This and this you must accept on faith; these are the עקרים, basic and sacrosanct, we ask in the trenchant words of Job to his friends:

> Do you mean to defend falsehood in behalf of God?
> Or to uphold untruth for His sake?
> Will you be partial to Him?
> Will you defend God?
> Will it be well with you when He searches you out?
> Or do you think that you could deceive Him as you can men?   (13:7–9)

We have been willing, indeed we are persistently willing, to question and to doubt. We consider doubt a value; we do not shrink from searching. We ask our questions and we trust the answers that we find—the educated answers (note this well)—not random but educated answers. We trust the answers that we find or if we find no answers we live at peace with our uncertainties.

We do not know where or when our search will end. But we do know and we put in fervent words our wished-for goal: that this native American Jewry, conscious, coming of age and unencumbered, will find itself, will discover its authentic self, and then accept that self and grow enduringly in ever deepening vision and ever expanding compassion. To such a goal we dedicate our labors as we turn to the business of this new year. So may our work bear fruit.

Spoken in the Scheuer Chapel on June 7, 1967— the Close of the "Six Day War"

We are tearfully grateful, soberly jubilant.
Discipline, vigor, the will to survive, have triumphed.
Israel's arms have swept on to victory; open before
   us lie new vistas of greatness.
In ancient boundaries we may yet sit under vine and fig—
   with none to make afraid.

In the heroism of our brothers we are immeasurably proud.
We thank them for doing a job.
We grieve for all who bled and died.
And with word and deed we stand ready to show that their
   cause is our cause.

But for the achievement of great ends we know that vision
   is no less vital than action.
And we remember that he is truly a hero who succeeds in
   making a friend of his enemy.
I invite you to ponder with me this question—in the
   moments, and the weeks, that lie ahead:
What vision can we bring to bear on the titanic task of
   winning now the confidence of an enemy—a defeated
   enemy?

To Care Enough

"Vietnam Commencement," University of Cincinnati, May 23, 1968.
Honoring those who signed the "We won't go" pledge: "Our war in Vietnam is unjust and immoral. As long as the United States is involved in this war, I will not serve in the armed forces."

I have to confess, ladies and gentlemen, that since I received your invitation to speak here tonight I have been experiencing something of an identity crisis. I will tell you some more about my troubles in a little while, but first a different word about me and you and what we are doing here.

I am here as a private citizen. My words are my own and I represent no one but myself. And when I say "you" I have in mind the principals in this ceremony, those of you within this gathering who think of this occasion as a special stage in your commencement. I have been told what you intend, and I have been trying to think myself into your place.

In one respect I find it quite simple to think myself into your place. Precisely 50 years ago, at the end of May in the year 1918, I was where you now are—expecting in a couple of weeks to receive my degree from this same University. As now, then too a war was to fight. I graduated on this campus half a year before the end of the First World War. So I can think myself, in that particular, into your place.

But there the similarity ends. After graduation I went into military service, starting at U.C. in a student army training corps and going on to an officers school. Before I saw active duty the war was over, and the only scar I bear I received right here where now I stand. I can almost see the X that marks the spot. Before this Student Union building was erected this area was only a mud lot, and the army built barracks here in that summer of 1918. I was assigned to the wheelbarrow detail; I was hauling cinders to make a company street when I slipped and cut my lip on the barrow for my only scar.

The fifty years between then and now have made more than merely physical changes on this beloved campus and in my person. They have made more than physical changes. And this is the point where my identity problem moves onto the scene. I indeed see changes in myself—but I am not all that sure just what I see. I was not then and I am not now a brave man. I do not think that I am a conscientious objector to all wars, If I were to say that I am a pacifist I would have difficulty in convincing even myself. Pacifism is not a state of mind; it is a type of action. I can not know whether I am a pacifist until I have been tried. If I were to say that I advocate civil disobedience I would discount that remark at once and observe that I am a model of a law-abiding citizen. And such counselling as I do is of the non-directive variety. I mostly try to understand another preson and maybe try to help him understand himself. So I may have my identity problem, but I am not really here to talk about that.

Nor am I here to urge on you a certain course of action. The most that I want out of this evening's experience is a measure of understanding. The least we in my generation can do for you is to try to understand you. Now to the extent that I *can* think myself (whoever I am) into your position I find myself suspecting (1) that you are probably a little bit frightened, (2) that you are finding it hard to make plans for your future and (3) that you know what you have to do, and are saying to yourselves:

> Sometimes a man has to be himself, come what may.

If I suggest that you may be a bit frightened I am not suggesting that you are without courage. If a man is not frightened he has no need for courage. The courageous are they who do what they must do, frightened or not.

And why may you have reason for fear? Because you are few. A scary kind of loneliness goes with being among the few. Of course, you are not so few as a year ago you would have been, and things look better now in May than they looked in March—two months ago. If—a year ago—in May of 1967, that year's Senior men had taken the step that you are taking now they would have been "like all alone." *Still* the road is thinly populated, but now in May of 1968 you are not all that lonely.

If the climate for your action has at all changed, that is largely because in the months between then and now the voice of dissent has added some decibels. What started little more than a year ago as a murmur of dissatisfaction swelled to a diapason and surely helped the President decide to start to talk with the enemy. That is the virtue of dissent. A raised voice destroys the illusion that a majority is a totality. An articulate minority is a collection point for silent others, who find support in the evidence that good men share their convictions. Dissent can subtly influence the broader climate of opinion and in time it can create a setting for action.

You are not so alone as you would have been a year ago. But it is no small thing that you are undertaking, as you yourselves are well aware. The worst of it is that you can not see the shape of your future. All life is like that, to be sure, but you have found the added courage to steam up the glasses through which you scan the way ahead—and to move on despite the poor visibility.

There are two kinds of patriots, I have heard say: there are those who care, and there are those who care enough. I suspect that you are doing what you propose to do because you care enough.

You care enough for America to want it true. You care enough to believe without cynicism in the high principles on which our nation was founded. You care enough for the ideals which we historically profess that you can not see them betrayed nor yourselves betray them. You care indeed about our national self-interest, but you care even more—you care enough to care about our national conscience. You care enough to risk your future. We must respect you because you dare to care enough.

And finally, if I have thought myself into your mind and mood you are saying that you know what you have to do. My specialty is the Hebrew Bible, and my specialty within my specialty is the Hebrew prophets. I think that my prophet friends would have phrased in different terms what I have just said you are saying. They did not say that a man must do what he must do; they said that a man must obey the voice of God. The prophets thought that they heard the voice of God. We are more inclined to say—with the same meaning—that we know some things with peremptory authority. We enjoy an argument of course, but when we get through talking and sit quietly alone we know. We know some things to be right, and true, and good—not simply practical or strategic, or politic or diplomatic, but morally right and true and just, not to be negated by considerations of hurt or advantage, of caution or expediency. Of these things we say: This I must do because I must.

Should all of us not thank the Lord? Should we not thank the Lord for brave men who will not kill, for men with reverence for life who will not kill, who look on the face of the enemy and see a human visage, who look at the enemy and see only men and women and children, with flesh that will burn and with bodies that will bleed? We thank the Lord for men who can not learn to hate and will not kill. We thank the Lord for brave men who care enough.

Spoken in the Scheuer Chapel, October 1969: Vietnam Moratorium Day

I was still a student when Abraham Cronbach came here to teach. First he was my teacher—then, when I returned to H.U.C. as an instructor, we were colleagues on this Faculty for many years. I never knew a more dedicated pacifist then Abraham Cronbach. I have only a passing acquaintance with Dr. Spock and with Steward Meacham. I have a great deal of respect for Michael Robinson whom you have invited here as a speaker. But Abraham Cronbach is the person who most influenced my thinking in this matter of peace. When Myron asked me to speak here this morning I thought of that man and his works—and especially of an essay on "War and Peace in Jewish Tradition." He wrote it on invitation for the CCAR and read it at the Cape May convention in 1936. If any of you ever has to do what we are doing here on this panel, run to that paper for help. It is a treasury of source material and analysis of attitudes on war and peace. You will find it in the 1936 Yearbook of the CCAR or reprinted in a volume of his essays titled *The Jewish Peace Book*.

I am going to start where he does. He constructs a scale—a horizontal scale (characteristically he made the scale horizontal not vertical so that it should be descriptive not evaluative): *Absolute militarism* at one end, *absolute pacifism* at the other—with all the gradations of attitudes towards war and peace taking their positions on the scale between the two extremes. Let me list his stations from 5 at one end to zero at the other. It will help us.

5. Absolute militarism—war is *good in itself*—intrinsically joyous and glorious.
4. If not good in itself at least *useful*—good for certain purposes—acquisitions and protections ... territorial, economic, political.
3. *Aggression* is not good but *defensive wars* are—good and necessary. We can not let them massacre our women and children. We can not let them desecrate our flag.
2. There are certain *alternatives to war* that may be healthier for children and other living things. We should try *by means other than war* to secure the advantages of a war.
1. It is a mistake to assume that war confers advantages or defends. If it did we might find a defensive war justifiable. No war defends. Wars imperil every one and protect no one.
0. Absolute pacifism. There are spiritual values that rank higher even than self-defense, so war is never justifiable.

That is the scale from A. Cronbach "War and Peace in Jewish Tradition" in the *CCAR Yearbook* XLVI (1936) p. 198 ff., reprinted in *The Jewish Peace Book*. Now try it out with a recent striking statement by that remarkable woman, Golda Meir. The *New York Times* (9/28/69) reported her saying "When peace finally comes as it must, it may be easier for us to forgive the Arabs for *killing us* than for the fact that *they made us kill them*"—a striking statement, indeed, and I think the other panelists will agree with me that it has a distinctively "Jewish" flavor. Where does it fit on the scale? Not at 0, I think; it is not absolute pacifism—more nearly at point 3—"defensive or preventive wars only"—"they made us kill them."

So now to the Bible and to my special part in this discussion: War and Peace in the Bible. The Cronbach paper will still help me here.

Let me first remind you that biblical man regarded peace as the greatest gift which God could bestow on man—the ultimate blessing. It is no chance that the threefold priestly blessing ends with the word on which we love to linger as we pronounce it from our pulpits: the euphonious word שלום. "The Lord bless thee and keep thee," we say, and in conclusion we repeat "The Lord lift up his countenance upon thee, and give thee peace," יאר י' פניו אליך וישם לך שלום.

Now I suspect that you would like to hear me say that biblical views on war and peace consistently emphasize the virtue of peace, that they are massively arrayed at the zero end of the militarist-pacifist scale—approaching, if not indeed expressing, the absolutely pacific position. But I suspect also that your own knowledge of the Bible and your trust in my integrity prevent you from expecting me in fact to say that they are. No, the variety of views that we might find within the population of a contemporary American community can be matched by the assortment of views which we find between the covers of the *Tanach;* and the distribution is probably similar in the two places, despite the passage of over 25 centuries.

We may, of course, derive some satisfaction from the fact that in that ancient time and place the ideal of the peaceable co-existence of the families of men was not simply present but found substantial—indeed notable—representation. At that stage in the evolution of conscience it might have been simply absent. But no—it is distinctly visible.

And yet—if you think of yourself as a pacifist and set out to defend that position, let me advise you not to say: "I am a pacifist because I believe in the Bible." It would be too easy for your interlocutor to remind you of the exultation of Moses and Miriam at the Red Sea, Joshua's ruthless conquest of Canaan, the Song of Deborah, the wars for added territory projected in Deuteronomy, the mandatory hatred for Amalek, and of many similar biblical expressions glorifying war and celebrating victories. And you could not help yourself by observing, for example, that not Moses but God drowned Pharaoh's army. By such a maneuver you only add to the glory of war; you only make war holy, כביכול. And you would find certain biblical accounts of the treatment of conquered peoples and prisoners of war more than a little embarrassing.

Somewhat nearer the peaceable end of the scale, but still not pacifistic is the passage in Deuteronomy 20 (10 ff.) which appears to offer an alternative to war. The Hebrew text reads: כי תקרב אל עיר להלחם עליה וקראת אליה לשלום and this sounds pretty good—until you look more closely at it and read a bit further. The new JPS translation puts it so: "When you approach a town to attack it, you shall offer it terms of peace" (which means: "you shall call on it to surrender"). "If it responds peaceably and lets you in, all the people present there shall serve you at forced labor. If it does not . . . " the dire consequences then are listed: you shall put all its males to the sword . . . take as booty the women, the children, the livestock . . . all its spoil . . . . Taken as a whole the alternative is hardly a live option—and there is small comfort here for the pacifist who leans on Scripture.

But his prospect is not wholly bleak. At or near the zero or the war-no-more end of the scale we find a substantial cluster of unambiguous aspirations. The Psalms and the Prophets are the major sources.

I am not disturbed by the fact that these sources nowhere mention Vietnam by name—or Nasser either for that matter. I am quite aware that at this end of the scale they deal in the broadest generalities—but it is that very fact that keeps them timeless and immutably pertinent. They are beacons always beyond our reach—the hopes and the promises that goad us into action.

From another great Jewish thinker whose life, like the life of Abraham Cronbach, was a total expression of his religious concerns, from Leo Baeck the inspired leader of German Jewry who never abandoned his people in their need and yet miraculously survived Theresienstadt—from his words and his works I learned the principle which I am about to apply to the most quoted passage in our portfolio—I learned from him that "Hope is duty." Now to apply that principle to the most quoted passage in our portfolio.

I said "most quoted"; perhaps I should have said "most frequently misquoted"—but the principle almost justifies the modification. You will recognize the passage in the command "Beat your swords into plowshares and your spears into pruning hooks."

There is no need to read the whole passage. Most of us know it by heart. But when you go over it again, do look at it closely. In the original it is of course no command at all—it is a gleaming promise. God does not ask us to *do* anything—he tells what he is going to do. *He* will do it. It is to comfort us in time of trouble—to give us hope in a time of despair. If it is a command as we read it today we have made it so. On the principle that hope is a duty and with our good old Jewish humanism we have taken on the task of converting a promise into a reality. So—go on and say it—say it with a good conscience—issue your command to the nations—say:

> Beat your swords into plowshares
> and your spears into pruning hooks.
> Let man not lift up sword against man
> and let them learn war no more.

I do not mean even to attempt to cover my subject in 15 minutes. I want to refer only briefly to two other aspects of the theme, as illustrations of what might yet be said:

When the Psalmist wrote צדק ושלום נשקו "Righteousness and peace will kiss each other" (85.11) he suggested the answer to the quest for the *prerequisites* of peace. That is the *prophetic* road to peace. In Isaiah we read: והיה מעשה הצדקה שלום "The effect of righteousness will be peace" (Isa. 32.17). And in two passages descriptive of the messianic king, his righteousness is, as it were, the precondition of the reign of peace on earth.

> His waist will be girt with righteousness, and faithfulness will be the girdle of his loins . . .

and *then*

> Men will not work harm or destruction in all of my holy mountain.

This is from Isaiah 11 and in the 9th chapter we read

> ... Peace will be limitless on the throne of David and throughout his kingdom To establish it and to sustain it in justice and righteousness, from now on and forever.

—Always the bond between righteousness and peace!

Does this seem somewhat remote from the activity of this day of Moratorium? We who are here, along with the youth of America, and not the youth only, are hoping today to bring influence to bear upon the rulers of this state to move them towards peace. Many of us, if not all, are giving expression to our dissatisfaction with things as they are. We are putting on record our dissent. That is perhaps the point at which we here most nearly approach the position of the Hebrew prophets. They were the dissidents of their time—of all times, refusing to accept as inevitable the status quo. They dared to ask questions quite as we do today, and hoped by so doing to help shape a future—a future.

"The Voice of Mirth and the Voice of Gladness, the Voice of the Bridegroom and the Voice of the Bride"

Founders' Day Address, Cincinnati, 1970

קול ששון וקול שמחה קול חתן וקול כלה, "the voice of mirth and the voice of gladness, the voice of the bridegroom and the voice of the bride." Breaking with custom, my friends, I am about to interpret my text *in its context*. I am *not* going to pull it out of its frame and impose a meaning on it; I am going to interpret it *according to* its context. And I do not mean the context of the seventh *berakah* of the wedding ceremony or any such pleasant location. I mean the *pasuk* in its place in the seventh chapter of Jeremiah. "The voice of mirth and the voice of gladness, the voice of the bridegroom and the voice of the bride," lovely, isn't it? Makes you feel good, like, you know, like biology and evolution, "all's well with the world," and, you know, springtime and the Song of Songs, being sociable and all those nice things. That's when you take it *out* of context. But as it was read for us we heard it in context: "Behold, the days come, saith the Lord, that it shall no more be called Topheth, nor The Valley of the son of Hinnom, but The valley of slaughter; for they shall bury in Topheth, for lack of room. And the carcasses of the people shall be food for the fowls of the heaven, and for the beasts of the earth; and none shall frighten them away. Then will I cause to cease from the cities of Judah, and from the streets of Jerusalem, the voice of mirth and the voice of gladness, the voice of the bridegroom and the voice of the bride; for the land shall be desolate." "The land shall be desolate"—silent the voice of mirth and the voice of gladness, that is the shuddering context of the lovely words. And that is where I must start.

I must not overstate my intention to stay within the context. I do not intend to be *only* literal. I shall indeed leave the gem in its abrasive matrix and let it mean what it means—only more so. I shall understand (הארץ) "the land" along with "Judah and Jerusalem," to be this planet Earth, and understand all their inhabitants to be all of the species man. Read it so and sense the horror.

> Then will I cause to cease from this planet
> the voice of mirth and the voice of gladness,
> the voice of the bridegroom
> and the voice of the bride;
> for the earth—the earth shall be desolate.

Hear the silence; feel the unproductive void. That is what I want to talk about. On this afternoon in the Spring of nineteen hundred seventy I mean to speak about the possibility of non-survival.

I have acknowledged my perfidy and now I turn to my theme.

Yes, we are in the decade of the seventies, the nineteen hundred and seventies. Isaac M. Wise founded the Hebrew Union College in the eighteen hundred seventies nearly a century ago, ninety-five years, to be precise, in 1875. He did not speak of the possibility of non-survival. He put on record his confident expectations:

> It is a great mistake (he wrote) to believe, that mankind can retrograde again . . . when the atmosphere is pregnant with progressive ideas, new inventions and discoveries, and the telegraphs carry far and wide every idea sent into the world. (That was in May of 1875.)

> Before our very eyes (he said) the world moves onward into the golden age of redeemed humanity and the fraternal union of nations, as our prophets thousands of years ago have predicted (Dena Wilensky, *Sinai to Cincinnati*, p. 34).

You heard that reference to "the predictions of our prophets," there in the predictions of Dr. Wise, and you were aware that he was being selective—as all of us are when we speak of (quotes) "our prophets." He chose to refer to Malachi and to Isaiah (or to Micah, if you prefer) and to what they said about our having all one father, and beating swords into plowshares. Fine! Those predictions indeed are there. But our founder could equally well have chosen to speak of other predictions in other prophets. One of those same prophetic books—Isaiah—contains apocalypse too. And apocalypse is roughly the same as what I am calling "the possibility of non-survival." That is the alternate prophetic mood that I am dragging into the observance of this Founders' Day of the nineteen seventies.

But am I "dragging it in?" Is it not already here? My friends, a dread is at large in our world—the apocalyptic mood. I saw it expressed not long ago (and I would quote the writer by name but my note is incomplete; it only says "*Saturday Review*, February 1963"). Whoever it was who wrote it asked a question and gave his own answer. "Question: Where does one go from a world of insanity? Answer: Somewhere on the other side of despair." No, I am not introducing the mood of apocalypse; I am simply acknowledging its presence.

So let's talk about Samson. (What? Another text for the sermon? My last homiletical atrocity, I hope.) Let's talk about Samson. You remember him. In his vocabulary "Philistine" was another word for "trouble." In his language "Here come the Philistines" meant "Oh, oh! here comes trouble" or "Here come de Judgment Day." But Samson was audacious and he had met up with trouble before and he knew quite well that Philistines were not for real. Samson played with crises like a bear with dogs until he'd had enough and then he laughed and shook them off. He always led a charmed life—always, until the last time—after he'd had the barber in. But that last time, when Delilah said "Hey, Samson, better wake up; here come the Philistines" and he woke up and thought "I'll just go out as always and shake myself free of this trouble"—that last time it just was not so. It was not "as always," כפעם בפעם, and there was a dread in his heart.

The story of Samson is a parable for our day. It illustrates the two moods that dominate the current scene—the two moods in tension. It is stylish to call this tension a "generation gap"—but we know that the gap is not simply a matter of chronological or physical age. Gray beards mingle with black on the one shore, and the yet beardless consort with the bald on the other. The tension is in the outlook, confidence and smug self-assurance on one side, doubt and downright fear on the opposite.

And who of us are the Samson people? Those among us who have grown up with Samson's persuasion that crises come and crises go, and we go merrily on forever—such among us are the Samson people. Those of us whom the shoe fits have in mind our personal experiences, our own narrow escapes from dissolution (here we are, you see?) and we have also read the Bible, and the history books. Individually, and as a people of Jews, and as a nation of Americans, we have good reason to feel secure, however lowering the clouds.

The record is there for all to read. As a people have we not met one crisis after another—and survived? There has always been a Noah. The exodus followed on the bondage of Egypt, the promised land opened before the desert wanderers, Samaria fell but Jerusalem survived, Jerusalem fell but the *golah* lived on by the rivers of Babylon, Romans destroyed the rebuilt Temple but a diaspora became fruitful and multiplied, German Jewry all but perished and Israel was born. Yes, so it has been down the colonnade of centuries. We the proud community of American Jews along with the stubborn newborn State of Israel are living witnesses to the fact that, Samson-like, we always outlive the crises that menace our being.

America, our country, is equally secure. These United States have survived repeated threats. No foe has ever invaded our borders; we have never lost a war. Militarily, technologically, in terms of both human and natural resources, we are at the same time the wealthiest and the most powerful of all the nations of this earth. We are invulnerable—like Samson. Who then are the Samson people? These are the Samson people: the muscular with their sense of power, the successful undefeated, the men of faith, *sure* that what has been will be, the contented apathetic.

But unfortunately—"unfortunately" is a long word and I may want to drop one syllable before I am through—unfortunately those others, the unSamson people over there on the other shore of the gap, those people not ancient enough to know or sophisticated enough to have our knowledge, they are unaware of the fact that we always escape disaster and that of course "it can't happen here." And that is why they are scared, incontinently scared. And dammit! Maybe they've a right to be scared.

Yes, there is a dread at large in our world, like the dread in the heart of the giant Samson when he woke up and shook himself not knowing "that the Lord was departed from him." The Philistines now are upon us, and we run—run in hurtling traffic on a one-way road to disaster.

Consider: Anyone of several, or any combination of threats that are presently abroad could mean that mankind has run out of time.

Consider: We may breed ourselves out of space and resources on a lean and limited planet.

Consider: We can blast ourselves to extinction with our growing nuclear arsenal.

Consider: We can loose on the world strains of viruses and bacteria or vapors of toxins and chemicals fatal to life—and destroy ourselves in the doing.

Consider: We can choke and suffocate our kind with fouled water, contaminated soil and used up air,

Consider: Our communications media have developed the satanic capacity to bring on an epidemic insanity—such madness as would make all things possible, non-survival among them.

And none of these potencies are fantasies of a diseased mind; they are simply sober fact.

Consider again: These threats are new; they have never stalked our earth before, never within historical times. Those threats are also as wide as this earth. Their magnitude puts them in a wholly new category.

A hundred years too soon Walt Whitman wrote: "Never were such sharp questions ask'd as this day" *(Leaves of Grass)*.

It is essential that we should recognize this new phenomenon for what it is. These are not threats which menace one people or nation alone; not the people of Israel alone, no one corner of the earth; not the American nation alone, no one nation only. They threaten the survival of all earthly life and the species man in particular. We are becoming aware of a new possibility—the real possibility of non-survival. Our planet may well have contracted a terminal illness; we may have shaped for ourselves an irreversible course.

> Only, (Beloved) remember, that a frame may be thrown
> down in much less time than it was set up . . .
> A childe, an ape can give fire to a cannon; and a
> vapour can shake the earth: and these fires and
> these vapours can throw down cities in minutes.

These words are taken from a sermon which John Donne preached to King Charles I at the Court in the sixteen twenties. I wonder what his stately prose would have made of the possibilities which confront the nineteen seventies.

At any rate, let us drop the otiose syllable: do not say "unfortunately"; say "fortunately"—fortunately the unSamson people over there are scared. Without the defense of delusions, distrustful of others' ways, unsure, sure only of now, needing to live now, the unSamson people are frightened. Fortunately too they are frightening the rest of us, arousing us, waking us up—in time, we hope—before our hair is cut and we find ourselves too weak to shake off the snarling menace.

I must be briefly autobiographical. I have always taught, always believed in, the reality of Israel's mission. Starting with a firm belief in the perfectibility of man I have always thought and taught that, by reason of his tradition and his history, the Jew has a place and a role in the achievement of a harmonious, a nobler human brotherhood. For decades I have subscribed substantially to the hope and faith of the eighteen seventies, as Dr. Wise set them forth: "the golden age of a redeemed humanity and the fraternal union of nations." I know that we are custodians of saving truths and that it is our proud duty to disseminate these truths by word and deed among mankind. This has been my faith.

But frankly—and in the vernacular—now "I am being somewhat shooken." I too have a queasy feeling that time is running out. There may not even be a tomorrow—a twenty-first Christian century.

Furthermore, (but speaking now in symbols), I have always been sustained and comforted by the conviction that having created this world out of a chaos a purposeful creator cannot permit it to relapse and return into that primal state of *tohu va-vohu*. But I have now grown less secure also in that comfort.

And there is something odd about this change which I observe in my thinking. As I contemplate the change I seem to wonder whether what has happened in me is all bad. Maybe the world would be safer with the unsafe people. Maybe I needed to be "shooken." Maybe I had slipped into the perilous mood which Israel's prophets discovered in our people in ages past—and mercilessly condemned. Those prophets cast massive doubt upon the comforting inherited delusions which sustained their trustful contemporaries: "With us is God (עמנואל)"; "no evil can befall us." In God we trust. You know, like those slogan makers האומרים שלום שלום ואין שלום—who say "after the Vietnam war" and say it often enough to make it sound like "the day after tomorrow."

To be sure, I knew and appreciated the sequel. I know that those prophets also condemned those soothing slogans, branded them the opiate that numbed the public senses against dangers abroad in the world. The assurance that all is well, that very assurance, they suggested, makes all *not* well. I also know the length to which Jeremiah went in the extension of this thought. A large factor in the shaping of my present view has surely been my preoccupation with Jeremiah. He was one prophet who ended "somewhere on the other side of despair."

A few minutes ago I compared the contemporary mood to the dark and violent mood of apocalypse. But as I think of the comparison I realize that it is not entirely sound. The darkness and the violence are indeed a common denominator and they justify the comparison. But also there are at least two significant differences in substance between apocalypse and our estate.

One is the matter of: how total is total? We have been contemplating a grim prospect unrelieved by any gleam of hope: the possibility of non-survival, the end of life on earth. But apocalypse is less than total. The day of final judgment at the end of time according to the Isaiah apocalypse, for example, the cosmic catastrophe that turns the earth over to spill out its inhabitants and shakes the stars from their courses, is likened to the deluge at the beginning of time, and, even as the family and pets of the righteous Noah survived to seed the future, a people few in number rides out the apocalyptic fury.

The source of this feature in apocalypse may be the writings of Jeremiah whose thinking made room for the all-but-total—the concept of the lone survivors, the unSamson people—as we shall yet see.

But we face the possibility of non-survival, unless . . . The word "unless" introduces the second, the more significant difference. Apocalypse is only God's doing. It is a cataclysmic irruption of the divine into history. That is not characteristic of our thinking today. We do not hold God responsible for the fouling of our environment, the runaway population of our planet or the nuclear threat. I doubt that we think today of God as the agent of our destruction. He is neither doing it—nor, note well! is he preventing it. We have no one to blame for the threat but ourselves. And to say it in good Americanese "Hain't no one else gonna get us out of this mess." It is suicide, self-destruction—and only the subject can refrain.

I get another message from Jeremiah. Like the Psalmist the prophet too sank in the mire where there was no foothold. The unwanted expected was happening and the end of his world was drawing near. The iron ring of the Chaldeans was closing in on his people and Jerusalem. And the prophet screamed their danger to them.

It is not strange that they took him for an enemy agent, an outside agitator demoralizing the defenders of Zion and inciting them to mutiny; what he asked of his people invited that suspicion, and indeed the people acted on it and lowered him now in grim fact into the cistern, that he might sink into the mire and die there, a fit end for a traitor.

What had he asked of his people? Jeremiah had priorities, and life came first. He asked the defenders of the city to choose to live—to live even at the cost of national prestige, even at the price of liberty, even in captivity. "I offer you a way of life," he said for God, "and a way of death. Whoever remains in this city will die by sword, by famine, or by disease. But whoever goes over to the Chaldeans will live and his life will be his boon." If any were to hear him they would be the unSamson people—those with no illusions of security, those who could apprehend, internalize (according to the jargon), act on, the certain possibility of non-survival. What shreds of hope Jeremiah could gather he placed on those rare few with opened eyes who admitted no hope but who could not accept non-survival as an option. The significant point is that with this challenge Jeremiah made survival a human undertaking. This is not the apocalyptic mode, but it has vast meaning for our time.

When Attorney Kunstler recently, explained the behavior of certain persons as a "'deadly serious attempt by deadly serious men' to make the nation conscious 'of the realities before it's too late,'" he could as well have been speaking of the enterprise of Jeremiah among the Hebrew prophets (*Cincinnati Enquirer* March 4, 1970.)

One final thought. Apocalypse and a certain well-known promise stand at opposite poles. On the day of the Vietnam Moratorium last October when I was privileged to speak here on biblical attitudes towards war and peace, I made inevitable reference to that gleaming promise, which we lovingly repeat: "And they shall beat their swords into plowshares and their spears into pruning hooks; nation shall not lift up sword against nation; neither shall they learn war anymore." I observed that this passage in Isaiah (and Micah) is a promise—nothing more. Like apocalypse it is a divine undertaking, an irruption of God into human history. That much it has in common with apocalypse, despite the vast difference. God here asks nothing of man; he tells what he will do—what God will do "in the end of days." But I also observed then that we with our good old Jewish humanism have taken on the task of converting an ancient promise into a present program. As we have adapted this promise for use in the *Union Prayer Book* (p. 41) it reads: "*Let them* beat their swords into plowshares . . . *let* nation not lift up sword against nation nor learn war anymore." And recently a colleague here, Robert Katz, in a service designed for this Chapel (like last night's special service) included this same passage and with fine discrimination entitled it a "prayer." It is a natural progression: from prophetic promise, through program, to prayer—that is, provided you accept my understanding of prayer as that which after deep searching a man who prays resolves himself to do.

So threat and promise merge in human undertaking.

Shall I say it again—in one sentence? What hope may yet remain for the species man on earth may reside with the unsure generation, with that growing number of disillusioned and resolute men and women—of whatever age—who are loving enough to refuse non-survival, clear-eyed and young enough to know—to know and to act on the knowledge, that only they can preserve this earth—preserve its living sights and sounds: "the voice of mirth and the voice of gladness, the voice of the bridegroom and the voice of the bride, sound of mill and light of lamp."

A Frontier Is a Lonely Place
Ordination Address, 1971

Mr. President, Colleagues, Ladies and Gentlemen:

I am looking for a text. I am tempted to talk about the state of the world. But no; I look at the world and I decide: You shall be my text. You, the recipients of degrees—earned and honorary, you who are to be ordained here today—yes, you shall be my *Parashah* and my text: you in particular, the class of 1971, twenty-eight good men poised for the countdown; your wives nearby, holding your hands as it were, as they have done through these recent years but today with a reassuring squeeze; your children — that is to say your future; your parents and other family, with a lump in their throats, grateful for this moment of fulfillment and not a little proud ("my son the rabbi") — justifiably proud; fellow students, soon to be known as "the boys back there at the College," just now somewhat emphatically involved in this climactic ceremony; other friends of yours, among them this faculty — not terribly sorry to see the daily pressure of the academic tasks lightened as of tomorrow, and yet somewhat sad to lose contact with as fine a group of individualists and eager human beings as I for one have seen pass through this College in the span of a pretty long memory—somewhat sad but expecting great things of you and prayerfully wishing you well. Incidentally, it will not be unmanly if when you are "out there" you cast an occasional nostalgic thought in our direction too.

I cannot mention the faculty at these ordination services this year without a thought and a sigh for one who is not here to lay his hands on your shoulders, the gesture of *Semichah*—not here to name you "rabbi" with his blessing. The world of scholarship, the state of Israel, American Jewry, the city of Cincinnati, the Hebrew Union College on its four campuses, persons and organizations everywhere mourn the death of our late beloved president Nelson Glueck. But we here gathered have personal reason to grieve—I through nearly sixty years of warm association, you through fewer years but still a closeness—and our personal loss is particularly poignant here at this place and time. Our memory dwells on him now for a silent moment—

And turning to life and the future we greet another warm and welcome friend, the new president of the Hebrew Union College-Jewish Institute of Religion, Alfred Gottschalk, capable and learned, a friend of God and men. We are confident that his leadership will bring this institution to ever greater heights and we offer him our labors towards that end. It is he who will have the satisfaction of ordaining this class of 1971 and you will be known as the first class ordained by President Gottschalk; that is to be your honor.

Yes, not knowing very much about the world, I have decided to talk about you here this morning. I try to feel myself into your place and I suspect that two emotions may be in tension in your guts: exuberance and apprehension. Yes: apprehension. You have reached the frontier of a new life and a frontier is a lonely place.

You know, you have been spending a lot of years—four, five, six—some more, some less—gathering material, laying in supplies, reading, studying, cramming for exams, writing papers, conducting liturgies, teaching and preaching, serving bi-weekly congregations, organizing, protesting, counselling—accumulating more and more experience to sustain you—"out there," to be used when you become a rabbi. But listen: Now (or a few minutes from now) you will be just that—each one a rabbi and your experience account will be closed. You're there; and you are entitled to be apprehensive if you will, the while you are exuberant.

I can see you preparing to challenge a statement which I just made, and I welcome the challenge—as I have welcomed so many such challenges in the give and take of the classroom with you. I said that the experience account is closed, and you wonder whether it is so. Does learning stop with ordination? you ask. And I have to agree with the implications of your question; God help us if it does! And you are right to ask and I am guilty of dramatizing a thought at the cost of precision. It is time to draw on the experience account indeed—but not without replenishing it.

Most of your years at College were during the turbulent sixties. I want to call them frontier years. Amazing things have been happening—amazing things. Bear with me because in what I now say I will appear to be confused. I say: Our world has grown much larger. And I say: Our world has grown much smaller. And when I say this and when I say that I am not speaking about our world at all; I am still speaking about us. Bear with me.

Early in the sixties just over ten years ago—no longer than that—Alan Shepard spent fifteen minutes in an orbiting capsule—the first earth man to venture into outer space. At the end of that decade two earth men walked the surface of the moon; and now still on the threshold of the seventies we are set to map the planet Mars. With the rim of our sky receding at such speed who would say how far our world may reach before this decade ends. Our world is rapidly expanding.

With equal speed our world is shrinking; menacingly closing in. Suddenly it has all become visible and we can see it while it happens: round-eyed children with swollen bellies, awaiting death in Biafra; putrefying victims of nature's raging in the flooded delta in Pakistan; our flamethrowers burning down homes, our machine guns crumbling people in far-off Southeast Asia, or nearer home officers of the law clubbing the likes of you and me bloody in Washington—as these things happen we see them. They are with us in place of music at our dinner table. We view them while we "eat too well" and suddenly the laburnum seed tastes bitter. So small has our world grown that these scenes crowd in and jostle us and we are denied the comfort of a shrug. In a shrinking world we cannot say: "Oh, that's in Peru."

So we inhabit an explosively expanding, oppressively shrinking world. But when we have said that we also realize that we are not in fact talking about our world; we are talking about ourselves. Analogously, John Keats was not in fact talking about astronomers and discoverers when he wrote:

> Then felt I like some watcher of the skies
> When a new planet swims into his ken;

> Or like stout Cortez when with eagle eyes
> He stared at the Pacific—and all his men
> Look'd at each other with a wild surmise—
> Silent, upon a peak in Darien.

No, not of astronomers and discoverers (he would not have said Cortez when he meant Balboa). He was talking about himself. Consider the major clause in his sentence: "then felt I like some watcher of the skies"—"then felt I." Or consider the title which John Keats prefaced to his sonnet; it reads: "On First Looking into Chapman's Homer" and, not in fact concerned with discoverers and astronomers, the sonnet reveals what the magic of that Chapman translation (then two centuries old) did to him, the sensitive younger poet. The sonnet concerns him, his feelings. In just that way we now are speaking of our expanding-shrinking world only to ask ourselves what our experience of this world may be doing to our own moral emotive sensors.

That experience leaves us with "fear and trembling" (if you like the phrase). I am inclined to say "with awe and with horror," abandoned by standard rationalizations, suddenly lonely on an exposed frontier. Not all frontiers are geographic.

So what do we do? A great temptation beckons and not uncommonly we follow. The chair-desks in our classrooms can serve us as a symbol. I came to the College as a student in 1914. Well, when students nowadays visit and conversation lags someone is sure to look at my white hair and ask: Doctor, have you noticed any changes while you've been at the College? That's a standard opener, and what I sometimes say is: Yes, the Cincinnati Reds no longer hover around seventh place. But today I want to give a new answer. It is about those classroom chair-desks: they have broader, more accommodating seats than they used to have, a temptingly large area to settle down on—corresponding apparently to lower centers of gravity among the occupants, more weight on the status quo. You realize of course that now I am not talking about you of the class of 1971. That development occurred before you came; you found those seats there—and you scorned them. I mention them only as symbols of the great temptation which you successfully resisted: the settling down syndrome.

Suddenly lonely on an exposed frontier we are tempted to turn about and get back to settled land, to retreat, to return to the shallow security of familiar rituals and territorial sovereignties—to comfortable theological and political platitudes. The old certainties pose as better company than the new questions, and we want to go back. But that is the wrong direction today; we are tempted but we resist; or if we succumb it is a passing phase and we recover. For myself I prefer the wilderness—as you have done. Sure it's lonely—at first. But if the direction is right others also find their way there; frontiers are like that.

As I see this class before me, as I look again at my text and reflect on the years we have shared, I am powerfully reminded that not all your learning was done in the classroom. You have not been static; you are a class of movers and the College has changed by reason of the years that you have spent here. You have done some fruitful grumbling, and you have initiated some valid changes. The status quo will never be the same again.

Another word for grumbling is "dissent" or "protest." There are those among us who refuse to believe that our military presence in Southeast Asia is a furthering of the American dream and see it instead as a betrayal of that dream. Some of us felt sufficiently enraged by that betrayal three or four years ago, to raise our voices in dissent—before it was the thing to do on campus—though to be sure Berkeley was already there. The swelling tide of protest then was surely a factor in the political changes which followed. When the job is done—and it is far from done—do not say that we accomplished it; simply be satisfied that you were on the right side trying.

Do you have the feeling even now that people have scored one small gain? Did you once have the sickening sense—some few years ago—that you were only a statistic, a number on a computer card, voiceless, resourceless? That sense was epidemic then; I hope I am right when I say that it is subsiding now and people are finding a voice; Americans are beginning to stand tall again.

There are movers among you who worked for intramural change as well. You joined with those who saw inadequacies in the course of study, in the administrative structure, in the religious activities within the College community—and you worked effectively. Perhaps you were surprised to find that you were not voiceless. Your counsel was heard in the planning of curriculum changes. You were given seats as representatives of the Student Association on Board and Faculty committees. The Chapel was turned over to you with no requirements except that you should provide regularly scheduled worship services. This freedom has seemed at times to be a heavier burden than many had supposed but there is no measurable sentiment in favor of a return to the earlier program. Many feel that the search for more valid modes of worship, which this change has quickened in these latter years, is a positive advantage. It is a frontier.

Now, in spite of the fact that we can orbit the planet Mars (if we keep on trying)—in spite of the other fact that, exploring the infinitely minute we can unravel the secrets of the atom and the chromosome, there is still much more that we do not know—and we may do ourselves harm by acting as though we do know. לא ידע האדם, "A person can't know;" מי יגיד לו, "Who is there to tell him?" Koheleth said it like it is a long time ago (10.14).

There are some things (theologically speaking) that we tend to accept without evidence. But on today's frontier in growing numbers people are preferring not to count on them as sure. Some are even saying that we lead a healthier life if we reject the ancient unsupported axioms of faith. Consider two examples: life after death and retributive justice. We do not know, and no one can tell us of a life beyond this life. And we do ourselves no good by pretending otherwise. Twenty-five years ago our colleague Joshua Loth Liebman said it incisively in his book *Peace of Mind* (on p. 106). He said in effect, that failure to admit the finality of death can diminish "the life hunger in the hearts of the living"—"the life hunger in the hearts of the living." Better, then, to accept its limits and employ for its maximum good this gift of life.

Also we do not know and no one can tell us that in fact God rewards the deserving and chastens the undeserving, either in this life or in an after life, if any. The doctrine of retributive justice is an unsupported postulate. And we are not the first of the Jews to say so. The man who wrote the book of Job and the author of the seventy-third Psalm both expressed their agonized doubt. Malachi scolded contemporary skeptics troubled in their mind, and the man who called himself Koheleth frankly said that evidence against the postulate mightily challenges its validity. It is indeed a fading fancy in our day—but we do not mourn its passing.

For, what is our human condition once we abandon the notion? Is it not simply this? that we are left to reach our decisions without the customary prods and carrots. The responsible party is man and he must assume his rightful stature. It is an exposed position on a lonely frontier—but, more than that, it is a strategic post in man's war for survival on a crumbling planet.

As I think of what I have said—and I am through now—it seems to me that I am asking you—each one of you—not to recoil from the venture, not to turn back and bleat. You have shown your mettle; you have demonstrated your precious individuality. So stand your ground. No, don't stand; don't sit; get on with the job. Go out to a people perplexed and waiting. Be their guide.

And may God bless you, each and all!

"Know Before Whom Thou Standest"

Once when the great rabbinic authority Rabbi Eliezer was ill his disciples came to visit him, and when they asked of him rules for proper living this was among the precepts he gave them: כשאתם מתפללים דעו לפני מי אתם עומדים "Know when you pray before whom you stand." This story is told in the Talmud (Ber. 28b). There, the expression "When you pray" (כשאתם מתפללים) probably means "when you recite the תפלה-prayer, the 'eighteen benedictions,' of the daily service." Rabbi Eliezer was telling his younger colleagues "offer these prayers with the full awareness that you are in the divine presence." Commenting on this rabbi's words Rashi adds the obvious: "so that you pray with reverence and with intent (ביראה ובכונה)." However narrowly he meant it Rabbi Eliezer's word has become a classic. In a somewhat shorter form and personalized we find it carved on many an ark in many a synagogue throughout the land, to be seen by Jewish worshippers at prayer: דע לפני מי אתה עומד—"Know before whom thou standest." It is a basic thought and Rashi is surely right when he refers to כונה, intent—but there is more to be said.

Have you thought of the difference between praying and daydreaming? I suggest that the difference is the address on the envelope. Prayers have an address, daydreams have none. Daydreams are diffuse, undirected; prayers are focused, directed. He who prays knows before whom he stands. And this is a significant distinction. Nothing limits or defines, refines or selects the chaotic substance of our daydreams; but the fact that prayer is directed—that fact itself imposes limitations, and the fact that the one addressed in prayer is God obliges him who prays to select and refine the substance of his recitation. The address puts the thoughts into a context.

This may sound too manifest to mention, but the address is in truth an essential fact—a by no means unimportant fact concerning prayer. It is evident, of course, you have only to listen to hear the address. "O Lord," we say, "O Lord, our God, and God of our fathers." Or we say, "Our Father," "Our Father, our King." "Blessed art Thou, O Lord," we say; or we say, "Dear God," "Our heavenly Father," "Lord of all worlds." We have many terms to use but they all have one meaning. They mean that we are directing our thoughts to God.

He who prays comes before the divine presence, stands there and speaks in that context. And his sense of being in the holy presence has certain results. Consequences flow from his very sense of being there.

Are you asking what I mean by "there"? What do I mean when I say he comes before the divine presence and stands there? No, I do not mean a certain locality—not necessarily. I do decidedly believe that the quiet of a sanctuary furthers the prayerful mood—that the fellowship of a congregation contributes to the context of prayer. A synagogue is a good place for prayer. It is a good place, but it is not the only place. When a student asked the other day whether what I meant by prayer could not take place in the midst of a symphony I said that indeed it could—and in other places as well. When another student said at another time that a man should have in his home a corner set aside especially for meditation and for prayerful thoughts, again I agreed. Remember the liturgical selection which begins: "Thou shalt love the Lord thy God." Meditation is commended there "when thou sittest in thy house, when thou walkest by the way, when thou liest down and when thou risest up." And as with meditation so with prayer. The locality is not essentially significant, and the word "there" is not geographical. Where I am when I call upon God, there I am in his presence; and consequences flow from my sense of being there.

When a man prays, the fact that he is in God's presence has this first result: that it disposes him to drop his pretenses, to recognize sham. The mask that he wears in society—comes off. The front that he puts up in his business or profession—falls. The veils that hide him—and hide him even from himself—dissolve. In the very process of bringing his thoughts to God a man becomes honest. Express it colloquially in good American slang: after all, who's he kidding? The sense of standing in God's presence makes a man less artificial, more sincere, more open and honest. Prayer at its best is a moment of *truth*.

Compared again to daydreams, prayers are disciplined. This is a second consequence of tle context of prayer. In dreams we give full rein to our wishes and to thoughts of their realization—let the consequences be what they may. But when we pray, our sense of being in the presence of God makes us more selective—not indeed because certain subjects are taboo or profane and thus not appropriate in a prayer—nothing should be taboo, all life is appropriate—but rather in the way that power, at its best, makes for responsibility. The feeling, when we are linked with God in prayer, that we are all-powerful, omnipotent, dictates caution. Conceiving the possibility that unlike our dreams our prayer wishes may be realized, we pray with heightened responsibility. We sift our wishes and in the process learn what it is that we really want—rejecting a selfish thought in favor of a generous impulse, finding a remote goal more desirable than a present good, recognizing the tawdry, choosing the worthy. So does the context discipline prayer.

And now a metaphor: You own a valuable canvas. You want to hang it to advantage, but it lacks a frame. You take it to a studio and with an artist's skillful aid design a frame. The frame is good; it picks up a highlight here, a shadow there, here and there a color, and you see on the canvas suddenly what you never saw before. Prayer is such a frame; it can do for your thoughts what the frame does for the canvas. This happens in prayer, and you see your life in a new way, your life with all its varied colors, lights and shades. This is a third consequence. Sorrows and joys assume their right proportion, troubles appear in truer perspective, the frame brings out the values.

Abandon the metaphor and imagine an example. You are a good man and want to do what is right—and now the time has come when you must make a moral decision. Your friends have had their say, considerations of status and profit have been weighed, but the balance is delicate and you still are not sure. It may just be that clarity will come and with it a resolve, if only you review the argument in the context of prayer, aware before whom you stand.

Review the argument. A prayer that tells a story is not to be despised. State the case; it is good to tell the story in that holy presence. It does not matter that the God whom we address in prayer is, as we conceive him, all-knowing, that nothing is hid from his gaze, that our telling is no more than a reminding. It does not matter; there is a virtue in the simple telling, because as we put our concerns into words and array our complaints and demands, doing this there in that presence, something inevitably happens. Affairs appear in a proper proportion; the significant is suddenly significant and the trivial trivial. And other distinctions emerge as well—the distinction between what can yet be restored since hope remains, and what is over and done where only acceptance is in place, the distinction between what we are powerless to effect and what is in fact our own responsibility. In the telling in that presence we discover our course, whether resignation or resolve. Review the argument, tell the story, yes—.

But still nothing happens in prayer unless we listen. A vastly significant part of the prayer experience is the listening. There are, to be sure, different kinds of listening. One kind is passive, another active. Active listening characterizes the Jewish prayer experience—not a languid openness to sound, but an active creative listening—a dialogue. No narcotic element is present; we are alert, listening even to our own words, to the words we pray—and to the silences between the words. Jewish prayer is a reaching—a reaching and a grasping. We listen as we pray alone in silence. And as at Sinai—something happens.

"I suggest," a rabbinical friend* has said to his congregation, "that you do at times what I do frequently: come into this synagogue when there is no one around, when the sun pours its light in through the windows, and sit quietly in your pew. Sit quietly, humbly, alone—alone with your God. Forget your appointments . . . forget your peeves and your ambitions—just sit here alone, quietly, reverently. Something will happen to you."

I agree with this friend's conclusion: something will happen to you as you sit there "alone with your God." It has happened to me. First as student and then as teacher at the Hebrew Union College, now for a great number of years I have been in and out of the chapel there and have heard and joined in, and have myself prayed, many a prayer in that place. And things have happened. I have done some of my best growing there between the words of the prayers. While the student choir was singing some response some of my worst confusions have somehow got unconfused and bits and pieces have fallen into place. Some of my better impulses during some silent meditation have reached the stage of resolve, have hardened into resolution. We learn in prayer what it is *we* have to do.

Yes, something often happens in those moments there in that presence. And again I should say that the geographical locality is not the important thing. My friend was talking of his Sanctuary, I was speaking of my Chapel. But the localities, Chapel, or Sanctuary, Cincinnati, or somewhere else, are incidental—incidental—yes, but not wholly irrelevant. My long association with that Chapel has made it my spiritual home. My friend's long association with his congregation and his Temple made them his family and the place his home. We will not deny that years have a meaning and a room has a relevance. They too, are context, a frame and a setting for prayers. And still I say the place is not the one essential element. Knowing before whom you stand is what truly matters.

*Beryl D. Cohon in *My King and My God*, New York, 1964, p. 223.

Spoken at the Memorial Service for Merle Marcus, 1965

A light is dimmed; a voice is stilled. One whom we loved has gone too soon. Suddenly we see the slippery path of life. Surely man is grass.

Meaning is gone and we are brought low; we are emptied clean.

And yet we turn in prayer to Thee, our loving Father and our God. Futility is not our final word.

In this time of deep darkness we grope towards a light; in the unreason of accident we probe after reason. Buffeted by evil chance we run to shelter; in a reeling world we hold to the steady center. Creatures of a moment, we turn longing eyes on eternity; in our confusion we reach for a goal. We resolutely clutch at hope in despair; we scan a hostile crowd for the face of a friend.

All of these art Thou, O Lord. Thou art light and reason, with Thee are shelter and stability; Thou art both goal and eternity, we find hope in the certainty of Thy love. For what Thou art to us we reach unceasingly, and so find comfort in our grief, strength in our weakness, solace in our disappointment, meaning in unreason.

Even now we turn to Thee with prayerful gratitude. For the life that was Merle Marcus we are endlessly grateful. For the life of this daughter, our friend, we thank Thee. We thank Thee for the warmth and joy, the laughter and the music of her years, for the cheer and comfort that her great heart brought to others—and for what others—for what we could do, and did, to bring joy to her short life, as well.

For all her happiness that mingled with inevitable pain, for all the satisfactions that compensated for her discontent, for her surpassing courage, Lord, we thank Thee. Since we cannot know what the future held in store we do not murmur at that which has been. ד' נתן וד' לקח יהי שם ד' מברך The Lord gave and the Lord hath taken away; blessed be the name of the Lord.

We are grateful, Lord, and yet we grieve; and we bring to Thee our need. This man—our brother, colleague, teacher, friend—be Thou his comfort. This father, with his sorrow and his suffering—put Thine arm about his shoulders. Give him assurance of a lasting memorial, and help him to see beyond his grief.

O Thou who bringest comfort, grant also us understanding. Give us courage and strength, and lead us in the way of consolation.

Spoken at the Special Convocation Honoring Robert Frost, 1960

אדני שפתי תפתח ופי יגיד תהלתך

Teach us to praise Thee, Lord, with the flute of our lips.
May our mouth become an instrument of joyous song
And may our speech serve Thy widening purpose.
Bless Thou the words of our mouth.

Lend us the wit, O Lord, to speak the lean and simple word;
Give us the strength to speak the found word, the meant word;
Grant us the humility to speak the friendly word, the answering word.

And oh, make us sensitive, Lord—
Sensitive to the sound of the words which other men speak—
Sensitive to the sound of their words—and to the silences between.

The Sukkah
Its History and Promise

I saw the moon a bright disc and did a hasty calculation. This many full moons ago, I thought, we celebrated with a Seder service the spring festival of Passover; that many full moons from now we will say the blessings in our Sukkah, observing the autumn festival of Tabernacles—the two seasonal festivals just six full moons apart. By that moon, which city lights have dimmed and tall buildings have eclipsed in urban centres, our people have reckoned through the centuries their religious seasons.

Our Jewish calendar has a complex history. Men did not turn in Bible times to a printed table or a parchment chart to find a date. They observed the moon—and the sun. They watched the sun as well as the moon and fixed on those two points in the solar year when daytime equals night-time, the spring equinox and the autumnal equinox, and they started their year with one of these, but not always with the same one. We would probably say, if anyone asked us, that the Jewish year begins in the autumn—on Rosh Hashanah, the New Year's Day. And that is right, but still it is hard to explain why then it appears in our calendars at the first day of the *seventh* month—in our calendars and in the Bible. The same biblical source reserves a date in the *first* month for the spring festival of Passover. Not one but two or more systems of reckoning left their mark on the Bible, and the study of the ancient calendars is a science in itself. No modern scholar has done more to clear up this complicated history than the revered President Emeritus of the Hebrew Union College, Dr. Julian Morgenstern.

One probability which he observes is that the holy day which we now call Sukkot was once the most important day of the religious year. Only the three festivals are mentioned in the earliest biblical lists, and the festival of Sukkot occupies a special place. Pesach, Shavuot and Sukkot appear on the lists, but not the two *yamim nora'im*, 'the awesome days', which later attained and retained the greatest significance. The New Year's Day and the Day of Atonement were late arrivals.

Sukkot had a special importance. The three more ancient sacred days were known as 'festivals', *chaggim*; but one of these was called *he-chag*, 'the festival', or 'the Lord's festival'. This one day which did not need to be named because it could be described simply as 'the festival' was Sukkot, the feast of Tabernacles. Quite possibly as a consequence of certain calendar changes the one original Sukkot festival became fragmented yet in Bible times into the cluster of sacred days which now we call collectively the autumn Holy Days.

Sukkot is not the earliest name of this autumn festival. The *chag* in earliest times was referred to as "the festival of ingathering at the end of the year when you gather in from the field the fruit of your labour" (Exod. 23:16), or as "the festival of ingathering at the turn of the year" (Exod. 34:22). The New Year's element seems to show through the phrases "at the end, or turn, of the year"; but more significant for the character of this festival are the allusions to the harvest. It was undoubtedly a farmers' holiday, a time when they rejoiced and gave thanks to God because he had blessed and rewarded their labours. Significant too is the fact that annually on this 'Lord's festival' maidens danced a mating dance in the vineyards at Shiloh. The biblical book of Judges speaks of it, and the Mishnah also knows of it but, confusingly, as a festivity on the Day of Atonement!

The harvest, the merrymaking, the mating rituals, all suggest an original association of this cluster of sacred autumn days with the rites of agriculture. But Israel's origin was not agricultural; it was nomadic and pastoral. In all probability then the Sukkot festival grew up not in the desert but on the soil of Canaan and was there for Israel to adopt when the people settled on the land.

Like other institutions, and especially among them the other festivals, Sukkot underwent a change, already in Bible times, but it never lost its original flavour. Even in the Mishnah almost everything related to Sukkot can be viewed as an aspect of the farmer's life and concern. The ceremony of water drawing and libations of water and wine, associated in rabbinic sources with this feast, suggest the rainfall which is of course a prime concern of all who cultivate the land. The branches of palm, myrtle and willow, freshly cut and bound together to make the green bundle, the *lulav*, to be carried and shaken on the days of the festival, and the citron fruit, the *etrog*—these represent all that grows in forest, field and orchard. The *hallel* psalms prescribed for those days are quite as much prayer as thanksgiving; they indeed praise God for his multiple favours but they entreat him as well to continue his blessing:"We beseech thee, O Lord, save now *(hoshi'ah-na)*! We beseech thee, O Lord, make us now to prosper!"

The booth or *sukkah* itself is an agricultural or horticultural motif. When the time of harvest and vintage drew near, the grower built out of such materials as were at hand, in olive grove, vineyard or orchard, 'rude shelters' where a man might be stationed to guard from birds, beasts, or human trespassers, the ripening fruits. These *sukkot* were 'frail booths', temporary, not intended to last beyond the limited period of their usefulness. The Hebrew word *sukkah* suggests a 'covering', a roof of twigs and branches loosely interlaced, to provide some seasonal shade and shelter. It seldom rained in Palestine during the time of harvest.

The ceremonies of Sukkot, then, are quite consistently related to the concerns, the anxieties and the satisfactions of men who cultivate the soil and look to the yield of the vineyard, garden, orchard and field. The rites are designed to promote the yield of all planting, and when hazards are past, toil completed and fruits stored in barn and bin, the rituals also express man's thanks to "the Creator of the fruit of the ground," who "brings forth bread from the earth."

Those buildings that curtain off the sun and the moon also contain us within city limits, and mostly we know of growing things after they are processed and packaged on shelves and in freezers. Our role is to consume. Cushioned against the fears and uncertainties as against the rewards and satisfactions which the farmer knows, we are out of touch; and if it did nothing more, the Sukkot celebration would at least remind us of those vital processes without which all freezers and shelves would remain empty containers. It can give us back the feel of life and growing things.

So we may properly call Sukkot a harvest feast reminiscent of an agricultural stage in our Jewish development. But having called it a harvest feast we at once remember something about dwelling in booths for those forty years in the wilderness after Egypt, and we say: "But that is by no means the same as a shelter in an olive grove." Our recollection, of course, is right and we have a biblical precept to confirm it: " . . . seven days in the year . . . Israel shall dwell in booths; that your generations may know that I made the children of Israel dwell in booths when I brought them out of the land of Egypt, I the Lord your God" (Lev. 23:42 f.). Yes, this is not simply and only a harvest feast.

And when we think some more about it the very idea of such booths in the *desert* appears rather startling; we wonder about all that greenery! *sukkot* for all those people! at the end of scorching wilderness summers! We want to explain: "But you see . . . " and "Well, of course . . . " and that indeed is the right explanation. The booths in the wilderness are not made of poles and branches; their poles are constancy, and concern is the covering. God's constancy and faithfulness are the pledges of his promise, and his people will inherit the land. God's concern is the shelter and shade that sustain them on the desert way.

Once a pastoral-agricultural observance, Pesach became a reminder of God's redeeming his people from Egyptian bondage; once a tribute of first fruits, Shavuot became a reminder of the covenant of Sinai; once a harvest feast, Sukkot became a recollection of God's provident concern—that and a token for the future. In words now found in the book of Isaiah, a messianic allegorist projected the distant past on the distant future, comparing the goal of Israel's history with its ancient source. He spoke of a *sukkah* which God will once again provide—a shade and refuge for a new Jerusalem. In language not always lucid but indeed allusive and nostalgic for the one-time sheltering "glory of God" on the way through the wilderness, this dreamer said:

> The Lord will create over the whole habitation of mount Zion, and over her assemblies, a cloud and smoke by day, and the shining of a flaming fire by night; for the glory [of God] shall be a canopy *(chuppah)* over all. And it shall be a pavilion *(sukkah)* for a shadow in the day-time from the heat and for a refuge and for a covert from storm and from rain (Isa. 4.5 f.).

A new value is added. The *sukkah*, symbol of growth and bounty, has become an allegory also of the marvel of Israel's history and the promise of its destiny.

Bibliography of the Writings of Sheldon H. Blank

1920

Unpublished dissertation.
Kant, Croce and the a priori Synthesis.
A dissertation submitted in partial fulfillment of the requirements for the degree of Master of Arts, University of Cincinnati, April 1920.

Untermeyer and Co.
On the poets Untermeyer, James Oppenheim and Alter Brody
In: *Hebrew Union College Monthly*, Vol. VI, No. 5, March-April 1920, pp. 142–48.

1921

Review of Henry Berkowitz, *Intimate Glimpses of a Rabbi's Career*, Cincinnati, 1921.
In: *Hebrew Union College Monthly*, Vol. VIII, No. 1, November 1921, pp. 13–18.

1922

The Educational Theater and the Temple Center (in collaboration with S. Burnett Jordan)
In: *Hebrew Union College Monthly*, Vol. VIII, No. 3, January 1922, pp. 67–75.

A Play. The Dove—A Symbolic Tragedy.
In: *Hebrew Union College Monthly*, Vol. VIII, No. 6, April 1922, pp. 170–75.

1923

Unpublished dissertation.
The Organization of Jewish Communities in Tannaitic Times.
Thesis submitted in partial fulfillment of requirements for ordination, Hebrew Union College, Cincinnati, 1923.

Pulpit Freedom,
A compilation of opinions prepared for a class in social studies.
In: *Hebrew Union College Monthly*, Vol. IX, No. 6, April 1923, pp. 19–24.

1925

Unpublished dissertation
Das Wort תורה im Alten Testament.
Inaugural-Dissertation zur Erlangen der Doktorwürde bei der philosophischen Fakultät der Universität Jena, Jena 1925.

1929

Discussion. On "Recent Archaelogical Work in Palestine" by Nelson Glueck
In: *Central Conference of American Rabbis Yearbook*, Vol. XXXIX, 1929, pp. 29–31.

1930

The LXX Renderings of Old Testament Terms for Law.
In: *Hebrew Union College Annual*, Vol. VII, 1930, pp. 259–83.

1931

The Study of Hebrew Bible Manuscripts.
In: *Hebrew Union College Monthly*, Vol. XVIII, No. 5, April 1931, pp. 22–25.

"The Soul that Sinneth," A Sermon for Kol Nidre.
In: *A Set of Holiday Sermons*, 5692–1931, Cincinnati, pp. 25–31.

1932

A Hebrew Bible Ms. in the Hebrew Union College Library.
Paper presented at the Eighteenth Congress of Orientalists, Leiden, September 1931.
In: *Hebrew Union College Annual*, Vol VIII–IX, 1931–32, pp. 229–55.

1933

The Ben Naftali Bible Manuscripts.
In: *Hebrew Union College Monthly*, Vol. XX, No. 3, January 1933, pp. 7–9.

Jews in Nazi Germany.
In: *Hebrew Union College Monthly*, Vol. XXI, No. 1, October 1933, pp. 7–9.

1934

Palmyra and Petra (excerpts from travel letters, 1926).
In: *Hebrew Union College Monthly*, Vol. XXI, No. 3, February 1934, pp. 7–10.

1936

Glosses to the Old Testament from Lawrence's *Seven Pillars of Wisdom*.
In: *Hebrew Union College Monthly*, Vol. XXIII, No. 6, May 1936, pp. 7–10.

Studies in Post-Exilic Universalism.
In: *Hebrew Union College Annual*, Vol. XI, 1936, pp. 159–91.

1938

The Death of Zechariah in Rabbinic Literature.
In: *Hebrew Union College Annual*, Vol. XII–XIII, 1937–38, pp. 327–46.

A Blank Expression.

In: *Hebrew Union College Monthly*, Vol. XXV, No. 3, January 1938, p. 6.

Some Recent Archaeological Discoveries.
In: *Hebrew Union College Monthly*, Vol. XXV, No. 5, April 1938, p. 10.

Review of Joseph Reider, *The Holy Scriptures with Commentary: Deuteronomy*, New York, 1937.
In: *Journal of Biblical Literature*, Vol. LVII, Part II, 1938, p. 225.

1939

Sundry articles in the *Universal Jewish Encyclopedia*, Vols. 1—5, 1939—41.

1940

Studies in Deutero-Isaiah.
In: *Hebrew Union College Annual*, Vol. XV, 1940, pp. 1—46.

1945

Review of William A. Irwin, *The Problem of Ezekiel*, 1943.
In: *Journal of Jewish Bibliography*, Vol. V/VI, 1944/5.

Institutes on Judaism—One Man's Impressions
In: *Hebrew Union College Monthly*, Vol. XXXII, No. 5, June 1945, pp. 9, 20.

1946

The Dissident Laity in Early Judaism.
Expansion of Presidential address: "The Voice of the Laity in Early Post-Exilic Judaism" given at the meeting of the Middle West Branch of the American Oriental Society, April 1937.
In: *Hebrew Union College Annual*, Vol. XIX, 1945—46, pp. 1—42.

Beginning a New Era.
In: *Hebrew Union College Monthly*, Vol. XXXIII, No. 3, April 1946, p. 19.

1947

Julian Morgenstern, the Scholar.
In: *Hebrew Union College Monthly*, Vol. XXXIV, No. 5, April 1947, pp. 15, 22.

1948

The Confessions of Jeremiah and the Meaning of Prayer.
Presidential address given at the meeting of the Midwest Section of the Society of Biblical Literature.
In: *Hebrew Union College Annual*, Vol. XXI, 1948, pp. 331—54.

The Current Misinterpretation of Isaiah's *She'ar Yashub*.
In: *Journal of Biblical Literature*, Vol. LXVII, Part III, 1948, pp. 211–15.

Some Recent Trends in Bible Scholarship.
In: *Liberal Jewish Monthly*, Vol. 19, No. 5, London, 1948, pp. 50–51.

Dear Dr. Blank (a letter to, and the reply).
In: *Hebrew Union College Monthly*, Vol. XXXV, No. 5, Graduation 1948, pp. 12–13.

1949

The Mission of Israel: Biblical Origins.
In: *Report of the Sixth International Conference* (of the World Union for Progressive Judaism) held in London July 14th to July 19th, 1949. Paper read at conference as part of the program on The Mission of Judaism—Its Present Day Application.

1950

The Personal Aspect of Judaism.
1. In the Prophetic Writings
2. In the Psalms
In: *The Liberal Jewish Monthly*, London, March and April 1950, pages 35–37 and 55–56.

1951

Review of J. H. Greenstone, *The Holy Scriptures, Proverbs with Commentary*.
In: *Jewish Social Studies*, New York 1951, Vol. XIII, pp. 251–52.

The Curse, Blasphemy, the Spell and the Oath.
I: *Hebrew Union College Annual*, Vol. XXIII—Part One, 1950–51, pp. 73–95.

An Effective Literary Device in Job XXXI.
In: *The Journal of Jewish Studies*, Vol. II, No. 2, London, 1951, pp. 105–7.

1952

"And All Our Virtues"—An Interpretation of Isaiah 64.4b–5a.
In: *Journal of Biblical Literature*, Vol. LXXI, Part III, 1952, pp. 149–54.

Review of Robert Gordis: *Koheleth—the Man and his World*, New York, 1951.
In: *The Jewish Quarterly Review*, N.S. Vol. XLIII, 1952–53, pp. 93–96.

1953

Review of William A. Irwin, *The Old Testament: Keystone of Human Culture*, New York, 1952.
In: *Jewish Social Studies*, Vol. XV, No. 3–4, 1953, p. 303.

Men Against God, The Promethean Element in Biblical Prayer.
The Presidential Address delivered at the annual meeting of the Society of Biblical Literature and Exegesis in December 1952 at the Union Theological Seminary in New York.
In: *Journal of Biblical Literature*, Vol. LXXII, Part I, March 1953, pp. 1—13. Also reprint.

The Nearness of God and Psalm Seventy-three.
In: *To Do and To Teach*, essays in honor of Charles Lynn Pyatt, Lexington, The College of the Bible, 1953, pp. 1—13.

Review of *The Holy Bible, Revised Standard Version, Containing the Old and New Testaments*, 1952. (Only OT reviewed here.)
In: *Journal of Religion*, Vol. 33, No. 2, 1953, pp. 108—9.

1954

Immanuel and Which Isaiah?
In: *Journal of Near Eastern Studies*, Vol. XIII, No. 2, 1954, pp. 83—86.

Isaiah 52.5 and the Profanation of the Name.
In: *Hebrew Union College Annual*, Vol. XXV, 1954, pp. 1—8.

The Prophetic Element in Progressive Judaism.
In: *Aspects of Progressive Jewish Thought*, London, 1954, pp. 30—36.

1955

"Of a Truth the Lord Hath Sent Me." An Inquiry into the Source of the Prophet's Authority.
The Goldenson Lecture for 1955.
The first of the Goldenson Lectures: issued as a booklet in 1955, subsequently included as first in the collection of twelve Goldenson Lectures 1955—1966, published in book form as *Interpreting Prophetic Tradition*, Cincinnati, 1969, pp. 1—20.

"יאבד יום" (איוב ג׳, ג׳)—קללה המכוונת שלא למקומה.
Translation of paper "'Perish the Day!' A Misdirected Curse (Job iii, 3)," read at a meeting of the midwest Branch of the American Oriental Society, Cincinnati, April 1950.
In: *Bulletin of the Israel Exploration Society*, Vol. XIX, Nos. 1—2, 1955, pp. 65—9.

The Relevance of Prophetic Thought for the American Rabbi.
Also "preprinted and distributed by some friends and students of the author as a tribute . . ."
In: *Central Conference of American Rabbis Yearbook*, Vol. LXV, 1955, pp. 163—72.

"Doest Thou Well to be Angry?" A Study in Self-Pity.

Read at the meeting of the British Society for Old Testament Study in Edinburgh, 1954.
In: *Hebrew Union College Annual*, Vol. XXVI, 1955, pp. 29–41.

1956

Traces of Prophetic Agony in Isaiah.
In: *Hebrew Union College Annual*, Vol. XXVII, 1956, pp. 81–92.

Review of John Wolf Miller, *Das Verhältnis Jeremias und Hesekiels Sprachlich und Theologisch Untersucht*, Assen, Der Nederlande, 1955.
In: *Journal of Biblical Literature*, Vol. LXXV, Part III, 1956, pp. 260–61.

1958

Review of Arvid S. Kapelrud, *Central Ideas in Amos*, Oslo, 1956.
In: *Journal of Biblical Literature*, Vol. LXXVII, Part II, 1958, pp. 193–94.

Prophetic Faith in Isaiah.
Harper & Brothers Publishers, New York; also Adam & Charles Black, London. 1958, xii + 241 pp. Reprinted as paperback (Waynebook) with only minor emendations, Detroit, 1967.

Jewish Ways to Understanding.
High Holy Day address at Liberal Jewish Synagogue, St. Johns Wood Road, London.
In: *Liberal Jewish Monthly*, London, Vol. XXIX, No. 10, December 1958, pp. 148–51.

1959

Review of Josef Scharbert, *Solidarität im Segen und Fluch im Alten Testament und in seiner Umwelt, Band I: Väterfluch und Vätersegen*, Bonn, 1958.
In: *Journal of Biblical Literature*, Vol. LXXVIII, Part III, 1959, pp. 259–61.

Review of Joh. Lindblom, *A Study on the Immanuel Section in Isaiah*.
In: *Journal of Biblical Literature*, Vol. LXXVIII, Part IV, 1959, p. 372.

1960

"In Verita il Signore mi ha Mandato."
Translation of the Goldenson Lecture for 1955 (see above, pp. 11 ff.).
In: *La Voce della Unione Italiana per l'Ebraismo Progressivo*, Vol. II, part 7, April–June 1960, pp. 266–77.

What Do We Want Our Children to Know about the Bible? A Fresh Appraisal.
In: *The Jewish Teacher*, March 1960, pp. 15–19.

Review of Margaret B. Crook, *The Cruel God: Job's Search for the Meaning of Suffering*, Boston, 1959.
In: *Journal of Biblical Literature*, Vol. LXXIX, Part II, 1960, p. 191.

1961

Il Profeta e Dio.
Given (in English: The Prophet and God) at the University of Rome, March 1961.
In: *Studi e Materiali di Storia delle Religione*, Vol. 32, fasc. 1, Roma, 1961, pp. 3–20.

Some Observations Concerning Biblical Prayer.
In: *Hebrew Union College Annual*, Vol. XXXII, 1961, pp. 75–90.

The Dawn of Our Responsibility.
Paper read at conference as part of the program on Aspects of Progressive Judaism and Human Responsibility.
"Reprinted and distributed by some friends and pupils of the author as a tribute . . ."
In: *Report of the Twelfth International Conference* (of the World Union for Progressive Judaism) *held in London, July 6th to July 13th, 1961.*

Jeremiah, Man and Prophet.
Hebrew Union College Press, Cincinnati, 1961, xii + 260 pp.
"This book is a publication of the Alumni Association of the HUC-JIR."

1962

Entries in *The Interpreters Dictionary of the Bible*, New York, Nashville, 1962:

Age, old.
Ecclesiastes.
Fable.
Folly.
Friend, Friendship.
Happiness.
Kiss.
Proverb.
Proverbs, Book of.
Riddle.
Wisdom.
Youth.

Review of *Adam to Daniel—An Illustrated Guide to the Old Testament and its Background*, Gaalyahu Cornfeld, Editor, New York, 1961.
In: *The American Rabbi*, 1962.

1963

A Foundation is to Build
Given as Founders Day Address at Hebrew Union College, Cincinnati, March 1963.
In: *Central Conference of American Rabbis Journal*, Vol. XI, No. 2 June 1963, pp. 9–13, 25.

1965

Review of Christopher R. North, *The Second Isaiah: Introduction, Translation and Commentary to Chapters XL–LV*, Oxford, 1964.
In: *Journal of Biblical Literature*, Vol. LXXXIV, Part II, 1965, pp. 207 f.

Review of John Bright, *The Anchor Bible: Jeremiah*, New York, 1955 and Christopher R. North, *The Second Isaiah, Introduction, Translation and Commentary to Chapters XL–LV*, Oxford 1964.
In: *Central Conference of American Rabbis Journal*, Vol. XIII, No. 2, 1965, pp. 76–78.

1966

The Sukkah—its History and Promise.
In: *Pointer*, Quarterly Journal of the Union of Liberal and Progressive Synagogues, Vol. II, No. 1, London, Autumn 1966, pp. 4–5.

Prophetic Roots for a Liberal Religion.
In: *Dimension*, Vol. 1, No. 1, Fall 1966, pp. 3–5.

The Ten Commandments.
In: *The New Book of Knowledge*, Grolier, New York, 1966, pp. 72–73.

1967

The World a Stage and We the Players?
A sermon spoken at the Rockefeller Chapel of the University of Chicago, February 1963.
In: *Rockefeller Chapel Sermons of Recent Years*, University of Chicago Press, 1967.

Review of Claus Rietzschel, *Das Problem der Urrolle: ein Beitrag zur Redaktionsgeschichte des Jeremiabuches*, Gütersloh, 1966.
In: *Journal of Biblical Literature*, Vol. LXXXVI, Part IV, 1967, pp. 468–70.

Review of Brevard S. Childs, *Isaiah and the Assyrian Crisis*, Naperville, Ill., 1967.
In: *Journal of Biblical Literature*, Vol. LXXXVI, Part IV, 1967, pp. 466–67.

1968

The Theology of Jewish Survival According to Biblical Sources.
In: *Central Conference of American Rabbis Journal*, Vol. XV, No. 4, October 1968, pp. 22–31, 104.

1969

Review of Elias Bickerman, *Four Strange Books of the Bible*, New York, 1967.
In: *Dimensions*, Vol. III, No. 4, 1969, p. 48.

Understanding the Prophets.
Union of American Hebrew Congregations, New York, 1969, iv + 138 pp.

1970

Irony by Way of Attribution.
In: *Semitics*, Vol. I, University of South Africa, 1970, pp. 1–6.

Prolegomenon.
In: The reissue of *The Song of Songs and Coheleth*, by Christian D. Ginsburg, New York, 1970, pp. IX–XLIV.

1971

MMMM.
A story for grandchildren, written in Norway in 1961.
Privately printed, Boston, September 1971.

1972

Review of Hans Wildberger, *Biblischer Kommentar, Altes Testament, Jesaja*, fascicles 1–4, Neukirchen-Vluyn, 1965–69.
In: *Journal of Biblical Literature*, Vol. 91, No. 1, 1972, pp. 97–98.

1974

Isaiah.
In: the fifteenth edition of *Encyclopaedia Britannica*, 1974, Vol. 9, pp. 908–10.

The Prophet as Paradigm.
In: *Essays in Old Testament Ethics (J. Philip Hyatt, in Memoriam)*, New York, 1974, pp. 113–30.

1975

Review of Hans Wildberger, *Biblischer Kommentar, Altes Testament, Jesaja*, fascicles 5–6, Neukirchen-Vluyn, 1972–73.
In: *Journal of Biblical Literature*, Vol. 94, No. 2, June 1975, pp. 288–89.

1976

Notes on Jeremiah in *The New English Bible with the Apocrypha, Oxford Study Edition*, Oxford University Press, New York, 1976.

The Study of Bible in the College-Institute 1875–1975.
In: *Hebrew Union College-Jewish Institute of Religion at One Hundred Years*, Cincinnati, 1976, pp. 287–316.

Preparation for the Rabbinate Yesterday and Tomorrow
In: *Central Conference of American Rabbis Yearbook*, Vol. LXXXV, New York, 1976.

LIBRARY OF DAVIDSON COLLEGE